ISLAM ON MERCY AND COMPASSION

ISLAM ON MERCY AND COMPASSION

Shaykh-ul-Islam
Dr Muhammad Tahir-ul-Qadri

Author: Dr Muhammad Tahir-ul-Qadri

Published by
Minhaj-ul-Quran Publications
292–296 Romford Road
Forest Gate
London, E7 9HD
United Kingdom

All proceeds from the books, literature and audio-visual media (all multimedia) delivered by Dr Muhammad Tahir-ul-Qadri are entirely donated to Minhaj-ul-Quran International (MQI).

Research Assistants
Abdul Aziz Suraqah, Shaykh Abdul Aziz Dabbagh

A catalogue record for this book is available from the British Library.

Library of Congress Control Number: 2013952864

ISBN–13: 978–1–908229–17–5 (hbk)
ISBN–13: 978–1–908229–22–9 (pbk)

www.minhaj.org | www.minhajuk.org
www.minhajpublications.com

First published December 2013

Printed by Mega Printing, Turkey

بِسْمِ ٱللَّهِ ٱلرَّحْمَٰنِ ٱلرَّحِيمِ

In the name of God, Most Compassionate, Ever-Merciful

Saying of God ﷻ

﴿كَتَبَ رَبُّكُمْ عَلَىٰ نَفْسِهِ ٱلرَّحْمَةَ﴾

﴿Your Lord has made mercy incumbent upon Himself (as a gracious obligation).﴾

[Qurʾān 6:54]

Saying of the Prophet ﷺ

عَنْ أَبِـي هُرَيْرَةَ رضي الله عنه قَالَ: سَمِعْتُ رَسُوْلَ اللهِ ﷺ يَقُوْلُ: «جَعَلَ اللهُ الرَّحْمَةَ مِائَةَ جُزْءٍ. فَأَمْسَكَ عِنْدَهُ تِسْعَةً وَتِسْعِيْنَ جُزْءًا، وَأَنْزَلَ فِي الْأَرْضِ جُزْءًا وَاحِدًا».

Abū Hurayra رضي الله عنه reported that he heard Allah's Messenger ﷺ say, 'Allah created mercy in one hundred parts; He retained ninety-nine parts and sent one part to the earth.'

[Al-Bukhārī and Muslim]

Shaykh-ul-Islam Dr Muhammad Tahir-ul-Qadri

Shaykh-ul-Islam Dr Muhammad Tahir-ul-Qadri was born in 1951 in the city of Jhang, Pakistan, hailing from a family of Islamic saints, scholars and teachers. His formal religious education was initiated in Medina at the age of 12 in Madrasa al-ʿUlūm al-Sharʿiyya, a traditional school situated in the blessed house of the Companion of the Prophet Muhammad ﷺ, Abū Ayyūb al-Anṣārī ؓ. He completed the traditional studies of classical and Arabic sciences under the tutelage of his father and other eminent scholars of the time. He continued to travel around the Islamic world in the pursuit of sacred knowledge, and studied under many famous scholars of Mecca, Medina, Syria, Baghdad, Lebanon, the Maghreb, India and Pakistan, and received around five hundred authorities and chains of transmission from them in hadith and classical Islamic and spiritual sciences. Amongst them is an unprecedented, unique and highly honoured chain of authority which connects him, through four teachers, to Shaykh ʿAbd al-Razzāq, the son of Sayyidunā Shaykh ʿAbd al-Qādir al-Jīlānī al-Ḥasanī al-Ḥusaynī (of Baghdad), al-Shaykh al-Akbar Muḥyī al-Dīn b. al-ʿArabī [(the author of *al-Futūḥāt al-Makkiyya*) (Damascus)] and Imam Ibn Ḥajar al-ʿAsqalānī, the great hadith authority of Egypt. Through another chain he is linked to Imam Yūsuf b. Ismāʿīl al-Nabhānī directly via only one teacher. His chains of transmission are published in two of his *thabts* (detailed list): *al-Jawāhir al-Bāhira fī al-Asānīd al-Ṭāhira* and *al-Subul al-Wahabiyya fī al-Asānīd al-Dhahabiyya*.

In the academic sphere, Dr Qadri received a First Class Honours Degree from the University of the Punjab in 1970. After earning his MA in Islamic studies with University Gold Medal in 1972 and achieving his LLB in 1974, Dr Qadri began to practise law in the district courts of Jhang. He moved to Lahore in 1978 and joined the University of the Punjab as a lecturer in law and completed his doctorate in Islamic

Law. He was later appointed as a professor of Islamic Law and was head of the department of Islamic legislation for LLM.

Dr Qadri was also a jurist advisor to the Federal Shariat Court and Appellate Shariah Bench of the Supreme Court of Pakistan and advisor on the development of Islamic Curricula to the Federal Ministry of Education. Within a short span of time, Dr Qadri emerged as one of the Pakistan's leading Islamic jurists and scholars and one of the world's most renowned and leading authorities on Islam. A prolific author, researcher and orator, Dr Qadri has written around one thousand books, of which more than four hundred and fifty have been published, and has delivered over six thousand lectures (in Urdu, English and Arabic) on a wide range of subjects.

Shaykh-ul-Islam Dr Muhammad Tahir-ul-Qadri issued a historic fatwa on the vital matter of suicide bombings and terrorism carried out in the name of Islam. It is regarded as a significant and historic step, the first time that such an explicit and unequivocal decree against the perpetrators of terror has been broadcast so widely. The original fatwa was written in Urdu, and amounts to 600 pages of research and references from the Qur'ān, hadith, the opinions of the Companions رضي الله عنهم, and the widely accepted classical texts of Islamic scholarship. This historic work has been published in English and Indonesian, while translation into Arabic, Norwegian, Danish, Hindi and other major languages is also in process. Islamic Research Academy of Jamia al-Azhar Egypt wrote a detailed description of the fatwa and verified its contents as well.

Dr Qadri is also the founder and head of Minhaj-ul-Quran International (MQI), an organisation with branches and centres in more than ninety countries around the globe; he is the chairman of the Board of Governors of Minhaj University Lahore, which is chartered by the Government of Pakistan; he is the founder of Minhaj Education Society, which has established more than 600 schools and colleges in Pakistan; and he is the chairman of Minhaj Welfare Foundation, an organization involved in humanitarian and social welfare activities globally.

Transliteration Key

ا/آ/ى	ā	ظ	ẓ
ب	b	ع	ʿ
ت	t	غ	gh
ث	th	ف	f
ج	j	ق	q
ح	ḥ	ك	k
خ	kh	ل	l
د	d	م	m
ذ	dh	ن	n
ر	r	ه	h
ز	z	و	ū/w
س	s	ي	y/ī
ش	sh	ة	a
ص	ṣ	ء	ʾ
ض	ḍ	أ	a
ط	ṭ	إ	i

Formulaic Arabic Expressions

(*Subḥānahū wa taʿālā*) an invocation to describe the Glory of Almighty Allah: 'the Exalted and Sublime'

(*Ṣalla-llāhu ʿalayhi wa ālihī wa sallam*) an invocation of God's blessings and peace upon the Prophet Muhammad and his family: 'God's blessings and peace be upon him and his family'

(*ʿAlayhis-salām*) an invocation of God's blessings and peace upon a Prophet or an angel: 'May peace be upon him'

(*ʿAlayhas-salām*) an invocation of God's blessings and peace upon a Prophet's mother, wife, daughter and other pious woman: 'May peace be upon her'

(*ʿAlayhimus-salām*) an invocation of God's blessings and peace upon two Prophets or two angels: 'May peace be upon both of them'

(*ʿAlayhimus-salām*) an invocation of God's blessings and peace upon three or more Prophets: 'May peace be upon them'

(*Raḍiya-llāhu ʿanhu*) an invocation of God's pleasure with a male Companion of the Prophet: 'May God be pleased with him'

(*Raḍiya-llāhu ʿanhā*) an invocation of God's pleasure with a female Companion of the Prophet: 'May God be pleased with her'

(*Raḍiya-llāhu ʿanhumā*) an invocation of God's pleasure with two Companions of the Prophet: 'May God be pleased with both of them'

(*Raḍiya-llāhu ʿanhum*) an invocation of God's pleasure with more than two Companions of the Prophet: 'May God be pleased with them'

Contents

Part I

اَلْبَابُ الْأَوَّلُ

عَظَمَةُ رَحْمَةِ اللهِ تعَالَى

Chapter One

On the Infinite Mercy of Almighty Allah

The mercy of Allah ﷻ is vast and all-encompassing, for He made it incumbent upon Himself. That said, He has not extended its honour in the life to come to those who disbelieve in and reject Him—even though it is true that He shows mercy to them in this life. For such disbelievers, He shows mercy through provision, health, wealth, children, and so on. For this reason, the servants of Allah must show delight in Allah's mercy and must never despair of it, for none despairs of His mercy save the disbelievers.

The revealed texts that detail Allah's mercy, whether in the Holy Qur'ān or the noble Prophetic traditions, are vast in number. While unique points have been placed under a separate subheading to acquaint the reader and make it easy for him to memorize, a summary of the various manifestations of Allah's mercy has been given in the conclusion.

1.1 Allah Has Written Mercy upon Himself

Allah ﷻ has informed us that He has written mercy upon His Ineffable Self. Allah ﷻ said,

﴿قُل لِّمَن مَّا فِي ٱلسَّمَٰوَٰتِ وَٱلْأَرْضِ ۖ قُل لِّلَّهِ ۚ كَتَبَ عَلَىٰ نَفْسِهِ ٱلرَّحْمَةَ ۚ﴾

﴾*Ask (them this question): 'To whom belongs whatever is in the heavens and the earth?' And (then) proclaim (this as well): 'Allah's it is.' He has made mercy incumbent upon Himself (as a gracious obligation).*﴿[1]

He also said,

﴿وَإِذَا جَآءَكَ ٱلَّذِينَ يُؤْمِنُونَ بِـَٔايَٰتِنَا فَقُلْ سَلَٰمٌ عَلَيْكُمْ ۖ كَتَبَ رَبُّكُمْ
عَلَىٰ نَفْسِهِ ٱلرَّحْمَةَ أَنَّهُۥ مَنْ عَمِلَ مِنكُمْ سُوٓءًۢا بِجَهَٰلَةٍ ثُمَّ تَابَ مِنۢ بَعْدِهِۦ
وَأَصْلَحَ فَأَنَّهُۥ غَفُورٌ رَّحِيمٌ﴾

[1] Qur'ān 6:12.

﴾*And when those who believe in Our Revelations come to you, then say (affectionately): 'Peace be upon you!' Your Lord has made mercy incumbent upon Himself (as a gracious obligation). So whoever from amongst you commits some evil out of ignorance (or suspension of discretion) but later turns to (Allah in) repentance and amends (himself), then surely He is Most Forgiving, Ever-Merciful.*﴿[2]

Allah has made mercy incumbent upon Himself out of His Divine largesse, bounties, and grace for His creation.

1.2 Allah is the Lord of Mercy

Allah Most High also informed us that He is absolutely free of needs, independent of His creation, yet at the same time He is the Possessor of Mercy and is compassionate towards them and is the Lord of mercy. Allah Most High said,

﴿وَرَبُّكَ ٱلْغَنِيُّ ذُو ٱلرَّحْمَةِ﴾

﴾*And your Lord is Self-Sufficient, Lord of (great) mercy.*﴿[3]

He also said,

﴿وَرَبُّكَ ٱلْغَفُورُ ذُو ٱلرَّحْمَةِ لَوْ يُؤَاخِذُهُم بِمَا كَسَبُوا۟ لَعَجَّلَ لَهُمُ ٱلْعَذَابَ﴾

﴾*And your Lord is Most Forgiving, Full of Mercy. If He had to take them to task for their doings, He would certainly send the torment upon them quickly.*﴿[4]

In this verse, Allah mentioned the word mercy in the definite form with an *alif* and *lām* [*al-raḥma*] to show that He is the possessor of all forms of mercy.

1.3 Allah is the Owner of Mercy

One of the many manifestations of Allah's vast mercy is the fact that

---

[2] Ibid., 6:54.

[3] Ibid., 6:133.

[4] Ibid., 18:58.

He is Compassionate and the Owner of Mercy, and that no one else owns it. None owns its treasure-stores save Him, the Most High. It is uniquely His and no one can contend it with Him. There are numerous verses in the Qur'ān that bear this out. Allah Most High said,

﴿أَمْ عِندَهُمْ خَزَآئِنُ رَحْمَةِ رَبِّكَ ٱلْعَزِيزِ ٱلْوَهَّابِ﴾

﴾*Do they have the treasures of the mercy of your Lord, Who is the Almighty, the Most Benevolent?*﴿[5]

Just as He alone owns its treasure-stores, He bestows it upon whomever He wills among His servants. This is why He ascribed it to Himself in the verse,

﴿يَخْتَصُّ بِرَحْمَتِهِۦ مَن يَشَآءُ﴾

﴾*And Allah especially chooses whom He pleases for His mercy.*﴿[6]

He also said,

﴿مَا يَفْتَحِ ٱللَّهُ لِلنَّاسِ مِن رَّحْمَةٍ فَلَا مُمْسِكَ لَهَا﴾

﴾*Whatever of (the treasure of) His mercy Allah opens to mankind, there is none who can withhold it.*﴿[7]

1.4 Allah Shows Mercy to Whom He Wills

Since Allah ﷻ is the Owner of Mercy, He shows mercy to whom He wills and veils others from it as He wills. This is because Allah alone is the disposer of affairs who manages the cosmos, and it is based upon a wisdom that He knows. Allah said,

﴿رَّبُّكُمْ أَعْلَمُ بِكُمْ إِن يَشَأْ يَرْحَمْكُمْ أَوْ إِن يَشَأْ يُعَذِّبْكُمْ﴾

﴾*Your Lord is Well Aware of your state of affairs. If He wills, He may have mercy on you, or if He likes, He may*

[5] Ibid., 38:9.

[6] Ibid., 2:105.

[7] Ibid., 35:2.

torment you.﴾[8]

He also said,

﴿يُعَذِّبُ مَن يَشَآءُ وَيَرۡحَمُ مَن يَشَآءُۖ﴾

﴾*He torments whom He wills and shows mercy to whom He pleases.*﴿[9]

1.5 Allah is the All-Merciful, the Compassionate

To further explain Allah's infinite mercy, let us consider the fact that His names include the Most Compassionate (al-Raḥmān) and Ever-Merciful (al-Raḥīm). Although Allah ﷻ described His exalted Prophet ﷺ as Raḥīm, and also described other people as *raḥīm*, He uniquely possess the name al-Raḥmān. No one shares with Him in this name. There are numerous Qurʾānic verses that mention these two noble names.

The Name al-Raḥmān is mentioned by itself in the Qurʾān fifty-seven times, the name al-Raḥīm is mentioned by itself in the Qurʾān ninety-five times, and the quality *raḥīman* is mentioned twenty times. As for the combination of al-Raḥmān and al-Raḥīm, it occurs 113 times, corresponding to the number of chapters in the Qurʾān, apart from *Sūra Tawba*. How many times does the word occur if we are to include the word mercy (*raḥma*) and its derived forms? Undoubtedly, the number will increase, and all this proves the infinite mercy of Allah ﷻ.

And indeed, if the servants were to dedicate themselves to their Lord, they would find Him All-Forgiving, Most Merciful. Allah ﷻ said,

﴿وَمَن يَعۡمَلۡ سُوٓءًا أَوۡ يَظۡلِمۡ نَفۡسَهُۥ ثُمَّ يَسۡتَغۡفِرِ ٱللَّهَ يَجِدِ ٱللَّهَ غَفُورٗا رَّحِيمٗا﴾

﴾*And he who commits evil or wrongs his own soul and then*

---

[8] Ibid., 17:54.

[9] Ibid., 29:21.

seeks Allah's forgiveness will find Allah Most Forgiving, Ever-Merciful.﴾[10]

1.6 Allah is the Most Merciful of Those Who Show Mercy

Moreover, Allah ﷻ is the Most Merciful of those who show mercy. There is no one more merciful than Allah, and how could that be, when it is He who created the Creation, gave them that description, and sent down to them one part of the one hundred parts of His mercy in order for them to show mercy to one another.

Allah ﷻ said,

﴿وَقُل رَّبِّ ٱغْفِرْ وَٱرْحَمْ وَأَنتَ خَيْرُ ٱلرَّٰحِمِينَ﴾

﴿*And submit: 'O my Lord, forgive and have mercy, and You (alone) are the Best of those who have mercy.'*﴾[11]

This was clarified by all the Prophets and Messengers ﷺ, which is why they all addressed Allah with that formula. There are many Qur'ānic verses that mention this. Allah said,

﴿قَالَ رَبِّ ٱغْفِرْ لِى وَلِأَخِى وَأَدْخِلْنَا فِى رَحْمَتِكَ ۖ وَأَنتَ أَرْحَمُ ٱلرَّٰحِمِينَ﴾

﴿*Mūsā (Moses) said: 'O my Lord! Forgive me and my brother and admit us to (the Embrace of) Your Mercy and You are the Most Merciful of those who show mercy.'*﴾[12]

He also mentioned that Yaʿqūb ﷺ said,

﴿فَٱللَّهُ خَيْرٌ حَٰفِظًا ۖ وَهُوَ أَرْحَمُ ٱلرَّٰحِمِينَ﴾

﴿*Then Allah alone is the Best Protector, and He alone is the Most Merciful of all the merciful.*﴾[13]

---

[10] Ibid., 4:110.

[11] Ibid., 23:118.

[12] Ibid., 7:151.

[13] Ibid., 12:64.

He also said,

﴿وَأَيُّوبَ إِذْ نَادَىٰ رَبَّهُۥٓ أَنِّي مَسَّنِيَ ٱلضُّرُّ وَأَنتَ أَرْحَمُ ٱلرَّٰحِمِينَ﴾

﴾And (call to mind the account of) Ayyūb (Job) when he called out to his Lord: 'Misery has laid a hand on me, and You are the Most Merciful of all the merciful.'﴿ [14]

And the exalted Prophet ﷺ explained Allah's vast mercy and the fact that He is the most merciful of those who show mercy. There is a hadith reported from Abū Saʿīd al-Khudrī ؓ in which the Prophet ﷺ spoke about the believers' beatific vision of their Lord on the Day of Resurrection, and their intercession for their brethren who are in the Hellfire. At the end of the hadith, the Prophet ﷺ said,

فَيَقُولُ اللهُ: شَفَعَتِ الْـمَلَائِكَةُ وَشَفَعَ النَّبِيُّونَ وَشَفَعَ الْـمُؤْمِنُونَ، وَلَمْ يَبْقَ إِلَّا أَرْحَمُ الرَّاحِمِينَ.

So Allah ﷻ shall say, 'The angels have interceded, as have the Prophets and the believers, and their remains none but the Most Merciful of those who show mercy.[15]

This was narrated by Muslim.

Just as the noble Prophet and Chosen One ﷺ explained that Allah is the Most Merciful of those who show mercy, he also explained that Allah is more merciful to His creation than a mother is to her child. ʿUmar b. al-Khaṭṭāb ؓ said,

قَدِمَ عَلَى النَّبِيِّ ﷺ سَبْيٌ فَإِذَا امْرَأَةٌ مِنَ السَّبْيِ قَدْ تَحْلُبُ ثَدْيَهَا تَسْقِي. إِذَا وَجَدَتْ صَبِيًّا فِي السَّبْيِ أَخَذَتْهُ فَأَلْصَقَتْهُ بِبَطْنِهَا وَأَرْضَعَتْهُ. فَقَالَ لَنَا النَّبِيُّ ﷺ: أَتُرَوْنَ هَذِهِ طَارِحَةً وَلَدَهَا فِي النَّارِ؟ قُلْنَا: لَا، وَهِيَ تَقْدِرُ عَلَى أَنْ لَا تَطْرَحَهُ. فَقَالَ: لَلهُ أَرْحَمُ بِعِبَادِهِ مِنْ هَذِهِ بِوَلَدِهَا.

---

14 Ibid., 21:83.

15 Set forth by •Muslim in *al-Ṣaḥīḥ:* Bk.: *al-Īmān* [The Faith], Ch.: "Knowing the Routes of Transmission," 1:170 §302.

Captives came to the Prophet ﷺ among whom was a woman whose breast was oozing with milk. When she found a child among the captives, she took it and put it upon her breast to suckle. The Prophet ﷺ asked us, 'Do you think this woman would cast her child into the fire?' 'No' we said, 'she will not do that as long as she is able.' Allah's Messenger ﷺ said, 'Allah is more merciful to His servants than this woman is to her child.'[16]

This is agreed upon.

The phrase 'to His servants' refers to His believing servants, since there is another narration from Anas ﷺ of the same hadith in which the Prophet ﷺ said,

وَلَاءُ اللهِ لَا يُلْقِي حَبِيبَهُ فِي النَّارِ.

By Allah, He would never cast His beloved in the Fire.[17]

1.7 Allah's Mercy is Boundless and Encompasses All Things

Allah ﷻ has informed us that His mercy encompasses everything in existence—be it animate or inanimate—whether animal or human or angel or jinn. Allah said,

﴿فَإِن كَذَّبُوكَ فَقُل رَّبُّكُمْ ذُو رَحْمَةٍ وَاسِعَةٍ﴾

﴾*Should they belie you, then say: "Your Lord is the Lord of infinite mercy."*﴿[18]

Allah also recorded the angels' saying,

---

[16] Set forth by •al-Bukhārī in *al-Ṣaḥīḥ:* Bk.: *al-Adab* [The Manners], Ch.: "On Showing Mercy to a Child and Kissing and Hugging Him," 5:2235 §5653; •Muslim in *al-Ṣaḥīḥ:* Bk.: *al-Tawba*, [The Repentance], Ch.: "On Allah's Vast Mercy, and That is Precedes His Wrath," 4:2109 §2754.

[17] Set forth by •Aḥmad b. Ḥanbal, *al-Musnad*, 3:104, 235; •Abū Yaʿlā, *al-Musnad*, 6:397 §3747; •al-Ḥākim, *al-Mustadrak*, 1:126 §194, 4:195 §7374; •al-Haythamī, *Majmaʿ al-zawāʾid*, 10:213, 383.

[18] Qurʾān 6:147.

﴿رَبَّنَا وَسِعْتَ كُلَّ شَىْءٍ رَّحْمَةً وَعِلْمًا فَٱغْفِرْ لِلَّذِينَ تَابُوا۟ وَٱتَّبَعُوا۟ سَبِيلَكَ
وَقِهِمْ عَذَابَ ٱلْجَحِيمِ﴾

﴾O our Lord, You encompass everything in (Your) mercy and knowledge. So forgive those who turn to You in repentance and follow Your path and protect them from the torment of Hell.﴿[19]

So just as Allah ﷻ encompasses His Creation in knowledge, He swathes them in mercy. His mercy is infinite and cloaks the entire Creation.

1.8 Allah's Multiplied Mercy for the Believers

Allah ﷻ has honoured His believing servants who are Godfearing and who believe in His noble Messenger ﷺ by multiplying for them His mercy. Allah said,

﴿يَـٰٓأَيُّهَا ٱلَّذِينَ ءَامَنُوا۟ ٱتَّقُوا۟ ٱللَّهَ وَءَامِنُوا۟ بِرَسُولِهِۦ يُؤْتِكُمْ كِفْلَيْنِ مِن
رَّحْمَتِهِۦ وَيَجْعَل لَّكُمْ نُورًا تَمْشُونَ بِهِۦ وَيَغْفِرْ لَكُمْ ۚ وَٱللَّهُ غَفُورٌ
رَّحِيمٌ﴾

﴾O believers! Become Godfearing and believe in His (Esteemed) Messenger (ﷺ). He will bless you with two portions of His mercy and will bring about light for you to walk in (in the world and in the Hereafter) and will forgive you. And Allah is Most Forgiving, Ever-Merciful.﴿[20]

Indeed, Allah ﷻ has bestowed light and forgiveness on this community.

---

[19] Ibid., 40:7.

[20] Ibid., 57:28.

1.9 The Prophets ﷺ Supplicate Allah to Envelop Them in Mercy

The Prophets ﷺ are the most knowledgeable of the people when it comes to their Lord Most High and His vast mercy. This is why we find that they would often supplicate Allah, asking Him to envelop them in mercy. And Allah certainly responded to their supplications and they obtained the mercy they sought after. Allah ﷻ said,

﴿قَالَ رَبِّ ٱغْفِرْ لِى وَلِأَخِى وَأَدْخِلْنَا فِى رَحْمَتِكَ ۖ وَأَنتَ أَرْحَمُ ٱلرَّٰحِمِينَ﴾

﴾*Mūsā (Moses) said: "O my Lord! Forgive me and my brother and admit us to (the Embrace of) Your Mercy and You are the Most Merciful of those who show mercy."*﴿ [21]

Allah also said,

﴿وَأَيُّوبَ إِذْ نَادَىٰ رَبَّهُۥٓ أَنِّى مَسَّنِىَ ٱلضُّرُّ وَأَنتَ أَرْحَمُ ٱلرَّٰحِمِينَ﴾

﴾*And (call to mind the account of) Ayyūb (Job) when he called out to his Lord: "Misery has laid a hand on me, and You are the Most Merciful of all the merciful."*﴿ [22]

And He also said,

﴿وَقَالَ رَبِّ أَوْزِعْنِىٓ أَنْ أَشْكُرَ نِعْمَتَكَ ٱلَّتِىٓ أَنْعَمْتَ عَلَىَّ وَعَلَىٰ وَٰلِدَىَّ وَأَنْ أَعْمَلَ صَٰلِحًا تَرْضَىٰهُ وَأَدْخِلْنِى بِرَحْمَتِكَ فِى عِبَادِكَ ٱلصَّٰلِحِينَ﴾

﴾*And he (Sulaymān [Solomon]) submitted: "O Lord, keep me by Your bestowal firm on it that I remain ever-thankful for Your favour You have conferred on me and on my parents, and I do such pious deeds as You are pleased with, and admit me by Your mercy amongst Your pious slaves enjoying exceptional nearness to You."*﴿ [23]

---

[21] Ibid., 7:151.

[22] Ibid., 21:83.

[23] Ibid., 27:19.

Allah also said about some of His Messengers,

﴿وَأَدْخَلْنَٰهُمْ فِى رَحْمَتِنَآ ۖ إِنَّهُم مِّنَ ٱلصَّٰلِحِينَ﴾

﴾*And We admitted them to (the embrace of) Our mercy. Surely, they were of the pious.*﴿[24]

1.10 The Recipients of Mercy

It has been mentioned earlier how those who follow the exalted Prophet ﷺ have mercy written for them. Others who shall receive Allah's mercy are those who show mercy to other people, because they are the merciful servants in whose hearts Allah has placed mercy. Here some of the hadith reports that are mentioned speak of those on whom Allah ﷻ shall have mercy.

Usāma b. Zayd ﷺ reported in the story of the demise of the Prophet's ﷺ grandson,

فَرُفِعَ الصَّبِيُّ فِي حَجْرِ النَّبِيِّ ﷺ وَنَفْسُهُ جُئِثُ. فَفَاضَتْ عَيْنَا النَّبِيِّ ﷺ، فَقَالَ لَهُ سَعْدٌ: مَا هَذَا، يَا رَسُولَ اللهِ؟ قَالَ: هَذِهِ رَحْمَةٌ وَضَعَهَا اللهُ فِي قُلُوبِ مَنْ شَاءَ مِنْ عِبَادِهِ. وَلَا يَرْحَمُ اللهُ مِنْ عِبَادِهِ إِلَّا الرُّحَمَاءَ.

The child was placed in the Prophet's lap and its breathing was ragged. Tears fell from the eyes of the Prophet ﷺ and Saʿd asked, 'O Allah's Messenger! What is this?' 'This,' the Prophet ﷺ answered, 'is an aspect of mercy which Allah has put in the hearts of whomever He wishes of His slaves. Allah is only merciful to His slaves who are merciful.'[25]

This was narrated by al-Bukhārī.

It is also reported by Jarīr b. ʿAbd Allāh ﷺ that Allah's Messenger ﷺ said,

لَا يَرْحَمُ اللهُ مَنْ لَا يَرْحَمُ النَّاسَ.

---

[24] Ibid., 21:86

[25] Set forth by •al-Bukhārī in *al-Ṣāḥīḥ:* Bk.: *al-Marḍā* [Patients], Ch.: "Visiting Sick Children," 5:2141 §5331; •Muslim in *al-Ṣaḥīḥ:* Bk.: *al-Janāʾiz* [Funerals], Ch.: "Weeping over the Dead," §11.

Allah does not show mercy to those who do not show mercy to the people.[26]

Abū Hurayra ﵁ said,

قَبَّلَ رَسُوْلُ اللهِ ﷺ الْحَسَنَ بْنَ عَلِيٍّ ﵄ وَعِنْدَهُ الأَقْرَعُ بْنُ حَابِسٍ التَّمِيْمِيُّ جَالِسًا. فَقَالَ الْأَقْرَعُ: إِنَّ لِي عَشَرَةً مِنَ الْوَلَدِ. مَا قَبَّلْتُ مِنْهُمْ أَحَدًا. فَنَظَرَ إِلَيْهِ رَسُوْلُ اللهِ ﷺ، ثُمَّ قَالَ: مَنْ لَا يَرْحَمُ، لَا يُرْحَمُ.

Once, Allah's Messenger ﷺ kissed al-Ḥasan b. ʿAlī [his grandson] ﵄ and al-Aqraʿ b. Ḥābis al-Tamīmī was sitting in his presence. Al-Aqraʿ said, 'I have ten children and have not kissed a single one of them.' Upon hearing this, Allah's Messenger ﷺ looked at him and said, 'He who does not show mercy shall not receive mercy.'[27]

This is agreed upon.

ʿAbd Allāh b. ʿAmr ﵄ reported that Allah's Messenger ﷺ said,

اَلرَّاحِمُونَ يَرْحَمُهُمُ الرَّحْمٰنُ. اِرْحَمُوا أَهْلَ الْأَرْضِ، يَرْحَمْكُمْ أَهْلُ السَّمَاءِ.

Those who show mercy shall receive mercy from the All-Merciful; show mercy to those on earth and the Lord of the heavens shall show mercy to you.[28]

[26] Set forth by •al-Bukhārī in *al-Sāḥīḥ*: Bk.: *al-Tawḥīd*, [Divine Unity], Ch.: "On Allah's Saying, ﴾*Say, 'Call upon Allah or call upon the All-Merciful; whichever you call to Him belong the beautiful names.'*﴿, 6:2686 §6941; •Muslim in *al-Ṣaḥīḥ:* Bk.: *al-Faḍāʾil* [The Exemplary Virtues], Ch.: "On the Prophet's Mercy toward Children and Dependents," §66.

[27] Set forth by •al-Bukhārī in *al-Ṣaḥīḥ:* Bk.: *al-Adab* [The Proper Conduct], Ch.: Kind treatment of the child, kissing him and hugging him, 5:2235 §5651; •Muslim in *al-Ṣaḥīḥ:* Bk.: *al-Faḍāʾil* [The Virtues and Merits], Ch.: "Kind treatment of the family and humility is to your credit", 4:1808 §2315. Aḥmad b. Ḥanbal in *al-Musnad*, 2:241 §7287. Ibn Ḥibbān in *al-Ṣaḥīḥ*, 2:202 §457. al-Bukhārī in *al-Adab al-Mufrad*, 1:46 §91, 99. al-Bayhaqī in *al-Sunan al-Kubrā*, 7:100 §13354.

[28] Set forth by •Aḥmad b. Ḥanbal, *al-Musnad* (2:160); •Abū Dāwūd, *al-Sunan:* Bk.: *al-Adab* [Etiquette], Ch.: "On Etiquette," §1924; •al-Tirmidhī,

Reported by Aḥmad, Ibn Abī Shayba, al-Ḥumaydī, Abū Dāwūd, and al-Bayhaqī, and al-Tirmidhī, al-Ḥākim and al-Dhahabī declared it authentic.

1.11 Those Who Shall Triumph with Allah's Mercy

Since all the Creation is Allah's servants and He has free disposal over them, and because He commands them and forbids them with various things, the one who is divinely protected is the one who is enveloped in Allah's mercy—such a person is truly blessed and triumphant. This can only occur when Allah has mercy on someone. The disobedient person is the one who shuns this, and thus the divine mercy does not cover him, and he is the loser.

Allah ﷻ said,

﴿وَمَن تَقِ ٱلسَّيِّـَٔاتِ يَوْمَئِذٍ فَقَدْ رَحِمْتَهُۥ ۚ وَذَٰلِكَ هُوَ ٱلْفَوْزُ ٱلْعَظِيمُ﴾

﴿And the one You have saved from (the punishment of) sins that Day, You have indeed shown him great mercy. And that is great success indeed.﴾[29]

Allah mentioned the words of Prophet Nūḥ ﷺ who said as he was about to be overtaken by the flood,

﴿قَالَ لَا عَاصِمَ ٱلْيَوْمَ مِنْ أَمْرِ ٱللَّهِ إِلَّا مَن رَّحِمَ ۚ﴾

﴿Nūḥ (Noah) said: 'None can save today from Allah's punishment except someone to whom He (Allah) shows His mercy.﴾[30]

---

al-Sunan: Bk.: *al-Birr wa al-ṣila* [Piety and Familial Integration], Ch.: "What Has been Reported Regarding Mercy toward Muslims," §1924; •Ibn Abī Shayba, *al-Muṣannaf* (8:526); •al-Ḥumaydī, *al-Musnad* (2:269 §591); •al-Khaṭīb al-Baghdādī, *Tārīkh Baghdad* (3:260); •al-Bayhaqī, *al-Sunan al-kubrā* (9:41) and *al-Asmā' wa al-ṣifāt* (423); •Ibn Ḥajar al-ʿAsqalānī in *Fatḥ al-Bārī* (13:359). This hadith is known as *al-Musalsal bi al-awwaliyya* (the first hadith traditionally transmitted from teacher to student).

[29] Qur'ān 40:9.

[30] Ibid., 11:43.

He also said,

﴿وَلَوْ شَآءَ رَبُّكَ لَجَعَلَ ٱلنَّاسَ أُمَّةً وَٰحِدَةً ۖ وَلَا يَزَالُونَ مُخْتَلِفِينَ ﴿١١٨﴾ إِلَّا مَن
رَّحِمَ رَبُّكَ ۚ وَلِذَٰلِكَ خَلَقَهُمْ ۗ﴾

﴿*And had your Lord so willed, He would have made mankind one Umma (Community. But He has not done so by force. On the contrary, He has given free choice to all to adopt a religion.) And (now) these people will always hold divergent views, except for him on whom your Lord has bestowed His mercy, and that is what He has created them for.*﴾[31]

Prophet Yūsuf عليه السلام said,

﴿وَمَآ أُبَرِّئُ نَفْسِيٓ ۚ إِنَّ ٱلنَّفْسَ لَأَمَّارَةٌۢ بِٱلسُّوٓءِ إِلَّا مَا رَحِمَ رَبِّيٓ ۚ إِنَّ رَبِّي
غَفُورٌ رَّحِيمٌ﴾

﴿*And I do not (claim) absolution of my self. Certainly, the self commands much evil except the one on whom my Lord bestows mercy. Surely, my Lord is All-Forgiving, Ever-Merciful.*﴾[32]

Furthermore, all the people have a strong hope of Allah's mercy that they will be kept far from the torment on the Day of Resurrection. Allah سبحانه وتعالى said,

﴿قُلْ إِنِّيٓ أَخَافُ إِنْ عَصَيْتُ رَبِّي عَذَابَ يَوْمٍ عَظِيمٍ ﴿١٥﴾ مَّن يُصْرَفْ عَنْهُ
يَوْمَئِذٍ فَقَدْ رَحِمَهُۥ ۚ وَذَٰلِكَ ٱلْفَوْزُ ٱلْمُبِينُ﴾

﴿*Say: "Surely, I fear the Day of a mighty torment if I disobey my Lord. (So how is it possible?)" He from whom that (torment) is averted on that Day shall have been shown*

[31] Ibid., 11:118–119.

[32] Ibid., 12:53.

great mercy (by Allah). And it is this (deliverance on the Last Day) which is an evident success.﴾[33]

We notice that the places wherein mercy is mentioned are varied in their particulars, but they all share one thing in common: that the felicitous and triumphant person is the one who is wrapped in Allah's mercy, and that humans have no free disposal without the mercy of Allah ﷻ.

1.12 Taking Delight in Allah's Mercy

Allah ﷻ has sought from His blessed servants whom He has honored and graced with mercy to express delight in it. Allah informs that this is greater than the goods of the ephemeral world and all it contains. He said,

﴿قُلْ بِفَضْلِ ٱللَّهِ وَبِرَحْمَتِهِۦ فَبِذَٰلِكَ فَلْيَفْرَحُوا۟ هُوَ خَيْرٌ مِّمَّا يَجْمَعُونَ﴾

﴿*Say: "(All this) is due to the bounty and mercy of Allah (bestowed upon you through raising Muhammad [blessings and peace be upon him] as the exalted Messenger). So the Muslims should rejoice over it. This is far better than (all that affluence and wealth) that they amass."*﴾[34]

1.13 Those Whom Mercy Shall Encompass

The mercy of Allah ﷻ covers many types of Creation. It embraces the young as it does the old; it envelops the animal kingdom as it does humanity; and it encompasses the righteous in their myriad ranks and stations and every other creation, protecting them from mortal dangers. Now, considering that, it is difficult to delineate all of mercy's recipients. To approximate things, only a few categories from the various classes of believers have been mentioned.

1.14 The People who Possess Firm Faith

Allah said,

---

[33] Ibid., 6:15–16.

[34] Ibid., 10:58.

﴿يَـٰٓأَيُّهَا ٱلَّذِينَ ءَامَنُوا۟ ٱتَّقُوا۟ ٱللَّهَ وَءَامِنُوا۟ بِرَسُولِهِۦ يُؤْتِكُمْ كِفْلَيْنِ مِن رَّحْمَتِهِۦ وَيَجْعَل لَّكُمْ نُورًا تَمْشُونَ بِهِۦ وَيَغْفِرْ لَكُمْ ۚ وَٱللَّهُ غَفُورٌ رَّحِيمٌ﴾

﴾O believers! Become Godfearing and believe in His (Esteemed) Messenger (blessings and peace be upon him). He will bless you with two portions of His mercy and will bring about light for you to walk in (in the world and in the Hereafter) and will forgive you. And Allah is Most Forgiving, Ever-Merciful.﴿[35]

1.15 The People who Obey Allah ﷻ and His Noble Prophet ﷺ

Allah said,

﴿وَأَطِيعُوا۟ ٱللَّهَ وَٱلرَّسُولَ لَعَلَّكُمْ تُرْحَمُونَ﴾

﴾And persist in obedience to Allah and the Messenger (blessings and peace be upon him) so that you may be blessed with mercy.﴿[36]

1.16 The People who Follow the Qurʾān and Fear Allah ﷻ

Allah said,

﴿وَهَـٰذَا كِتَـٰبٌ أَنزَلْنَـٰهُ مُبَارَكٌ فَٱتَّبِعُوهُ وَٱتَّقُوا۟ لَعَلَّكُمْ تُرْحَمُونَ﴾

﴾And this (Qurʾān) is a Book which We have revealed full of blessings. So (now) follow it and fear (Allah) persistently so that you are shown mercy.﴿[37]

[35] Ibid., 57:28.

[36] Ibid., 3:132.

[37] Ibid., 6:155.

1.17 The People who are Committed to Spiritual Excellence

Allah said,

﴿إِنَّ رَحْمَتَ ٱللَّهِ قَرِيبٌ مِّنَ ٱلْمُحْسِنِينَ﴾

﴾Assuredly, Allah's mercy is near to those who are (spiritually excellent,) committed to doing pious works.﴿[38]

1.18 The Believers Who Hold Fast to Allah ﷻ

Allah said,

﴿فَأَمَّا ٱلَّذِينَ ءَامَنُواْ بِٱللَّهِ وَٱعْتَصَمُواْ بِهِۦ فَسَيُدْخِلُهُمْ فِى رَحْمَةٍ مِّنْهُ
وَفَضْلٍ وَيَهْدِيهِمْ إِلَيْهِ صِرَٰطًا مُّسْتَقِيمًا﴾

﴾So, those who believe in Allah and hold fast to His (embrace, Allah) will soon admit them to His (exceptional) mercy and grace and will show them the straight path to (reach) Him.﴿[39]

1.19 The People Who Consider What They Spend will Draw Them Near to Allah and Who Seek the Supplication of Allah's Messenger ﷺ

Allah said,

﴿وَمِنَ ٱلْأَعْرَابِ مَن يُؤْمِنُ بِٱللَّهِ وَٱلْيَوْمِ ٱلْءَاخِرِ وَيَتَّخِذُ مَا يُنفِقُ قُرُبَٰتٍ
عِندَ ٱللَّهِ وَصَلَوَٰتِ ٱلرَّسُولِ ۚ أَلَآ إِنَّهَا قُرْبَةٌ لَّهُمْ ۚ سَيُدْخِلُهُمُ ٱللَّهُ فِى رَحْمَتِهِۦٓ ۗ
إِنَّ ٱللَّهَ غَفُورٌ رَّحِيمٌ﴾

﴾And (yet) amongst these nomads there is (also) one who believes in Allah and the Last Day and considers whatever he spends (in the way of Allah) as a means of nearness to Allah and receiving (the merciful) supplications of the Messenger.

---

[38] Ibid., 7:56.

[39] Ibid., 4:175.

Listen! Assuredly, it is a source of nearness to Allah. Allah will soon admit them to His mercy. Surely, Allah is Most Forgiving, Ever-Merciful.﴿[40]

1.20 The People Who Pray, Pay Zakat and Obey Allah's Messenger ﷺ

Allah said,

﴿وَأَقِيمُوا۟ ٱلصَّلَوٰةَ وَءَاتُوا۟ ٱلزَّكَوٰةَ وَأَطِيعُوا۟ ٱلرَّسُولَ لَعَلَّكُمْ تُرْحَمُونَ﴾

﴾*And establish (the system of) prayers and (ensure) the payment of Zakat (the Alms-due) and accomplish (absolute) obedience to the Messenger (blessings and peace be upon him) so that you may be granted mercy (i.e., the blessings of sovereign rule, stability, peace and security may endure and continue).*﴿[41]

1.21 The People Who Exercise Piety for Fear of Torment

Allah said,

﴿وَإِذَا قِيلَ لَهُمُ ٱتَّقُوا۟ مَا بَيْنَ أَيْدِيكُمْ وَمَا خَلْفَكُمْ لَعَلَّكُمْ تُرْحَمُونَ﴾

﴾*And (recall) when it is said to them: "Fear that (torment) which is before you and which is behind you so that you may be shown mercy."*﴿[42]

1.22 The Believers Who Do Righteous Works

Allah said,

﴿فَأَمَّا ٱلَّذِينَ ءَامَنُوا۟ وَعَمِلُوا۟ ٱلصَّٰلِحَٰتِ فَيُدْخِلُهُمْ رَبُّهُمْ فِى رَحْمَتِهِۦ ۚ ذَٰلِكَ
هُوَ ٱلْفَوْزُ ٱلْمُبِينُ﴾

---

40 Ibid., 9:99.

41 Ibid., 24:56.

42 Ibid., 36:45.

﴾So those who believe and do good deeds, their Lord will admit them to His mercy. That is nothing but an evident success.﴿[43]

1.23 The People Who Listen to the Qur'ān with Extreme Respect

Allah said,

﴿وَإِذَا قُرِئَ ٱلْقُرْءَانُ فَٱسْتَمِعُوا۟ لَهُۥ وَأَنصِتُوا۟ لَعَلَّكُمْ تُرْحَمُونَ﴾

﴾And when the Qur'ān is recited, listen to it attentively, and observe silence so that mercy may be bestowed upon you.﴿[44]

1.24 The People Who Seek Allah's Forgiveness

Allah said,

﴿لَوْلَا تَسْتَغْفِرُونَ ٱللَّهَ لَعَلَّكُمْ تُرْحَمُونَ﴾

﴾Why do you not ask for forgiveness from Allah so that you are shown mercy?﴿[45]

1.25 The Believers Who Migrate and Strive Hard in the Cause of Allah

Allah said,

﴿ٱلَّذِينَ ءَامَنُوا۟ وَهَاجَرُوا۟ وَجَٰهَدُوا۟ فِى سَبِيلِ ٱللَّهِ بِأَمْوَٰلِهِمْ وَأَنفُسِهِمْ أَعْظَمُ
دَرَجَةً عِندَ ٱللَّهِ ۚ وَأُو۟لَٰٓئِكَ هُمُ ٱلْفَآئِزُونَ ﴿٢٠﴾ يُبَشِّرُهُمْ رَبُّهُم بِرَحْمَةٍ مِّنْهُ
وَرِضْوَٰنٍ وَجَنَّٰتٍ لَّهُمْ فِيهَا نَعِيمٌ مُّقِيمٌ﴾

﴾Those who have believed and have emigrated and have consistently toiled hard in the cause of Allah with their material and human resources enjoy a very high rank in

[43] Ibid., 45:30.

[44] Ibid., 7:204.

[45] Ibid., 27:46.

the presence of Allah, and it is they who have achieved the ultimate goal. Their Lord gives them glad tidings of mercy from Him and of (His) pleasure and of (those) Gardens for them in which there are eternal delights.﴾[46]

1.26 The People Who are Martyred in the Path of Allah

Allah said,

﴿وَلَئِن قُتِلْتُمْ فِي سَبِيلِ ٱللَّهِ أَوْ مُتُّمْ لَمَغْفِرَةٌ مِّنَ ٱللَّهِ وَرَحْمَةٌ خَيْرٌ مِّمَّا يَجْمَعُونَ﴾

﴿*And if you are slain in the cause of Allah or die, Allah's forgiveness and mercy is far better than that (wealth) which you accumulate.*﴾[47]

1.27 The People Who Are Well Endowed with Knowledge

Allah said,

﴿وَٱلرَّٰسِخُونَ فِي ٱلْعِلْمِ يَقُولُونَ ءَامَنَّا بِهِۦ كُلٌّ مِّنْ عِندِ رَبِّنَا ۗ وَمَا يَذَّكَّرُ إِلَّآ أُوْلُواْ ٱلْأَلْبَٰبِ ۝٧ رَبَّنَا لَا تُزِغْ قُلُوبَنَا بَعْدَ إِذْ هَدَيْتَنَا وَهَبْ لَنَا مِن لَّدُنكَ رَحْمَةً ۚ إِنَّكَ أَنتَ ٱلْوَهَّابُ﴾

﴿*And those who are perfectly firm in knowledge say: "We believe in it. The whole (Book) has been revealed by our Lord." And direction and guidance is the share of only those who possess wisdom and insight. (And they submit:) "O our Lord, let not our hearts deviate after You have honoured us with guidance, and grant us mercy especially from Your presence. Truly, You alone are the Great Bestower."*﴾[48]

---

[46] Ibid., 9:20–21.

[47] Ibid., 3:157.

[48] Ibid., 3:7–8.

1.28 The People Who Bring Peace between the Brothers

Allah said,

﴿إِنَّمَا ٱلْمُؤْمِنُونَ إِخْوَةٌ فَأَصْلِحُوا۟ بَيْنَ أَخَوَيْكُمْ ۚ وَٱتَّقُوا۟ ٱللَّهَ لَعَلَّكُمْ
تُرْحَمُونَ﴾

﴿The truth is that (all) believers are brothers (to one another). So make peace between your two brothers and always fear Allah, so that you may be shown mercy.﴾[49]

1.29 The People Who are Patient During Afflictions

Allah said,

﴿ٱلَّذِينَ إِذَآ أَصَٰبَتْهُم مُّصِيبَةٌ قَالُوٓا۟ إِنَّا لِلَّهِ وَإِنَّآ إِلَيْهِ رَٰجِعُونَ ﴿١٥٦﴾ أُو۟لَٰٓئِكَ
عَلَيْهِمْ صَلَوَٰتٌ مِّن رَّبِّهِمْ وَرَحْمَةٌ ۖ وَأُو۟لَٰٓئِكَ هُمُ ٱلْمُهْتَدُونَ﴾

﴿(They are the ones) who, when afflicted with some distress, say: "Indeed, to Allah we belong and to Him we shall return." It is they upon whom are bestowed successive blessings and mercy from their Lord. And it is they who are the guided ones.﴾[50]

1.30 The People Whose Faces would be Brightened because of Good Deeds

Allah said,

﴿وَأَمَّا ٱلَّذِينَ ٱبْيَضَّتْ وُجُوهُهُمْ فَفِى رَحْمَةِ ٱللَّهِ ۖ هُمْ فِيهَا خَٰلِدُونَ﴾

﴿But those with (glittering) white faces will be in Allah's mercy. Therein will they live forever.﴾[51]

---

[49] Ibid., 49:10.

[50] Ibid., 2:156–157.

[51] Ibid., 3:107.

1.31 The Believers Who Practise Good Moral and Spiritual Values

Allah said,

﴿وَٱلْمُؤْمِنُونَ وَٱلْمُؤْمِنَٰتُ بَعْضُهُمْ أَوْلِيَآءُ بَعْضٍ ۚ يَأْمُرُونَ بِٱلْمَعْرُوفِ وَيَنْهَوْنَ عَنِ ٱلْمُنكَرِ وَيُقِيمُونَ ٱلصَّلَوٰةَ وَيُؤْتُونَ ٱلزَّكَوٰةَ وَيُطِيعُونَ ٱللَّهَ وَرَسُولَهُۥٓ ۚ أُو۟لَٰٓئِكَ سَيَرْحَمُهُمُ ٱللَّهُ ۗ إِنَّ ٱللَّهَ عَزِيزٌ حَكِيمٌ﴾

﴾*The believers, men and women, are helpers and friends to one another. They command good and forbid evil and establish Prayer and pay Zakat (the Alms-due) and obey Allah and His Messenger (blessings and peace be upon him). It is they on whom Allah will soon shower His Mercy. Surely, Allah is Almighty, Most Wise.*﴿[52]

1.32 What Brings Mercy to Fruition?

There are many things that bring Allah's mercy such as obedience to Allah ﷻ and His noble Messenger ﷺ, Godfearingness, heeding the divine warning and acting accordingly, establishing the prayer and paying the Zakat, frequently remembering Allah ﷻ, seeking Allah's forgiveness, reciting the Qur'ān and listening to it, making peace between two parties, and so on. A few are mentioned here.

Allah ﷻ said,

﴿وَأَطِيعُوا۟ ٱللَّهَ وَٱلرَّسُولَ لَعَلَّكُمْ تُرْحَمُونَ﴾

﴾*And persist in obedience to Allah and the Messenger (ﷺ) so that you may be blessed with mercy.*﴿[53]

He also said,

﴿أَوَعَجِبْتُمْ أَن جَآءَكُمْ ذِكْرٌ مِّن رَّبِّكُمْ عَلَىٰ رَجُلٍ مِّنكُمْ لِيُنذِرَكُمْ وَلِتَتَّقُوا۟ وَلَعَلَّكُمْ تُرْحَمُونَ﴾

---

[52] Ibid., 9:71.

[53] Ibid., 3:132.

﴾*Do you wonder that direction and guidance from your Lord has come (on the tongue) of a man from amongst yourselves so that he may warn you (of the chastisement of Allah), and that you become Godfearing, and the purpose is that mercy may be shown to you?*﴿[54]

He also said,

﴿وَأَقِيمُوا۟ ٱلصَّلَوٰةَ وَءَاتُوا۟ ٱلزَّكَوٰةَ وَأَطِيعُوا۟ ٱلرَّسُولَ لَعَلَّكُمْ تُرْحَمُونَ﴾

﴾*And establish (the system of) prayers and (ensure) the payment of Zakat (the Alms-due) and accomplish (absolute) obedience to the Messenger (blessings and peace be upon him) so that you may be granted mercy (i.e., the blessings of sovereign rule, stability, peace and security may endure and continue).*﴿[55]

He also said,

﴿قَالَ يَٰقَوْمِ لِمَ تَسْتَعْجِلُونَ بِٱلسَّيِّئَةِ قَبْلَ ٱلْحَسَنَةِ ۖ لَوْلَا تَسْتَغْفِرُونَ ٱللَّهَ
لَعَلَّكُمْ تُرْحَمُونَ﴾

﴾*(Ṣāliḥ) said: "O my people, why do you hasten the evil (i.e., torment) before the good (i.e., mercy)? Why do you not ask for forgiveness from Allah so that you are shown mercy?"*﴿[56]

He also said,

﴿وَإِذَا قِيلَ لَهُمُ ٱتَّقُوا۟ مَا بَيْنَ أَيْدِيكُمْ وَمَا خَلْفَكُمْ لَعَلَّكُمْ تُرْحَمُونَ﴾

﴾*And (recall) when it is said to them: "Fear that (torment) which is before you and which is behind you so that you may be shown mercy."*﴿[57]

---

54 Ibid., 7:63.

55 Ibid., 24:56.

56 Ibid., 27:46.

57 Ibid., 36:45.

He also said,

﴿إِنَّمَا ٱلْمُؤْمِنُونَ إِخْوَةٌ فَأَصْلِحُوا۟ بَيْنَ أَخَوَيْكُمْ ۚ وَٱتَّقُوا۟ ٱللَّهَ لَعَلَّكُمْ تُرْحَمُونَ﴾

﴿The truth is that (all) believers are brothers (to one another). So make peace between your two brothers and always fear Allah, so that you may be shown mercy.﴾[58]

1.33 The Loser is the One Who Does Not Gain Allah's Mercy

Since mercy is from Allah ﷻ and He is the Most Compassionate, Ever-Merciful Whose mercy encompasses everything, it follows that the real loser is the one who is not enveloped in this mercy due to him not deserving it. Allah mentioned the supplication of Ādam and Ḥawwā ﵉,

﴿قَالَا رَبَّنَا ظَلَمْنَآ أَنفُسَنَا وَإِن لَّمْ تَغْفِرْ لَنَا وَتَرْحَمْنَا لَنَكُونَنَّ مِنَ ٱلْخَٰسِرِينَ﴾

﴿Both of them submitted: "O our Lord! We have wronged our souls. And if You do not forgive us and have mercy on us, we shall certainly be amongst the losers."﴾[59]

Allah also mentioned the prayer of Prophet Nūḥ ﵇,

﴿قَالَ رَبِّ إِنِّىٓ أَعُوذُ بِكَ أَنْ أَسْـَٔلَكَ مَا لَيْسَ لِى بِهِۦ عِلْمٌ ۖ وَإِلَّا تَغْفِرْ لِى وَتَرْحَمْنِىٓ أَكُن مِّنَ ٱلْخَٰسِرِينَ﴾

﴿Nūḥ (Noah) submitted: "O my Lord, I seek refuge with You from asking You that of which I have no knowledge. And if You forgive me not and bestow (not) mercy on me,

---

[58] Ibid., 49:10.

[59] Ibid., 7:23.

(then) I shall be of the losers."﴿[60]

Allah ﷻ also said,

﴿فَلَوْلَا فَضْلُ ٱللَّهِ عَلَيْكُمْ وَرَحْمَتُهُۥ لَكُنتُم مِّنَ ٱلْخَـٰسِرِينَ﴾

﴾*So, had there not been Allah's bounty and His mercy upon you, you would have been wrecked indeed.*﴿[61]

Allah addressed those who were participants in the slander of Sayyida ʿĀʾisha (رضي الله عنها),

﴿وَلَوْلَا فَضْلُ ٱللَّهِ عَلَيْكُمْ وَرَحْمَتُهُۥ فِى ٱلدُّنْيَا وَٱلْـَٔاخِرَةِ لَمَسَّكُمْ فِى مَآ أَفَضْتُمْ فِيهِ عَذَابٌ عَظِيمٌ﴾

﴾*And had there not been Allah's grace upon you and His mercy in this world and in the Hereafter, severe torment would have afflicted you for promoting that (slander) into which you rushed headlong.*﴿[62]

1.34 Allah's Mercy is the Source of Salvation

Allah's mercy is the Creation's source of mercy, so whoever is averted from the divine punishment—whatever form it takes—and honoured, he is the truly fortunate person. And the one from whom it is not averted has failed and lost. The Qurʾān has revealed,

﴿إِنَّ ٱلنَّفْسَ لَأَمَّارَةٌۢ بِٱلسُّوٓءِ إِلَّا مَا رَحِمَ رَبِّىٓ ۚ إِنَّ رَبِّى غَفُورٌ رَّحِيمٌ﴾

﴾*And I do not (claim) absolution of my self. Certainly, the self commands much evil except the one on whom my Lord bestows mercy. Surely, my Lord is All-Forgiving, Ever-Merciful.*﴿[63]

He also said,

---

[60] Ibid., 11:47.

[61] Ibid., 2:64.

[62] Ibid., 24:14.

[63] Ibid., 12:53.

﴿مَن يُصْرَفْ عَنْهُ يَوْمَئِذٍ فَقَدْ رَحِمَهُ﴾

﴿He from whom that (torment) is averted on that Day shall have been shown great mercy (by Allah).﴾[64]

Allah mentioned the statement of Prophet Nūḥ ﷺ,

﴿قَالَ سَآوِي إِلَىٰ جَبَلٍ يَعْصِمُنِي مِنَ ٱلْمَآءِ ۚ قَالَ لَا عَاصِمَ ٱلْيَوْمَ مِنْ أَمْرِ ٱللَّهِ إِلَّا مَن رَّحِمَ﴾

﴿He (Nūḥ's son) said: "(Instead of embarking on the Ark) I shall just now take shelter on some mountain. That will save me from the Deluge." Nūḥ (Noah) said: "None can save today from Allah's punishment except someone to whom He (Allah) shows His mercy."﴾[65]

Allah also said,

﴿وَلَوْ شَآءَ رَبُّكَ لَجَعَلَ ٱلنَّاسَ أُمَّةً وَٰحِدَةً ۖ وَلَا يَزَالُونَ مُخْتَلِفِينَ ﴿١١٨﴾ إِلَّا مَن رَّحِمَ رَبُّكَ﴾

﴿And had your Lord so willed, He would have made mankind one Umma (Community. But He has not done so by force. On the contrary, He has given free choice to all to adopt a religion.) And (now) these people will always hold divergent views, except for him on whom your Lord has bestowed His mercy.﴾[66]

Allah mentioned that the angels say when supplicating for the believers,

﴿وَقِهِمُ ٱلسَّيِّـَٔاتِ ۚ وَمَن تَقِ ٱلسَّيِّـَٔاتِ يَوْمَئِذٍ فَقَدْ رَحِمْتَهُۥ ۚ وَذَٰلِكَ هُوَ ٱلْفَوْزُ ٱلْعَظِيمُ﴾

---

[64] Ibid., 6:16.

[65] Ibid., 11:43.

[66] Ibid., 11:118–119.

﴿And save them from (the punishment of) sins. And the one You have saved from (the punishment of) sins that Day, You have indeed shown him great mercy. And that is great success indeed.﴾[67]

1.35 The Believers' Prayer for Mercy

No created being can stand without need of Allah's mercy. The entire Creation stands in need of it, whether it explicitly states that or not. This is why there are many supplications from the Prophets and Messengers, as well as the righteous people after them, supplicating Allah ﷻ for mercy.

Allah ﷻ mentioned that Prophet Mūsā عليه السلام said,

﴿تُضِلُّ بِهَا مَن تَشَآءُ وَتَهۡدِي مَن تَشَآءُۖ أَنتَ وَلِيُّنَا فَٱغۡفِرۡ لَنَا وَٱرۡحَمۡنَاۖ وَأَنتَ خَيۡرُ ٱلۡغَٰفِرِينَ﴾

﴿(This is just a trial from You) by which You hold astray whom You will and guide whom You desire. You alone are our Guardian, so forgive us and have mercy on us. And You are the Best of those who forgive.﴾[68]

Allah also mentioned that the believers pray,

﴿وَٱعۡفُ عَنَّا وَٱغۡفِرۡ لَنَا وَٱرۡحَمۡنَآۚ أَنتَ مَوۡلَىٰنَا فَٱنصُرۡنَا عَلَى ٱلۡقَوۡمِ ٱلۡكَٰفِرِينَ﴾

﴿And overlook (our sins), and forgive us and have mercy on us. You alone are our Master and Helper. So grant us victory over the disbelievers.﴾[69]

Allah said, addressing the pious child who treats his parents well,

﴿وَٱخۡفِضۡ لَهُمَا جَنَاحَ ٱلذُّلِّ مِنَ ٱلرَّحۡمَةِ وَقُل رَّبِّ ٱرۡحَمۡهُمَا كَمَا رَبَّيَانِي

---

67 Ibid., 40:9.

68 Ibid., 7:155.

69 Ibid., 2:286.

﴿صَغِيرًا﴾

﴾And always lower your wings of submissiveness and humility out of soft-heartedness for both of them, and keep supplicating (Allah): "O my Lord, have mercy on both of them as they brought me up in (my) childhood (with mercy and clemency)."﴿[70]

And Allah said, addressing His noble Prophet ﷺ,

﴿وَقُل رَّبِّ ٱغْفِرْ وَٱرْحَمْ وَأَنتَ خَيْرُ ٱلرَّٰحِمِينَ﴾

﴾And submit: "O my Lord, forgive and have mercy, and You (alone) are the Best of those who have mercy."﴿[71]

This verse, although addressing the Prophet ﷺ, is an instruction for all the believers.

1.36 Who Despairs and Loses Hope of Allah's Mercy?

Since Allah's mercy encompasses everything, and He is the Most Compassionate, Ever-Merciful, no one despairs of it or loses hope save the disbelievers. Allah ﷻ mentioned that Prophet Ibrāhīm ﷺ said,

﴿قَالَ وَمَن يَقْنَطُ مِن رَّحْمَةِ رَبِّهِۦٓ إِلَّا ٱلضَّآلُّونَ﴾

﴾Ibrāhīm (Abraham) said: "Who can lose hope of his Lord's mercy except the strayed ones?"﴿[72]

Allah ﷻ also said,

﴿وَٱلَّذِينَ كَفَرُوا۟ بِـَٔايَٰتِ ٱللَّهِ وَلِقَآئِهِۦٓ أُو۟لَٰٓئِكَ يَئِسُوا۟ مِن رَّحْمَتِى وَأُو۟لَٰٓئِكَ لَهُمْ عَذَابٌ أَلِيمٌ﴾

[70] Ibid., 17:24.

[71] Ibid., 23:118.

[72] Ibid., 15:56.

﴾*And those who reject Allah's Revelations and deny meeting with Him, they despair of My mercy. And it is they for whom there is painful punishment.*﴿[73]

Furthermore, Allah ﷻ instructed His servants—righteous or otherwise—never to despair of His mercy. He said,

﴿قُلْ يَٰعِبَادِىَ ٱلَّذِينَ أَسْرَفُوا۟ عَلَىٰٓ أَنفُسِهِمْ لَا تَقْنَطُوا۟ مِن رَّحْمَةِ ٱللَّهِ ۚ إِنَّ ٱللَّهَ يَغْفِرُ ٱلذُّنُوبَ جَمِيعًا ۚ إِنَّهُۥ هُوَ ٱلْغَفُورُ ٱلرَّحِيمُ﴾

﴾*Say: "O servants of Mine who have wronged their souls, do not lose hope of Allah's mercy. Assuredly, Allah forgives all sins (and excesses). He is certainly Most Forgiving, Ever-Merciful."*﴿[74]

1.37 The Disbeliever Does Not Merit Allah's Mercy

Humankind has agreed to bear the trust and has taken the solemn covenant and witnessed in the presence of their Lord Most High that they will be believers. And Allah ﷻ has erected proofs for His existence and unicity, and sent Messengers to remind humanity of the covenant, the trust and faith, so that no one may have any argument. For this reason, whoever disbelieves is undeserving of mercy because he has cast his own self into destruction after the establishment of evidence.

Allah ﷻ said,

﴿وَإِنَّ ٱلَّذِينَ لَا يُؤْمِنُونَ بِٱلْءَاخِرَةِ عَنِ ٱلصِّرَٰطِ لَنَٰكِبُونَ ﴿٧٤﴾ وَلَوْ رَحِمْنَٰهُمْ وَكَشَفْنَا مَا بِهِم مِّن ضُرٍّ لَّلَجُّوا۟ فِى طُغْيَٰنِهِمْ يَعْمَهُونَ﴾

﴾*And surely, those who do not believe in the Hereafter remain deviated from the (straight) path. And if We have mercy on them and remove the distress that has (afflicted) them, they will become hardened in their transgression,*

---

[73] Ibid., 29:23.

[74] Ibid., 39:53.

wandering disorientated.﴾[75]

And Allah said,

﴿وَإِذَآ أَذَقۡنَا ٱلنَّاسَ رَحۡمَةٗ مِّنۢ بَعۡدِ ضَرَّآءَ مَسَّتۡهُمۡ إِذَا لَهُم مَّكۡرٞ فِيٓ ءَايَاتِنَاۚ
قُلِ ٱللَّهُ أَسۡرَعُ مَكۡرًاۚ﴾

﴿*And when We make the people relish (Our) mercy after they are afflicted with distress, their plotting immediately begins against Our signs (consigning Our favour to oblivion). Say: "Allah is Swift to punish intrigues."*﴾[76]

1.38 Various Manifestations of Allah's Vast Mercy

There are numerous manifestations of Allah's vast mercy. There are so many, in fact, that we are unable to enumerate. However, let us cite ten manifestations to infer the rest.

1.38.1 Allah Conditioned the Punishment and Torment with the Sending of Messengers

Allah ﷻ said,

﴿وَمَا كُنَّا مُعَذِّبِينَ حَتَّىٰ نَبۡعَثَ رَسُولٗا﴾

﴿*And We do not torment (any people) at all until We send a Messenger (to them).*﴾[77]

And He said,

﴿وَمَا كَانَ رَبُّكَ مُهۡلِكَ ٱلۡقُرَىٰ حَتَّىٰ يَبۡعَثَ فِيٓ أُمِّهَا رَسُولٗا﴾

﴿*And your Lord does not destroy the towns until He sends to their capital city a Messenger.*﴾[78]

---

[75] Ibid., 23:74–75.

[76] Ibid., 10:21.

[77] Ibid., 17:15.

[78] Ibid., 28:59.

1.39 Allah Has Not Burdened a Soul with More Than it can Bear, and He Has Pardoned Them for What They are Unable to Do

Allah ﷻ said,

﴿لَا نُكَلِّفُ نَفْسًا إِلَّا وُسْعَهَا﴾

﴾*We do not burden any soul beyond its ability to bear it.*﴿[79]

There are many legal rulings in the Holy Qur'ān and Prophetic Sunna that indicate this lightening of burden; however, a few are mentioned here to elaborate the concept.

Dry ablution [*tayammum*] is one example. It is performed when water is absent or difficult to use. There is also the allowance to shorten the prescribed prayers during a journey, the dispensation to pray while sitting for one who is unable to stand, the dropping of the obligation to pray for women during menstruation, as well as the allowance to break the fast during travel and sickness and the obligation to perform the Hajj provided one is capable, and, in general, the lifting of constraint from the blind, the cripple and the ill.

Allah ﷻ said,

﴿لَّيْسَ عَلَى ٱلْأَعْمَىٰ حَرَجٌ وَلَا عَلَى ٱلْأَعْرَجِ حَرَجٌ وَلَا عَلَى ٱلْمَرِيضِ حَرَجٌ﴾

﴾*There is no restriction on the blind, nor any blame on the lame, nor is there any sin on the sick.*﴿[80]

In addition, Allah has lifted constraint generally from the one who is obliged. Allah ﷻ said,

﴿فَمَنِ ٱضْطُرَّ غَيْرَ بَاغٍ وَلَا عَادٍ فَلَآ إِثْمَ عَلَيْهِ﴾

﴾*But he who is forced by necessity and is neither disobedient nor transgressing will not incur any sin on himself (if he eats*

---

[79] Ibid., 6:152.

[80] Ibid., 24:61.

that much which is required to survive).﴾[81]

Allah ﷻ declared that this entire religion is free of constraint, burden and constriction:

﴿مَا يُرِيدُ ٱللَّهُ لِيَجْعَلَ عَلَيْكُم مِّنْ حَرَجٍ﴾

﴾*Allah does not want to make things hard for you.*﴿[82]

Another manifestation of Allah's mercy is that He does not hold the *Umma* to account for what they think inside of themselves, and He does not take them to task for innocent mistakes and forgetfulness and what they are coerced to do. In addition, He does not take a sleeping person, a young child or an insane person to account. All of this is established in the Sunna.

Another manifestation of Allah's mercy is that He forgives all sins with the exception of disbelief and associating partners with Him. Allah said,

﴿قُلْ يَٰعِبَادِىَ ٱلَّذِينَ أَسْرَفُوا۟ عَلَىٰٓ أَنفُسِهِمْ لَا تَقْنَطُوا۟ مِن رَّحْمَةِ ٱللَّهِ ۚ إِنَّ
ٱللَّهَ يَغْفِرُ ٱلذُّنُوبَ جَمِيعًا ۚ إِنَّهُۥ هُوَ ٱلْغَفُورُ ٱلرَّحِيمُ ﴿٥٣﴾﴾

﴾*Say: "O servants of Mine who have wronged their souls, do not lose hope of Allah's mercy. Assuredly, Allah forgives all sins (and excesses). He is certainly Most Forgiving, Ever-Merciful."*﴿[83]

Allah also said,

﴿إِنَّ ٱللَّهَ لَا يَغْفِرُ أَن يُشْرَكَ بِهِۦ وَيَغْفِرُ مَا دُونَ ذَٰلِكَ لِمَن يَشَآءُ ۚ وَمَن
يُشْرِكْ بِٱللَّهِ فَقَدِ ٱفْتَرَىٰٓ إِثْمًا عَظِيمًا﴾

﴾*Surely, Allah does not forgive setting up of partners with Him, and He forgives (any other sin) lesser in degree for*

81 Ibid., 2:173.

82 Ibid., 5:6.

83 Ibid., 39:53.

> *whom He wills. And whoever sets up partners with Allah certainly fabricates a horrible sin.*﴾[84]

1.40 ALLAH FORGIVES WHO REPENTS OF HIS ERROR

One of the elements of this is that Allah accepts the repentance of the penitent unless his sin is polytheism. It also indicates that the door to repentance shall remain open until the sun rises from the west. This also indicates that Allah will grant His servant reprieve in order that he repents of his error.

According to ʿAbd Allāh b. ʿUmar ﷺ, Allah's Messenger ﷺ said,

إِنَّ اللهَ يَقْبَلُ تَوْبَةَ الْعَبْدِ مَا لَمْ يُغَرْغِرْ.

> Indeed, Allah accepts the repentance of the servant so long as he is not in the gargling throes of death.[85]
>
> Reported by Aḥmad, al-Tirmidhī (who declared it fine), as well as Ibn Mājah (who declared it authentic), Ibn Ḥibbān and al-Ḥākim.

According to Abū Hurayra ﷺ, Allah's Messenger ﷺ said,

مَنْ تَابَ قَبْلَ أَنْ تَطْلُعَ الشَّمْسُ مِنْ مَغْرِبِهَا، تَابَ اللهُ عَلَيْهِ.

> Whoever repents before the sun rises from the west, Allah will turn to him in mercy.[86]
>
> Reported by Muslim.

Moreover, Allah ﷻ gives reprieve to the wrongdoer so that he turns to Allah in repentance. This is why Allah ordains the angels to

---

[84] Ibid., 4:48.

[85] Set forth by •Aḥmad in *al-Musnad*, 2:132; 3:425; •al-Tirmidhī in *al-Sunan:* Bk.: *al-Daʿawāt* [The Supplications], Ch.: "On the Virtue of Repentance and Seeking Forgiveness," 5:547 §3537; •Ibn Mājah in *al-Sunan:* Bk.: *al-Zuhd* [The Renunciation], Ch.: "Mention of Repentance," 2:1420 §4253; •al-Ḥākim in *al-Mustadrak*, 4:286 §§7659, 7661; •Ibn Ḥibbān in his *Ṣaḥīḥ* collection, 2:394–395 §628; •Ibn al-Jaʿd in *al-Musnad*, p. 489 §3404.

[86] Set forth by •Muslim in *al-Ṣaḥīḥ:* Bk.: *al-dhikr wa al-duʿā* [The Remembrance and Supplication], Ch.: "The Recommendation to Seek Forgiveness," 4:2076 §2703; •Aḥmad in *al-Musnad*, 2:395, 427, 495, 506.

delay their transcription of the names of the wrongdoers so that they may repent. This is not the case when it comes to good deeds. Allah also extends His Hand during the day for the wrongdoer of night to repent, and He extends His Hand by night for the wrongdoer of day to repent. Abū Mūsā al-Ashʿarī ☙ reported that the Prophet ☙ said,

إِنَّ اللهَ ﷻ يَبْسُطُ يَدَهُ بِاللَّيْلِ لِيَتُوبَ مُسِيءُ النَّهَارِ، وَيَبْسُطُ يَدَهُ بِالنَّهَارِ لِيَتُوبَ مُسِيءُ اللَّيْلِ، حَتَّى تَطْلُعَ الشَّمْسُ مِنْ مَغْرِبِهَا.

Indeed, Allah ﷻ outstretches His Hand during the night in order that the wrongdoer of day turns to Him in repentance, and He outstretches His Hand during the day in order that the wrongdoer of night turns to Him in repentance—and this will continue until the sun rises from the west.[87]

Reported by Muslim.

There are many Qur'ānic verses and hadith reports that speak about the encouragement and acceptance of repentance.

Another manifestation of Allah's mercy is that He informed us that His mercy precedes His wrath—so the beginning is with mercy. Abū Hurayra ☙ reported that the Prophet ☙ said,

إِنَّ اللهَ لَمَّا قَضَى الْخَلْقَ كَتَبَ عِنْدَهُ فَوْقَ عَرْشِهِ: إِنَّ رَحْمَتِي سَبَقَتْ غَضَبِي.

When Allah created the Creation, He wrote with Him over the Throne: 'My mercy precedes My wrath.'[88]

Agreed upon.

---

[87] Set forth by •Muslim in al-Ṣaḥīḥ: Bk.: al-dhikr wa al-duʿā [The Remembrance and Supplication], Ch.: "The Recommendation to Seek Forgiveness," 4:2113 §2759; •Aḥmad in al-Musnad, 4:395.

[88] Set forth by •al-Bukhārī in al-Ṣaḥīḥ: Bk.: al-Tawḥīd [Divine Unity], Ch.: "[And His Throne Was on Water, and He is the Lord of the Mighty Throne]," 6:2700 §6986; •Muslim in al-Ṣaḥīḥ: Bk.: al-Tawba [Repentance], Ch.: "The Vastness of Allah's Mercy and That His Mercy Precedes His Wrath," §2751; •al-Nasāʾī in al-Sunan al-kubrā, 4:418 §7757.

And since Allah ﷻ made His Prophet a Seal with mercy, not punishment, this means that the beginning and the end of existence are with mercy.

1.41 How are Good and Bad Deeds Dealt with?

Another manifestation of Allah's mercy for His servants is His pity and kindness toward them, His call for them to turn themselves wholly to Him, and His encouragement for them to repent and seek His nearness. This should not be surprising, since of Allah's names is al-Raʾūf (the One Who Shows Pity); this name appears eleven times in the Holy Book of Allah. There are numerous hadith reports that explain the extent of Allah's mercy to His servants and show how He is swifter in turning to His servant with mercy than the servant is in turning to Him in repentance. There are hadith reports that show how Allah is more delighted with the servant's repentance than a rider who loses his riding animal with his belongings and despairs of finding it, only to discover it after losing hope.

Abū Hurayra رضي الله عنه reported that Allah's Messenger ﷺ said,

> يَقُولُ اللهُ تَعَالَى: أَنَا عِنْدَ ظَنِّ عَبْدِي بِي وَأَنَا مَعَهُ إِذَا ذَكَرَنِي. فَإِنْ ذَكَرَنِي فِي نَفْسِهِ ذَكَرْتُهُ فِي نَفْسِي، وَإِنْ ذَكَرَنِي فِي مَلَاءٍ ذَكَرْتُهُ فِي مَلَاءٍ خَيْرٍ مِنْهُمْ. وَإِنْ تَقَرَّبَ إِلَيَّ بِشِبْرٍ تَقَرَّبْتُ إِلَيْهِ ذِرَاعًا. وَإِنْ تَقَرَّبَ إِلَيَّ ذِرَاعًا تَقَرَّبْتُ إِلَيْهِ بَاعًا. وَإِنْ أَتَانِي يَمْشِي، أَتَيْتُهُ هَرْوَلَةً.

> Allah ﷻ says, 'I am as My servant thinks of Me, and I am with him when he mentions Me. If he mentions Me in himself, I mention him in Myself, and if he mentions Me in a gathering, I mention him in a gathering better than his. If he seeks to draw near to Me by a hand span, I will draw near to him an arm's length. If he seeks to draw near to Me by an arm's length, I will draw near to him a fathom. And if he comes to Me walking, I will come to him jogging.'[89]

---

[89] Set forth by •al-Bukhārī in *al-Ṣaḥīḥ:* Bk.: *al-Tawḥīd* [The Affirmation of Oneness], Ch.: Allah's ﷻ saying: ﴾And Allah warns you to beware of Himself

Agreed upon.

In another narration of Muslim from Abū Dharr ﷺ:

وَمَنْ لَقِيَنِي بِقُرَابِ الْأَرْضِ خَطِيئَةً لَا يُشْرِكُ بِي شَيْئًا، لَقِيتُهُ بِمِثْلِهَا مَغْفِرَةً.

And whoever brings to Me an earth full of sins, but has not associated anything with Me, I will bring him an equal amount of forgiveness.

ʿAbd Allāh b. Masʿūd ﷺ said,

سَمِعْتُ رَسُوْلَ اللهِ ﷺ يَقُوْلُ: لَلّٰهُ أَفْرَحُ بِتَوْبَةِ عَبْدِهِ مِنْ رَجُلٍ نَزَلَ مَنْزِلًا، وَبِهِ مَهْلَكَةٌ، وَمَعَهُ رَاحِلَتُهُ عَلَيْهَا طَعَامُهُ وَشَرَابُهُ. فَوَضَعَ رَأْسَهُ، فَنَامَ نَوْمَةً، فَاسْتَيْقَظَ وَقَدْ ذَهَبَتْ رَاحِلَتُهُ، حَتَّى إِذَا اشْتَدَّ عَلَيْهِ الْحَرُّ وَالْعَطَشُ. قَالَ: أَرْجِعُ إِلَى مَكَانِيَ الَّذِي كُنْتُ فِيهِ. فَأَنَامُ حَتَّى أَمُوتَ. فَوَضَعَ رَأْسَهُ عَلَى سَاعِدِهِ لِيَمُوتَ، فَاسْتَيْقَظَ وَعِنْدَهُ رَاحِلَتُهُ، وَعَلَيْهَا زَادُهُ وَطَعَامُهُ وَشَرَابُهُ. فَاللهُ أَشَدُّ فَرَحًا بِتَوْبَةِ الْعَبْدِ الْمُؤْمِنِ مِنْ هَذَا بِرَاحِلَتِهِ وَزَادِهِ.

I heard Allah's Messenger ﷺ say, 'Certainly, Allah is more joyous with the repentance of His believing slave than a man who disembarks in a wasteland with his mount containing his food and drink, and takes a nap and wakes up to find that his mount is gone—(and after searching for it) and becoming more and more hungry and thirsty, says, "I will go back to my original place and go to sleep until I die," and then places his hands under his head on the ground and sleeps and waits

[*wa yuḥadhdhiru-kumu Allāh-u Nafsa-h*﴾." (Q.3:28), 6:2694 §6970; •Muslim, *al-Ṣaḥīḥ*: Remembrance [*Dhikr*], Supplication [*Duʿā*ʾ], Repentance [*Tawba*] and Seeking Forgiveness [*Istighfār*], Ch.: Urging the remembrance of Allah ﷻ, 4:2061 §2675; •Aḥmad b. Ḥanbal, *al-Musnad*, 2:413 §934; •al-Tirmidhī, *al-Sunan*: *al-Zuhd* [Abstinence] according to Allah's Messenger ﷺ], Ch.: Thinking well of Allah ﷻ, 5:581 §3603. Abū ʿĪsā said: "This is a fine authentic tradition." Ibn Mājah in *al-Sunan*: *al-Adab* [The Proper Conduct], Ch.: The excellent merit of work, 2:1255 §3822; •al-Nasāʾī, *al-Sunan al-Kubrā*, 4:412 §7730; •and al-Bayhaqī in *Shuʿab al-Īmān*, 1:406 §550.

for death, and after he wakes up, he finds his mount there before him with his provision, food and drink. Certainly, Allah is more joyous with the repentance of a servant than this man is with discovering his mount and provision.'[90]

Agreed upon.

Muslim added from the hadith of Anas ﷺ:

فَأَخَذَ بِخِطَامِهَا ثُمَّ قَالَ مِنْ شِدَّةِ الْفَرَحِ: اَللّٰهُمَّ، أَنْتَ عَبْدِي وَأَنَا رَبُّكَ. أَخْطَأَ مِنْ شِدَّةِ الْفَرَحِ.

And he took it by its reins and said mistakenly out of his extreme joy, 'O Allah! You are my servant and I am Your lord!'

1.42 Some other Manifestations of Allah's Mercy

Another manifestation of Allah's Lordly mercy is the fact that He divided mercy into one hundred parts and sent only one part down to the earth by which the Creation in their variety show mercy to one another—be it humans or animals—and left the remaining ninety-nine parts with Him. On the Day of Resurrection, the one part on earth will be added to the ninety-nine parts, returning to one hundred by which He shows mercy to His Creation. All of this indicates the infinite mercy of Allah ﷻ. Abū Hurayra ﷺ reported that he heard Allah's Messenger ﷺ say,

جَعَلَ اللهُ الرَّحْمَةَ مِائَةَ جُزْءٍ. فَأَمْسَكَ عِنْدَهُ تِسْعَةً وَتِسْعِيْنَ جُزْءًا، وَأَنْزَلَ فِي الْأَرْضِ جُزْءًا وَاحِدًا. فَمِنْ ذَلِكَ الْجُزْءِ يَتَرَاحَمُ الْخَلْقُ حَتَّى تَرْفَعَ الْفَرَسُ حَافِرَهَا عَنْ وَلَدِهَا خَشْيَةَ أَنْ تُصِيبَهُ.

Allah created mercy in one hundred parts. He retained ninety-nine parts and sent one part to the earth. Due to this one part, the creation shows mercy to one another, so much

---

[90] Set forth by •al-Bukhārī in his *al-Ṣaḥīḥ:* Bk.: *al-daʿawāt* [The Supplications], Ch.: "On Repentance," 5:2324 §5949; •Muslim in *al-Ṣaḥīḥ:* Bk.: *al-tawba* [The Repentance], Ch.: "The Encouragement to Repent," 4:2103–2103 §§§2744, 2746–2747.

that the horse lifts up its hoof from its young colt lest she harm it.'[91]

Agreed upon.

And in another narration in Muslim's collection:

إِنَّ للهِ مِائَةَ رَحْمَةٍ. أَنْزَلَ مِنْهَا رَحْمَةً وَاحِدَةً بَيْنَ الْجِنِّ وَالْإِنْسِ وَالْبَهَائِمِ وَالْهَوَامِّ. فَبِهَا يَتَعَاطَفُوْنَ وَبِهَا يَتَرَاحَمُوْنَ وَبِهَا تَعْطِفُ الْوَحْشُ عَلَى وَلَدِهَا. وَأَخَّرَ اللهُ تِسْعًا وَتِسْعِيْنَ رَحْمَةً يَرْحَمُ بِهَا عِبَادَهُ يَوْمَ الْقِيَامَةِ.

Allah has one hundred parts of mercy. Of these, He sent one part that is shared between humankind and jinn and animals and insects. Because of this one part shared between them, they show mutual affection and mercy, and, due to it, the wild beast shows mercy to her young. Allah has reserved the remaining ninety-nine parts of mercy and will have mercy upon His servants with them on the Day of Resurrection.[92]

Reported by Muslim.

Another manifestation of Allah's mercy is the fact that He multiplies good deeds numerously while counting sins singly. Nay, the good deeds even erase the bad deeds, and whoever thinks of performing a good deed but did not do it, Allah writes a good deed for him, and if he does

---

[91] Set forth by •al-Bukhārī in *al-Ṣaḥīḥ:* Bk.: *al-Adab* [Good Manners], Ch.: "Allāh Made Mercy One Hundred Parts," 5:2236 §5654; •Muslim in *al-Ṣaḥīḥ:* Bk.: *al-Tawba* [Repentance], Ch: "The Vastness of Allāh's Mercy and That His Mercy Precedes His Wrath," 4:2108 §2752; •al-Dārimī in *al-Sunan*, 2:413 §2785; •Ibn Ḥibbān in *al-Ṣaḥīḥ*, 14:16 §6148; •al-Ṭabarānī in *al-Muʿjam al-awsaṭ*, 1:297 §991; •al-Bayhaqī in *Shuʿab al-īmān*, 7:457 §10975.

[92] Set forth by •Muslim in *al-Ṣaḥīḥ:* Bk.: *al-Tawba* [Repentance], Ch.: "The Vastness of Allah's Mercy and That His Mercy Precedes His Wrath," 4:2108 §2752; •Aḥmad b. Ḥanbal in *al-Musnad*, 2:434 §9607; •al-Tirmidhī in *al-Sunan:* Bk.: *al-Daʿawāt ʿan Rasūl Allāh* ﷺ [The Invocations from Allāh's Messenger ﷺ], Ch.: "Allāh Created One Hundred Mercies," 5:549 §3541; •Ibn Mājah in *al-Sunan:* Bk.: *al-Zuhd* [The Renunciation], Ch.: "Hope for Allāh's Mercy on the Day of Resurrection," 2:1435 §4293; •Ibn Ḥibbān in *al-Ṣaḥīḥ*, 14:15 §6147; •Ibn al-Mubārak in *al-Musnad*, 1:20 §35; •Abū Yaʿlā in *al-Musnad*, 11:328 §6445.

it, Allah writes for him ten to seven hundred or more good deeds. And whoever thinks of doing a bad deed but does not do it Allah will write for him one good deed, and if he does it, He will write against him only one bad deed. Almighty Allah says,

﴿مَن جَآءَ بِٱلۡحَسَنَةِ فَلَهُۥ عَشۡرُ أَمۡثَالِهَاۖ وَمَن جَآءَ بِٱلسَّيِّئَةِ فَلَا يُجۡزَىٰٓ إِلَّا مِثۡلَهَا وَهُمۡ لَا يُظۡلَمُونَ ١٦٠﴾

﴾*Whoever brings one good deed will have to his credit (as a reward) ten more like it, and whoever brings an evil deed will not be punished for more than one similar (evil deed). And no injustice will be done to them.*﴿[93]

Moreover, Allah ﷻ replaces the sins of the wrongdoer and turns them into good deeds if the sinner repents. Allah ﷻ said,

﴿إِنَّ ٱلۡحَسَنَٰتِ يُذۡهِبۡنَ ٱلسَّيِّـَٔاتِۚ﴾

﴾*Surely, good actions erase the evil ones.*﴿[94]

And He said,

﴿فَأُوْلَٰٓئِكَ يُبَدِّلُ ٱللَّهُ سَيِّـَٔاتِهِمۡ حَسَنَٰتٖۗ﴾

﴾*So these are the people whose evil deeds Allah will change into good ones.*﴿[95]

Another manifestation of Allah's mercy is the fact that He made His entire Book a mercy, guidance, light and healing. Allah ﷻ said,

﴿إِنَّ هَٰذَا ٱلۡقُرۡءَانَ يَقُصُّ عَلَىٰ بَنِيٓ إِسۡرَٰٓءِيلَ أَكۡثَرَ ٱلَّذِي هُمۡ فِيهِ يَخۡتَلِفُونَ ٧٦ وَإِنَّهُۥ لَهُدٗى وَرَحۡمَةٞ لِّلۡمُؤۡمِنِينَ﴾

﴾*Surely, this Qur'ān expounds to the Children of Israel most of the things in which they differ. And verily, it is guidance*

---

[93] Qur'ān 6:160.

[94] Ibid., 11:114.

[95] Ibid., 25:70.

and mercy for the believers.﴿[96]

Allah also said,

﴿الٓمٓ ① تِلْكَ ءَايَٰتُ ٱلْكِتَٰبِ ٱلْحَكِيمِ ② هُدًى وَرَحْمَةً لِّلْمُحْسِنِينَ﴾

﴾*Alif, Lām, Mīm. (Only Allah and the Messenger ﷺ know the real meaning.) These are Verses of the Book of Wisdom, Guidance and mercy for the pious.*﴿[97]

He also said,

﴿وَلَقَدْ جِئْنَٰهُم بِكِتَٰبٍ فَصَّلْنَٰهُ عَلَىٰ عِلْمٍ هُدًى وَرَحْمَةً لِّقَوْمٍ يُؤْمِنُونَ﴾

﴾*And surely, We have brought them such a Book (the Qur'ān) that We have elucidated on (the basis of Our) knowledge, a guidance and a mercy for those who believe.*﴿[98]

And,

﴿وَنَزَّلْنَا عَلَيْكَ ٱلْكِتَٰبَ تِبْيَٰنًا لِّكُلِّ شَىْءٍ وَهُدًى وَرَحْمَةً وَبُشْرَىٰ لِلْمُسْلِمِينَ﴾

﴾*And We have revealed to you that Glorious Book which is a clear exposition of everything and is guidance, mercy and glad tidings for the believers.*﴿[99]

And,

﴿وَنُنَزِّلُ مِنَ ٱلْقُرْءَانِ مَا هُوَ شِفَآءٌ وَرَحْمَةٌ لِّلْمُؤْمِنِينَ﴾

﴾*And We are sending down in the Qur'ān what is healing*

---

[96] Ibid., 27:76–77.

[97] Ibid., 31:1–3.

[98] Ibid., 7:52.

[99] Ibid., 16:89.

and mercy for the believers.﴾[100]

Allah ﷻ also revealed the Torah to Prophet Mūsā ﵇—the original Scripture, not the current altered version—a mercy. Allah ﷻ said,

﴿ثُمَّ ءَاتَيۡنَا مُوسَى ٱلۡكِتَٰبَ تَمَامًا عَلَى ٱلَّذِيٓ أَحۡسَنَ وَتَفۡصِيلٗا لِّكُلِّ شَيۡءٖ وَهُدٗى وَرَحۡمَةٗ لَّعَلَّهُم بِلِقَآءِ رَبِّهِمۡ يُؤۡمِنُونَ﴾

﴿*Then We gave Mūsā (Moses) the Book to complete (the favour) on him who would become pious, and (revealed it) as explanation of everything and as guidance and mercy, so that they might believe in meeting with their Lord (on the Day of Resurrection).*﴾[101]

Another manifestation of Allah's infinite mercy is the fact that He does not take the servants to account for what He has given them and honoured them with, for if He were to demand of them what is commensurate with His bounties, no one would be able to bear it. Abū Hurayra ﵁ reported,

سَمِعْتُ رَسُولَ اللهِ ﷺ يَقُولُ: لَنْ يُدْخِلَ أَحَدًا عَمَلُهُ الْجَنَّةَ. قَالُوا: وَلَا أَنْتَ، يَا رَسُولَ اللهِ؟ قَالَ: لَا، وَلَا أَنَا إِلَّا أَنْ يَتَغَمَّدَنِي اللهُ بِفَضْلٍ وَرَحْمَةٍ.

I heard Allah's Messenger ﷺ say, 'None of you shall enter Paradise by virtue of his works.' The Companions asked, 'Not even you, O Allah's Messenger?' 'Not even me,' the Messenger ﷺ said, 'unless Allah envelops me in His bounty and mercy.'[102]

Agreed upon.

---

[100] Ibid., 17:82.

[101] Ibid., 6:154.

[102] Set forth by •al-Bukhārī in *al-Ṣaḥīḥ:* Bk.: *al-Marḍā* [The Patients], Ch.: "On the Sick Person Wishing for Death," 5:2147 §5349; •Muslim in *al-Ṣaḥīḥ:* Bk.: *Ṣifāt al-munāfiqīn* [On the Traits of the Hypocrites], Ch.: "No One Shall Enter Paradise by Virtue of His Deeds; It is Only by Allah's Mercy," 4:2064 §2680.

In addition, Allah ﷻ does not judge the servants according to His knowledge of their works; rather, He judges them on the basis of compatibility of their actions with the divine command and prohibition. So the one whose actions correspond to the divine command will be honoured, and the one whose actions breach the Lordly prohibition will be punished.

A similar example of Allah's mercy to His servants is that He conceals them in this life and does not expose them in the Hereafter. He only exposes those who announce their sins. Abū Hurayra ؓ reported that the Prophet ﷺ said,

لَا يَسْتُرُ اللهُ عَلَى عَبْدٍ فِي الدُّنْيَا إِلَّا سَتَرَهُ اللهُ يَوْمَ الْقِيَامَةِ.

> Allah does not veil a servant in this life [of sins] save that He will also veil him on the Day of Resurrection.[103]
>
> Reported by Muslim.

Abū Hurayra ؓ also reported that he heard Allah's Messenger ﷺ say,

كُلُّ أُمَّتِي مُعَافًى إِلَّا الْـمُجَاهِرِينَ. وَإِنَّ مِنَ الْـمُجَاهَرَةِ أَنْ يَعْمَلَ الرَّجُلُ بِاللَّيْلِ عَمَلًا، ثُمَّ يُصْبِحَ وَقَدْ سَتَرَهُ اللهُ، فَيَقُولَ: يَا فُلَانُ، عَمِلْتُ الْبَارِحَةَ كَذَا وَكَذَا، وَقَدْ بَاتَ يَسْتُرُهُ رَبُّهُ، وَيُصْبِحُ يَكْشِفُ سِتْرَ اللهِ عَنْهُ.

> My entire community is pardoned save the 'announcers'. Indeed, it is a form of announcing when a man commits an evil deed by night and says upon waking—even though Allah veiled him: 'O So-and-so! Last night I did such-and-such,' even though he spent the night veiled by his Lord, but woke up removing Allah's veil that covered him.[104]

---

103 Set forth by •Muslim in *al-Ṣaḥīḥ:* Bk.: *al-Birr wa al-ṣila* [The Piety and Familial Integration], Ch.: "The Glad Tidings for the One Whose Faults Allah Conceals in the World That His Fault Will Be Concealed in the Hereafter," 4:2002 §2590.

104 Set forth by •al-Bukhārī in *al-Ṣaḥīḥ:* Bk.: *al-Adab* [Manners], Ch.: "A believer concealing himself", 5:2254 §5721; •Muslim in *al-Ṣaḥīḥ:* Bk.: *al-Birr wa al-ṣila* [Piety and Familial Integration], Ch.: "The Glad Tidings for the One

Agreed upon.

Whose Faults Allah Conceals in the World That His Fault Will Be Concealed in the Hereafter," 4:2291 §2990.

اَلْبَابُ الثَّانِي

اَلْإِسْلَامُ دِيْنُ الرَّحْمَةِ وَالْيُسْرِ وَالسَّمَاحَةِ

Chapter Two

Islam is the Religion of Mercy, Ease and Moderation

Almighty Allah informed us that His religion, Islam, is the seal of all heavenly revealed religions, just as His Beloved Prophet ﷺ is the seal of all Prophets and Messengers عليهم السلام. Moreover, He made this religion, with its structures of clarity and comprehensiveness, and its overall applicability and conformity with the primordial nature, general and inclusive of all facets of worldly and Afterworldly life, and He made it compatible with and relevant to every time and place.

For this reason, Allah عز وجل has said that He is pleased with this religion:

﴿إِنَّ ٱلدِّينَ عِندَ ٱللَّهِ ٱلۡإِسۡلَٰمُۗ﴾

﴾*Truly, Islam is the only Dīn (Religion) in Allah's sight.*﴿[105]

He does not accept for anyone to embrace any other faith besides it, and He has informed us that whoever does so is among the losers:

﴿وَمَن يَبۡتَغِ غَيۡرَ ٱلۡإِسۡلَٰمِ دِينٗا فَلَن يُقۡبَلَ مِنۡهُ وَهُوَ فِي ٱلۡأٓخِرَةِ مِنَ ٱلۡخَٰسِرِينَ﴾

﴾*And whoever seeks a dīn (religion) other than Islam that shall not at all be accepted from him, and he will be amongst the losers in the Hereafter.*﴿[106]

2.1 Islam Desires Ease and Removal of Hardships

This religion corresponds to the innate, primordial nature with which Allah created man. This is why there are no burdensome difficulties, unbearable obligations, or commands to do the impossible.

Just as Almighty Allah made His Exalted Prophet ﷺ a mercy and sent him as the Prophet of Mercy, He also made his religion one of mercy. Islam is a faith of ease without difficulty, glad tidings without

---

105 Qur'ān 3:19.

106 Ibid., 3:85.

making people feel aversion, good without evil, gentleness without coarseness, light without burden, freedom without shackles, mercy without oppression, justice without transgression, guidance without disbelief or ingratitude, balance without extremism, and moderation without excessiveness. This lies in stark contrast to the previously revealed heavenly religions.

Because of this religion's ease, Allah has removed difficulty and burden and made things easy for the *Umma*. Allah desires ease for it and does not desire difficulty. He has made lawful the pure things and removed from the *Umma* the shackles that were upon the bygone nations. With respect to the previous communities, these shackles were decreed and His commands were good for them and the things He forbade were vile and bad for them; however, He has replaced those shackles with what is better than them. Allah سبحانه وتعالى said,

﴿يُرِيدُ ٱللَّهُ بِكُمُ ٱلْيُسْرَ وَلَا يُرِيدُ بِكُمُ ٱلْعُسْرَ﴾

﴿*Allah desires ease for you and does not desire hardship for you.*﴾[107]

The entire religion of Islam is structured upon ease and the removal of difficulty. Allah سبحانه وتعالى said,

﴿هُوَ ٱجْتَبَىٰكُمْ وَمَا جَعَلَ عَلَيْكُمْ فِى ٱلدِّينِ مِنْ حَرَجٍ﴾

﴿*He has chosen you, and has not laid upon you any hardship or constriction (in the matter of) Dīn (Religion).*﴾[108]

He also said,

﴿مَا يُرِيدُ ٱللَّهُ لِيَجْعَلَ عَلَيْكُم مِّنْ حَرَجٍ وَلَٰكِن يُرِيدُ لِيُطَهِّرَكُمْ وَلِيُتِمَّ نِعْمَتَهُۥ عَلَيْكُمْ لَعَلَّكُمْ تَشْكُرُونَ﴾

﴿*Allah does not want to make things hard for you, but He wants to purify you, and complete the bestowal of His*

[107] Ibid., 2:185.
[108] Ibid., 22:78.

favour upon you so that you may become grateful.﴿[109]

2.2 Islam Lightens the Burden of Obligations

Since Allah ﷻ knows the weakness of this *Umma*—because it is the last of the communities—He has lightened for it the legal responsibilities and lessened from it the obligations that it would not be able to fulfil. Allah said,

﴿يُرِيدُ ٱللَّهُ أَن يُخَفِّفَ عَنكُمْۚ وَخُلِقَ ٱلْإِنسَٰنُ ضَعِيفًا﴾

﴾*Allah intends to lighten your burden. And man has been created weak (and infirm).*﴿[110]

He also said,

﴿ٱلْـَٰٔنَ خَفَّفَ ٱللَّهُ عَنكُمْ وَعَلِمَ أَنَّ فِيكُمْ ضَعْفًاۚ﴾

﴾*Allah has, at present, lightened the burden (of His commandment) on you. He knows that there is (some degree of) weakness in you.*﴿[111]

Allah ﷻ informed us that His exalted Prophet ﷺ is a mercy and sent with mercy, and that not only is he the Prophet of Mercy, he is the embodiment of mercy from Allah to the worlds also. Allah ﷻ addressed His noble Prophet:

﴿فَبِمَا رَحْمَةٍ مِّنَ ٱللَّهِ لِنتَ لَهُمْۖ وَلَوْ كُنتَ فَظًّا غَلِيظَ ٱلْقَلْبِ لَٱنفَضُّوا۟
مِنْ حَوْلِكَۖ﴾

﴾*(O My Esteemed Beloved!) What a mercy of Allah that you are lenient with them! Had you been stern and hard-hearted, people would have deserted, scattering away from around you.*﴿[112]

---

[109] Ibid., 5:6.

[110] Ibid., 4:28.

[111] Ibid., 8:66.

[112] Ibid., 3:159.

This also forms a part of the Prophet's description found in the Torah. ʿAbd Allāh b. ʿAmr ﵄ was once asked about the description of the Prophet ﷺ in the Torah. He said, "Yes. By Allah, he is described in the Torah with some of his qualities mentioned in the Qurʾān,

﴿يَـٰٓأَيُّهَا ٱلنَّبِيُّ إِنَّآ أَرۡسَلۡنَـٰكَ شَـٰهِدٗا وَمُبَشِّرٗا وَنَذِيرٗا﴾

﴾*O (Esteemed) Prophet! Surely, We have sent you as a Witness (to the truth and the creation), a Bearer of glad tidings (of the beauty of the Hereafter) and a Warner (of the torment in the Hereafter).*﴿[113]

You are My slave and Messenger. I have named you al-Mutawakkal [the trustworthy one] who is neither coarse nor harsh, nor loud in the markets. He does not respond to a wrong action with a wrong action; rather he pardons and forgives."[114]

Allah also made the Prophet ﷺ a mercy to the believers in a particular way. Allah said,

﴿وَمِنۡهُمُ ٱلَّذِينَ يُؤۡذُونَ ٱلنَّبِيَّ وَيَقُولُونَ هُوَ أُذُنٞۚ قُلۡ أُذُنُ خَيۡرٖ لَّكُمۡ يُؤۡمِنُ بِٱللَّهِ وَيُؤۡمِنُ لِلۡمُؤۡمِنِينَ وَرَحۡمَةٞ لِّلَّذِينَ ءَامَنُواْ مِنكُمۡۚ وَٱلَّذِينَ يُؤۡذُونَ رَسُولَ ٱللَّهِ لَهُمۡ عَذَابٌ أَلِيمٞ﴾

﴾*And amongst these (hypocrites) are also those who hurt (the Esteemed) Messenger (blessings and peace be upon him) and say: "He is only an ear (believes everything he hears)." Say: "He is all ears to what is good for you; he believes in Allah and has faith in (what) the believers (say) and is mercy for those of you who have embraced faith. And those who hurt the Messenger of Allah (by means of their evil beliefs, doubts and foul statements), for them there is grievous torment."*﴿[115]

---

[113] Ibid., 33:45.

[114] Set forth by •al-Bukhārī in *al-Ṣaḥīḥ:* Bk.: *al-Buyūʿ* [Transactions], Ch.: "The Prohibition of Being Loud and Boisterous in the Marketplace," 2:747 §2018.

[115] Qurʾān 9:61.

He also made the Prophet ﷺ a mercy to the worlds, believers or otherwise, which sets him apart from all other Messengers عليهم السلام. Allah said,

﴿وَمَآ أَرۡسَلۡنَٰكَ إِلَّا رَحۡمَةٗ لِّلۡعَٰلَمِينَ﴾

﴾*And, (O Esteemed Messenger,) We have not sent you but as a mercy for all the worlds.*﴿[116]

And Allah made the Prophet ﷺ especially clement and merciful toward the believers:

﴿لَقَدۡ جَآءَكُمۡ رَسُولٞ مِّنۡ أَنفُسِكُمۡ عَزِيزٌ عَلَيۡهِ مَا عَنِتُّمۡ حَرِيصٌ
عَلَيۡكُم بِٱلۡمُؤۡمِنِينَ رَءُوفٞ رَّحِيمٞ﴾

﴾*Surely, a (Glorious) Messenger from amongst yourselves has come to you. Your suffering and distress (becomes) grievously heavy on him* ﷺ. *(O mankind,) he is ardently desirous of your (betterment and guidance. And) he is most (deeply) clement and merciful to the believers.*﴿[117]

One of Allah's mercies to us is that He made one of the Prophet's primary concerns the lifting and removal of the burdens that existed among the previous nations. Allah said,

﴿ٱلَّذِينَ يَتَّبِعُونَ ٱلرَّسُولَ ٱلنَّبِيَّ ٱلۡأُمِّيَّ ٱلَّذِي يَجِدُونَهُۥ مَكۡتُوبًا عِندَهُمۡ فِي
ٱلتَّوۡرَىٰةِ وَٱلۡإِنجِيلِ يَأۡمُرُهُم بِٱلۡمَعۡرُوفِ وَيَنۡهَىٰهُمۡ عَنِ ٱلۡمُنكَرِ وَيُحِلُّ لَهُمُ
ٱلطَّيِّبَٰتِ وَيُحَرِّمُ عَلَيۡهِمُ ٱلۡخَبَٰٓئِثَ وَيَضَعُ عَنۡهُمۡ إِصۡرَهُمۡ وَٱلۡأَغۡلَٰلَ ٱلَّتِي
كَانَتۡ عَلَيۡهِمۡۚ﴾

﴾*(They are the people) who follow the Messenger, the Prophet (titled as) al-Ummī (who imparts to the people from Allah the news of the unseen and knowledge and secrets of socio-economic disciplines of life without himself being taught by*

---

[116] Ibid., 21:107.

[117] Ibid., 9:128.

any human in the world); whose (eminent attributes and exquisite powers) these people find written in the Torah and the Injīl (Gospel); who enjoins on them virtues and forbids them vices, declares wholesome things lawful and impure ones unlawful for them and removes from them their heavy burdens and yokes (i.e., shackles) weighing upon them (due to their acts of disobedience and blesses them with freedom).﴾[118]

2.3 Islam Teaches Easiness and does not Approve of Harshness

The Prophet ﷺ informed us that he was sent to bring ease and not difficulty. Ease is the implication of mercy, for if it were not, things would not have been made easy. Jābir ؓ reported in the hadith about the Mothers of the Believers and their request to Allah's Messenger to increase in his spending upon them, and his withdrawal from them for one month and the revelation of the verse giving him a choice and his recitation of the verse to ʿĀʾisha ؓ. In it, the Prophet ﷺ said,

إِنَّ اللهَ لَمْ يَبْعَثْنِي مُعَنِّتًا وَلَا مُتَعَنِّتًا، وَلَكِنْ بَعَثَنِي مُعَلِّمًا مُيَسِّرًا.

Indeed, Allah did not send me to be harsh or cause harm; He sent me to teach and make things easy.[119]

Reported by Muslim.

The Prophet's Companions ؓ have related that one of his noble characteristics was that he made things easy and did not make things difficult. They related how he loved to lighten the *Umma*'s burdens. This is only because the Prophet ﷺ was a mercy sent with mercy, and with a religion of mercy that brings ease. Al-Arzaq b. Qays related a hadith that he heard during the battle against the Ḥarūriyya at Ahwāz. He mentioned that Abū Burza al-Aslamī ؓ said,

---

[118] Ibid., 7:157.

[119] Set forth by •Muslim in *al-Ṣaḥīḥ:* Bk.: *al-Ṭalāq* [The Divorce], Ch.: "Merely Giving a Woman the Option of Divorce Does not Make the Divorce Effective, But Only When it is Actually Intended," 2:1104 §1478.

غَزَوْتُ مَعَ رَسُولِ اللهِ ﷺ سِتَّ غَزَوَاتٍ، أَوْ سَبْعَ غَزَوَاتٍ، وَثَمَانِيَ، وَشَهِدْتُ تَيْسِيرَهُ.

I have waged six, seven, or eight battles with Allah's Messenger ﷺ and I saw his way of making things easy.[120]

Reported by al-Bukhārī.

The Mother of the Believers, ʿĀisha ◌, said,

وَالَّذِي ذَهَبَ بِهِ، مَا تَرَكَهُمَا حَتَّى لَقِيَ اللهَ، وَمَا لَقِيَ اللهَ تَعَالَى حَتَّى ثَقُلَ عَنِ الصَّلَاةِ، وَكَانَ يُصَلِّي كَثِيرًا مِنْ صَلَاتِهِ قَاعِدًا — تَعْنِي الرَّكْعَتَيْنِ بَعْدَ الْعَصْرِ — وَكَانَ النَّبِيُّ ﷺ يُصَلِّيهِمَا، وَلَا يُصَلِّيهِمَا فِي الْـمَسْجِدِ، مَخَافَةَ أَنْ يُثْقَلَ عَلَى أُمَّتِهِ، وَكَانَ يُحِبُّ مَا يُخَفَّفُ عَنْهُمْ.

By the One Who took him, he did not leave it until he met Allah, and he did not meet Allah until the prayer became heavy for him. He would pray many of his prayers sitting down [i.e., the two units after the ʿAṣr prayer]. He would pray them at home and would not pray them at the Mosque, for fear of making things hard for his *Umma*. He used to love that which made things lightened for them.[121]

Reported by al-Bukhārī.

2.4 THE HOLY PROPHET ﷺ CHOSE THE EASIER OF THE TWO OPTIONS

One of the many manifestations of the Prophet's mercy, and one which is an example for the believers to follow, is that he was never presented two options except that he would choose the easier of the two, so long as it was not a sin. If it was a sin, he would be the farthest of people

---

[120] Set forth by •al-Bukhārī in *al-Ṣaḥīḥ*: Bk.: *al-ʿAmal fī al-ṣalāt* [On Extraneous Actions Performed in the Prayer], Ch.: "When One's Animal Runs Away During the Prayer," 1:405 §1153.

[121] Ibid., Bk.: *Mawāqīt al-ṣalāt* [The Timing of the Prayers], Ch.: "On the Missed Prayers that Can Be Prayed After the ʿAṣr Prayer," 1:213 §565.

from it. ʿĀʾisha ﵁ said,

مَا خُيِّرَ رَسُولُ اللهِ ﷺ بَيْنَ أَمْرَيْنِ، إِلَّا أَخَذَ أَيْسَرَهُمَا، مَا لَمْ يَكُنْ إِثْمًا. فَإِنْ كَانَ إِثْمًا كَانَ أَبْعَدَ النَّاسِ مِنْهُ، وَمَا انْتَقَمَ رَسُولُ اللهِ ﷺ لِنَفْسِهِ، إِلَّا أَنْ تُنْتَهَكَ حُرْمَةُ اللهِ، فَيَنْتَقِمَ لِلّٰهِ بِهَا.

Never was Allah's Messenger ﷺ presented with two options except that he would choose the easier of the two, so long as it was not a sin. If it was a sin, he would be the farthest of people from it. Never did Allah's Messenger ﷺ take revenge for himself. Vengeance would only be taken if the sanctities of Allah were violated.[122]

Agreed upon.

2.5 The Best of Your Religion is the Middle Course

Another manifestation of Allah's lordly mercy upon creation is the fact that He made this religion one of ease and moderation, and instructed its followers to have temperance and not to make things hard upon themselves. The extremist, we are informed, is overcome by the religion. Abū Hurayra ﵁ reported that Allah's Messenger ﷺ said,

إِنَّ الدِّينَ يُسْرٌ، وَلَنْ يُشَادَّ الدِّينَ أَحَدٌ إِلَّا غَلَبَهُ. فَسَدِّدُوا وَقَارِبُوا، وَأَبْشِرُوا وَاسْتَعِينُوا بِالْغَدْوَةِ وَالرَّوْحَةِ، وَشَيْءٍ مِنَ الدُّلْجَةِ.

Indeed, the religion is ease, and no one makes it hard on himself save that he will be overpowered. So direct yourselves to what is right, follow a middle course, be of good cheer, and seek help [by worshipping] in the morning, evening and some of the night.[123]

---

[122] Ibid., Bk.: *al-Manāqib* [The Exemplary Virtues], Ch.: "The Qualities of the Prophet ﷺ," 3:1306 §3367; •Muslim in *al-Ṣaḥīḥ:* Bk.: *al-Faḍāʾil* [Virtues], Ch.: "The Prophet's Distance Away from Sins," 4:1813 §2327.

[123] Ibid., Bk.: *al-Īmān* [The Faith], Ch.: "The Religion is Ease," 1:23 §39.

Reported by al-Bukhārī.

Abū Qatāda ☵ related from the Bedouin who heard Allah's Messenger ☵ say,

$$إِنَّ خَيْـرَ دِينِكُمْ أَيْسَرُهُ؛ إِنَّ خَيْـرَ دِينِكُمْ أَيْسَرُهُ.$$

Indeed, the best of your religion is the easiest of it; indeed, the best of your religion is the easiest of it.[124]

Reported by Aḥmad with an authentic chain.

ʿUrwa al-Fuqaymī ☵ said,

$$كُنَّا نَنْتَظِرُ النَّبِيَّ ﷺ، فَخَرَجَ رَجِلًا، فَخَرَجَ رَجِلًا، يَقْطُرُ رَأْسُهُ مِنْ وُضُوءٍ أَوْ غُسْلٍ،$$
$$فَصَلَّى. فَلَمَّا قَضَى الصَّلَاةَ، جَعَلَ النَّاسُ يَسْأَلُونَهُ: يَا رَسُولَ الله، أَعَلَيْنَا$$
$$حَرَجٌ فِي كَذَا؟ فَقَالَ رَسُولُ الله ﷺ: لَا، أَيُّهَا النَّاسُ، إِنَّ دِينَ الله فِي يُسْرٍ.$$

Once we were waiting for the Prophet ☵ and he suddenly came out wet with water dripping from his head from the ablution or bath [*ghusl*] and he began to pray. After he completed his prayer, some of the people asked him, 'O Allah's Messenger! Is there any problem with us doing this [i.e., offering prayers without wiping the ablution water or allowing it to dry]?' The Messenger ☵ said thrice, 'No, O people! The religion of Allah is found in ease.'[125]

Reported by Aḥmad, Ibn Abī ʿĀṣim, Abū Yaʿlā and al-Ṭabarānī. Al-Ḥāfiẓ Ibn Ḥajar declared this is an authentic tradition.

---

[124] Set forth by •Aḥmad b. Ḥanbal in *al-Musnad*, 3:479; •al-Haythamī in *Majmaʿ al-zawāʾid*, 1:61; and cited by •Ibn Ḥajar in *Fatḥ al-Bārī*, 1:94; while al-Ṭabarānī in *al-Muʿjam al-kabīr*, 18:230 §573; •Ibn Abī ʿĀṣim in *al-Āḥād wa al-mathānī*, 4:349 §2383; al-Quḍāʿī in *Musnad al-Shihāb*, 2:219–220 §§1224–1225; and al-Maqdisī in *al-Aḥādīth al-mukhtāra* (7:132 §2565).

[125] Set forth by •Aḥmad b. Ḥanbal in *al-Musnad*, 5:69; •al-Bukhārī in *al-Tārīkh al-kabīr*, 7:30–31 §135; •Ibn Abī ʿĀṣim in *al-Āḥād wa al-mathānī*, 2:397 §1190; •Abū Yaʿlā in *al-Musnad*, 12:274 §6863; •Ibn al-Qāniʿ in *Muʿjam al-Ṣaḥāba*, 2:262 §780; and cited by •al-Haythamī in *Majmaʿ al-zawāʾid*, 1:61–62.

2.6 Prohibition of Extremism and Commandment of Moderation

According to ʿAbd Allāh b. ʿAbbās ﵄, Allah's Messenger ﷺ said,

إِيَّاكُمْ وَالْغُلُوَّ فِي الدِّينِ، فَإِنَّمَا أَهْلَكَ مَنْ كَانَ قَبْلَكُمُ الْغُلُوُّ فِي الدِّينِ.

Beware of going to extremes in the religion, for the only thing that destroyed those before you was extremism in the religion.[126]

Reported by al-Nasāʾī, Ibn Mājah and Ibn Ḥibbān.

According to Burayda b. al-Ḥaṣīb ﵁, Allah's Messenger ﷺ said,

عَلَيْكُمْ هَدْيًا قَاصِدًا، عَلَيْكُمْ هَدْيًا قَاصِدًا، عَلَيْكُمْ هَدْيًا قَاصِدًا، فَإِنَّهُ مَنْ يُشَادَّ هَذَا الدِّينَ يَغْلِبْهُ.

Stick to the moderate way! Stick to the moderate way! Stick to the moderate way, for no one makes the religion hard on himself save that it will overcome him.[127]

Reported by Aḥmad and al-Ṭayālisī. Ibn Khuzayma and al-Ḥākim declared it authentic.

In addition to this, the Prophet ﷺ informed us that he was sent with the way of tolerance and moderation. And the most beloved of the religion in the sight of Allah ﷻ is the way of tolerance and moderation. Ibn ʿAbbās ﵄ narrated,

قِيلَ لِرَسُولِ اللهِ ﷺ: أَيُّ الْأَدْيَانِ أَحَبُّ إِلَى اللهِ؟ قَالَ: الْحَنِيفِيَّةُ السَّمْحَةُ.

A man asked Allah's Messenger ﷺ, 'What religion is the

---

[126] Set forth by •al-Nasāʾī, *al-Sunan*, 5:268 §3058; •Ibn Mājah, *al-Sunan*, 2:1008 §3029; •Ibn Ḥibbān, *al-Ṣaḥīḥ*, 9:183–184 §3871; •Abū Yaʿlā, *al-Musnad*, 4:316 §2427; •al-Ṭabarānī, *al-Muʿjam al-kabīr*, 12:156 §12747; •al-Bayhaqī, *al-Sunan al-kubrā*, 5:127.

[127] Set forth by •Aḥmad b. Ḥanbal, *al-Musnad*, 5:350, 361; •al-Ṭayālisī, *al-Musnad*, p. 109 §809; •Ibn Abī ʿĀṣim, *al-Sunna*, 1:46 §95; •Ibn Khuzayma, *al-Ṣaḥīḥ*, 2:199 §1179; •al-Ḥākim, *al-Mustadrak*, 1:457 §1176; •al-Bayhaqī, *al-Sunan al-kubrā*, 3:18.

most beloved in the sight of Allah?' The Messenger replied, 'The tolerant *ḥanafiyya* way.'[128]

Reported by al-Bukhārī in *al-Adab al-mufrad*, Aḥmad and ʿAbd b. Ḥumayd.

Here we see that Allah's Messenger was sent with the tolerant *ḥanafiyya* way, and that there is expansiveness in this religion, in contrast to the religion of the Jews and the Christians.

According to ʿĀʾisha ﵂, Allah's Messenger ﷺ said on the occasion of *ʿĪd*,

لَتَعْلَمُ يَهُودُ أَنَّ فِي دِينِنَا فُسْحَةً، إِنِّي أُرْسِلْتُ بِحَنِيفِيَّةٍ سَمْحَةٍ.

The Jews do know that our religion has expansiveness, and that I have been sent with the tolerant *ḥanafiyya* way.[129]

Reported by Aḥmad and al-Ḥumaydī. This is an authentic hadith whose origin is found in the collections of al-Bukhārī and Muslim from the story of the Abyssinians dancing in the Mosque.[130]

2.7 No Soul should be Burdened beyond its Ability

One of the manifestations of the tolerance and moderation of Islam is that Allah ﷻ does not burden a soul with more than it can bear, whether in acts of worship, interactions or other things.

Allah ﷻ said,

﴿لَا نُكَلِّفُ نَفْسًا إِلَّا وُسْعَهَا﴾

﴾*We do not burden any soul beyond its ability to bear it.*﴿[131]

---

[128] Set forth by •Aḥmad b. Ḥanbal, *al-Musnad*, 1:236; •ʿAbd b. Ḥumayd, *al-Musnad*, p. 199 §569; •al-Bukhārī, *al-Adab al-mufrad*, p. 108 §287.

[129] Set forth by •Aḥmad b. Ḥanbal, *al-Musnad*, 6:116, 233; •al-Ḥumaydī, *al-Musnad*, 1:123 §254; •Ibn Ḥajar, *Fatḥ al-bārī*, 2:444.

[130] Set forth by •al-Bukhārī, *al-Ṣaḥīḥ*, 1:173 §443 and 3:1063 §2745; •Muslim, *al-Ṣaḥīḥ*, 2:608–610 §892–893.

[131] Qurʾān 6:152.

﴿لَا يُكَلِّفُ ٱللَّهُ نَفْسًا إِلَّا وُسْعَهَا لَهَا مَا كَسَبَتْ وَعَلَيْهَا مَا ٱكْتَسَبَتْ

رَبَّنَا لَا تُؤَاخِذْنَا إِن نَّسِينَآ أَوْ أَخْطَأْنَا رَبَّنَا وَلَا تَحْمِلْ عَلَيْنَآ إِصْرًا كَمَا

حَمَلْتَهُۥ عَلَى ٱلَّذِينَ مِن قَبْلِنَا رَبَّنَا وَلَا تُحَمِّلْنَا مَا لَا طَاقَةَ لَنَا بِهِۦ وَٱعْفُ

عَنَّا وَٱغْفِرْ لَنَا وَٱرْحَمْنَآ أَنتَ مَوْلَىٰنَا فَٱنصُرْنَا عَلَى ٱلْقَوْمِ ٱلْكَٰفِرِينَ﴾

﴿*Allah does not put under stress any soul more than its
endurance. There is a reward for whatever good it has earned,
and there is torment for whatever evil it has perpetrated. "O
our Lord, do not take us to task if we forget or do some
mistake. O our Lord, lay not on us such a (heavy) burden
as You laid on those before us. O our Lord, put not on us
(also) the burden that we have not the strength to bear, and
overlook (our sins), and forgive us and have mercy on us.
You alone are our Master and Helper. So grant us victory
over the disbelievers."*﴾ [132]

Moreover, with every difficulty, Allah provides relief out of His
mercy and ease to His servants, lest they despair. Allah said,

﴿فَإِنَّ مَعَ ٱلْعُسْرِ يُسْرًا ۝ إِنَّ مَعَ ٱلْعُسْرِ يُسْرًا﴾

﴿*So surely ease (comes) with every hardship. Verily, with
(this) hardship (too) there is ease.*﴾ [133]

For this reason, one difficulty cannot overcome two eases.
According to Abū Hurayra 🙶, the Prophet 🙶 said,

دَعُونِي مَا تَرَكْتُكُمْ. إِنَّمَا هَلَكَ مَنْ كَانَ قَبْلَكُمْ بِسُؤَالِهِمْ وَٱخْتِلَافِهِمْ عَلَى

أَنْبِيَائِهِمْ. فَإِذَا نَهَيْتُكُمْ عَنْ شَيْءٍ فَٱجْتَنِبُوهُ، وَإِذَا أَمَرْتُكُمْ بِأَمْرٍ فَأْتُوا مِنْهُ مَا

ٱسْتَطَعْتُمْ.

Do not enquire of me so long as I leave you, for the people

[132] Ibid., 2:286.

[133] Ibid., 94:5–6.

before you were only destroyed due to their [incessant] questioning and differing with their Prophets. When I forbid you something, abstain from it, and when I command you to do something, do it as much as you are able.[134]

Agreed upon.

Whenever the Prophet ﷺ would take the pledge of fealty [*bayʿa*] from someone—man or women—he would always add at the end "as much as you are able." ʿAbd Allāh b. ʿUmar ﷺ said,

كُنَّا إِذَا بَايَعْنَا رَسُولَ اللهِ ﷺ عَلَى السَّمْعِ وَالطَّاعَةِ، يَقُولُ لَنَا: فِيمَا اسْتَطَعْتُمْ.

When we would pledge fealty to Allah's Messenger ﷺ that we would hear and obey, he would add, 'As much as you are able'.[135]

Agreed upon.

Jābir b. ʿAbd Allāh ﷺ said,

بَايَعْتُ النَّبِيَّ ﷺ عَلَى السَّمْعِ وَالطَّاعَةِ، فَلَقَّنَنِي: فِيمَا اسْتَطَعْتُ.

I pledged fealty to Allah's Messenger ﷺ with the condition that I hear and obey, and he added, 'As much as you are able.'[136]

Agreed upon.

Umayma b. Ruqayya ﷺ said,

---

[134] Set forth by •al-Bukhārī in *al-Ṣaḥīḥ:* Bk.: *al-Iʿtiṣām* [The Holding Fast to the Qurʾān and Sunna], Ch.: "Emulating the Sunnas of Allah's Messenger ﷺ," 6:2658 §6858; •Muslim in *al-Ṣaḥīḥ:* Bk.: *al-Faḍāʾil* [The Virtues], Ch.: "Respect for the Prophet ﷺ and Avoiding Frequent Questions Posed to Him as Long as There is No Harm," 4:1832 §2359.

[135] Ibid., Bk.: *al-Aḥkām* [The Legal Rulings], Ch.: "How the Imam is to Take the Pledge of Fealty from the People," 6:2633 §6776; •Muslim in *al-Ṣaḥīḥ:* Bk.: *al-Imāra* [The Leadership], Ch.: "Swearing fealty for listening to and obeying the orders of the leader as far as possible," 3:1490 §1867.

[136] Ibid., 6:2633 §6778; •Muslim in *al-Ṣaḥīḥ:* Bk.: *al-Īmān* [The Faith], Ch.: "Explanation that the Religion is Sincere Counsel," 1:75 §56.

أَتَيْتُ رَسُولَ اللهِ ﷺ فِي نِسْوَةٍ بَايَعْنَهُ عَلَى الْإِسْلَامِ. فَقُلْنَ: يَا رَسُولَ اللهِ، نُبَايِعُكَ عَلَى أَنْ لَا نُشْرِكَ بِاللهِ شَيْئًا وَلَا نَسْرِقَ وَلَا نَزْنِيَ وَلَا نَقْتُلَ أَوْلَادَنَا وَلَا نَأْتِيَ بِبُهْتَانٍ نَفْتَرِيهِ بَيْنَ أَيْدِينَا وَأَرْجُلِنَا وَلَا نَعْصِيكَ فِي مَعْرُوفٍ. قَالَ: فِيمَا اسْتَطَعْتُنَّ وَأَطَعْتُنَّ. قَالَتْ: فَقُلْنَا: اللهُ وَرَسُولُهُ أَرْحَمُ بِنَا مِنَّا بِأَنْفُسِنَا.

I went to Allah's Messenger with a group of women in order to pledge fealty to him on Islam. We said, 'O Allah's Messenger! We pledge our fealty to you that we will not associate any partner with Allah and that we will not steal, fornicate, kill our children, or bring calumny or disobey you in what is good.' Allah's Messenger ﷺ said, 'As much as you are able and can bear.' We said, 'Allah and His Messenger are more merciful to us than we are to ourselves!'[137]

Reported by Aḥmad and Mālik.

2.8 Things be Made Easy so that People may not Feel Aversion

The Prophet ﷺ encouraged his *Umma* to make things easy, not to make things difficult. He urged them to be of good cheer, not to drive people away.

According to Anas b. Mālik ﷺ, the Prophet ﷺ said,

يَسِّرُوا وَلَا تُعَسِّرُوا، وَبَشِّرُوا وَلَا تُنَفِّرُوا.

Make things easy and do not make things difficult. Give glad tidings and do not make people feel aversion.[138]

Agreed upon.

---

[137] Set forth by •Aḥmad b. Ḥanbal in *al-Musnad*, 6:357, 365; •Mālik in *al-Muwaṭṭa'*, 2:982 §1775.

[138] Set forth by •al-Bukhārī in *al-Ṣaḥīḥ:* Bk.: *al-ʿIlm* [Knowledge], Ch.: "On the Prophet ﷺ Being Careful about Giving People Admonition and Knowledge Lest They Feel Aversion to It," 1:38 §69; •Muslim in *al-Ṣaḥīḥ:* Bk.: *al-Jihād wa al-siyar* [The Striving and Military Expeditions], Ch.: "The Command to Make Things Easy and Not Making Others Feel Aversion," 3:1359 §1734.

According to Abū Burda 🙏, when the Prophet 🙏 sent Muʿādh b. Jabal and Abū Mūsā al-Ashʿarī 🙏 to Yemen, he said,

يَسِّرَا وَلَا تُعَسِّرَا، وَبَشِّرَا وَلَا تُنَفِّرَا، وَتَطَاوَعَا وَلَا تَخْتَلِفَا.

Make things easy and do not make things difficult. Give glad tidings and do not make people feel aversion. Obey one another and do not differ with each other.[139]

Agreed upon.

In another narration in Muslim's collection, Abū Mūsā al-Ashʿarī 🙏 said, "When Allah's Messenger 🙏 would dispatch one of his Companions he would say to him,

بَشِّرُوا وَلَا تُنَفِّرُوا، وَيَسِّرُوا وَلَا تُعَسِّرُوا.

'Give glad tidings and do not make people feel aversion. Make things easy and do not make things difficult.'"[140]

In this narration, the Prophet 🙏 used the verb in the plural form in order to indicate them and others.

Abū Hurayra 🙏 narrated in the story of the Bedouin who urinated in the Mosque, 'Allah's Messenger 🙏 said,

دَعُوهُ وَهَرِيقُوا عَلَى بَوْلِهِ سَجْلًا مِنْ مَاءٍ، أَوْ ذَنُوبًا مِنْ مَاءٍ؛ فَإِنَّمَا بُعِثْتُمْ مُيَسِّرِينَ، وَلَمْ تُبْعَثُوا مُعَسِّرِينَ.

"Leave him. Pour a bucket or pail of water on his urine. You were sent to make things easy and not to make things difficult."[141]

---

[139] Ibid., Bk.: al-Maghāzī [The Expeditions], Ch.: "Abū Mūsā al-Ashʿarī and Muʿādh's Mission to Yemen before the Farewell Pilgrimage," 3:1104 §2873; •Muslim in al-Ṣaḥīḥ, ibid., 3:1359 §1733.

[140] Set forth by •Muslim in al-Ṣaḥīḥ, ibid., 3:1358 §1732; •Abū Dāwūd in al-Sunan, 4:260 §4835.

[141] Set forth by •al-Bukhārī in al-Ṣaḥīḥ: Bk.: al-Wuḍūʾ [The Ablution], Ch.: "Pouring Water Over Urine in the Mosque," 1:89 §217; •Muslim in al-Ṣaḥīḥ: Bk.: al-Ṭahāra [The Purification], Ch.: "The Obligation to Wash Away Urine and Other Impurities," 1:236 §§284–285.

Agreed upon.

Had Allah's Messenger ﷺ only said 'make things easy' it would apply to anyone who received ease, even if that person experienced numerous difficulties after it; however, the Prophet ﷺ also said, 'and do not make things difficult,' which negates difficulties in all circumstances.

Allah's Messenger ﷺ explained the virtue of the one who makes things easy for servants who experience difficulty, and said that Allah ﷻ will in turn make things easy for him in this life and the Next. According to Abū Hurayra ؓ, Allah's Messenger ﷺ said,

مَنْ نَفَّسَ عَنْ مُؤْمِنٍ كُرْبَةً مِنْ كُرَبِ الدُّنْيَا، نَفَّسَ اللهُ عَنْهُ كُرْبَةً مِنْ كُرَبِ يَوْمِ الْقِيَامَةِ؛ وَمَنْ يَسَّرَ عَلَى مُعْسِرٍ، يَسَّرَ اللهُ عَلَيْهِ فِي الدُّنْيَا وَالْآخِرَةِ.

Whoever relieves a believer of a difficulty from the difficulties of this world, Allah shall relieve for him a difficulty from the difficulties of the Day of Resurrection. And whoever lightens the burden of someone in difficulty, Allah shall lighten his burden in this life and the Next.[142]

Reported by Muslim.

2.9 Prescription of a Balanced and Moderate Way of Life

Another manifestation of mercy for this *Umma* is the fact that the Prophet ﷺ made moderation and ease incumbent, and he made extremism, excessiveness and fanaticism forbidden in all things, whether in acts of worship, interactions or other facets of life. For this reason, there are numerous occasions where the Prophet ﷺ says,

عَلَيْكُمْ مِنَ الْأَعْمَالِ مَا تُطِيقُونَ، فَإِنَّ اللهَ لَا يَمَلُّ حَتَّى تَمَلُّوا، وَإِنَّ أَحَبَّ الْأَعْمَالِ إِلَى اللهِ مَا دُووِمَ عَلَيْهِ وَإِنْ قَلَّ.

[142] Set forth by •Muslim in *al-Ṣaḥīḥ:* Bk.: *al-Dhikr wa al-duʿā* [The Remembrance and Supplication], Ch.: "The Virtue of Congregating to Recite the Qurʾān and Invoke,' 4:1996 §2580.

> Stick to the actions you can bear, for Allah does not tire until you tire. Indeed, the most beloved of actions in the sight of Allah are those that are the most consistent, even if they are only a little.[143]

This hadith describes fasting and prayer and other acts of worship.

ʿAbd Allāh b. ʿAmr b. al-ʿĀṣ ﷺ married his son ʿAbd Allāh ﷺ to one of the noblewomen of Quraysh, but ʿAbd Allāh did not consummate the marriage with her because he was occupied with devotions, standing the night in prayer and shunning sleep, and fasting during the day and never breaking his fast. When ʿAmr informed Allah's Messenger ﷺ about his son's acts, the Messenger ﷺ forbade him and guided him to the path of moderation and balance, saying,

> فَإِنَّ لِـجَسَدِكَ عَلَيْكَ حَقًّا، وَإِنَّ لِعَيْنِكَ عَلَيْكَ حَقًّا، وَإِنَّ لِزَوْجِكَ عَلَيْكَ حَقًّا، وَإِنَّ لِزَوْرِكَ عَلَيْكَ حَقًّا.
>
> Indeed, your body has a right over you; your eyes have a right over you; your wife has a right over you; and your neighbour has a right over you.

In the narration of Muslim, it adds:

> إِنَّكَ لَا تَدْرِي لَعَلَّكَ يَطُولُ بِكَ عُمْرٌ.
>
> You do not know, perhaps you will live for a long time.

ʿAbd Allāh ﷺ said, 'When I grew older I wished that I had accepted the dispensation of Allah's Prophet ﷺ.'[144]

Agreed upon.

---

[143] Set forth by •al-Bukhārī in *al-Ṣaḥīḥ:* Bk.: *al-Īmān* [The Faith], Ch.: "The Most Beloved Element of the Religion in the Sight of Allah is the Most Consistent of It," 1:24 §43; •Muslim in *al-Ṣaḥīḥ:* Bk.: *Ṣalāt al-musāfirīn* [The Travelers' Prayer], Ch.: "The Virtue of Consistent Actions Such as Night Vigil Prayer and the Like,' 1:540 §782.

[144] Ibid., Bk.: *al-Ṣawm* [The Fasting], Ch.: "The Body's Right When Fasting," 2:697 §1874; •Muslim in *al-Ṣaḥīḥ:* Bk.: *al-Ṣiyām* [The Fasting], Ch.: "The Prohibition of Perpetual Fasts for Those Who are Harmed by Them," 2:812–817 §1159.

Allah's Messenger ﷺ also forbade ʿUthmān b. Maẓʿūn ؓ from celibacy. Saʿd b. Abī Waqqās ؓ said,

رَدَّ رَسُولُ اللهِ ﷺ عَلَى عُثْمَانَ بْنِ مَظْعُونٍ التَّبَتُّلَ، وَلَوْ أَذِنَ لَهُ لَاخْتَصَيْنَا.

The Prophet forbade ʿUthmān b. Maẓʿūn from celibacy, and had he permitted him, we would have castrated ourselves.[145]

Agreed upon.

Anas b. Mālik ؓ said,

جَاءَ ثَلَاثَةُ رَهْطٍ إِلَى بُيُوتِ أَزْوَاجِ النَّبِيِّ ﷺ يَسْأَلُونَ عَنْ عِبَادَةِ النَّبِيِّ ﷺ. فَلَمَّا أُخْبِرُوا كَأَنَّهُمْ تَقَالُّوهَا، فَقَالُوا: وَأَيْنَ نَحْنُ مِنَ النَّبِيِّ ﷺ قَدْ غُفِرَ لَهُ مَا تَقَدَّمَ مِنْ ذَنْبِهِ وَمَا تَأَخَّرَ؟ قَالَ أَحَدُهُمْ: أَمَّا أَنَا، فَإِنِّي أُصَلِّي اللَّيْلَ أَبَدًا. وَقَالَ آخَرُ: أَنَا أَصُومُ الدَّهْرَ وَلَا أُفْطِرُ. وَقَالَ آخَرُ: أَنَا أَعْتَزِلُ النِّسَاءَ، فَلَا أَتَزَوَّجُ أَبَدًا. فَجَاءَ رَسُولُ اللهِ ﷺ إِلَيْهِمْ، فَقَالَ: أَنْتُمُ الَّذِينَ قُلْتُمْ كَذَا وَكَذَا؟ أَمَا وَاللهِ إِنِّي لَأَخْشَاكُمْ لِلهِ وَأَتْقَاكُمْ لَهُ. لَكِنِّي أَصُومُ وَأُفْطِرُ، وَأُصَلِّي وَأَرْقُدُ، وَأَتَزَوَّجُ النِّسَاءَ. فَمَنْ رَغِبَ عَنْ سُنَّتِي فَلَيْسَ مِنِّي.

A group of three people went to the Prophet's wives and asked them about his worship. After they were informed of his devotions, they seemed to consider it small. They said, 'How can we possibly compare to the Prophet ﷺ when Allah has forgiven all the earlier and later sins (of all the people of your *Umma*)?' One of them said, 'As for me, I shall always pray the entire night.' Another said, 'As for me, I shall fast perpetually and never break my fast.' And the last one said, 'As for me, I shall shun women and never marry.' Thereafter the Prophet ﷺ came to them and asked, 'Do you say such-and-such? As for me, by Allah, I have the most fear of Allah

[145] Set forth by •al-Bukhārī in *al-Ṣaḥīḥ:* Bk.: *al-Nikāḥ* [Marriage], Ch.: "The Prohibition celibacy and castration," 5:1952 §4786; •Muslim in *al-Ṣaḥīḥ:* Bk.: *al-Nikāḥ* [Marriage], Ch.: "Fasting of that who is unable to support and marry," 2:1020 §1402.

and awe of Him, yet I fast and break my fast, I pray and take rest, and I marry women. Whoever shuns my Sunna is not from me.'[146]

Agreed upon.

Once the Prophet ﷺ saw an elderly man being carried between his two sons. The Prophet ﷺ asked, "What is the matter with him?" The Companions ﷺ replied, "He vowed to walk [in the pilgrimage]." The Prophet ﷺ said, "Indeed, Allah has no need of this man's self-torture," and then he ordered the man to mount a riding animal.[147]

When ʿUqba b. ʿĀmir ﷺ asked the Prophet ﷺ for a verdict concerning his sister's vow to perform the Hajj barefooted, the Prophet ﷺ said, "Let her walk and ride."[148]

Allah's Messenger ﷺ commanded us to deal with matters using gentleness, softness and ease, and he cautioned us against force lest people despair. Further, the Prophet ﷺ informed us that for every servant or action there is a period of activity followed by a period of inactivity, and that the best of all things are those in accordance with his Sunna. Anas ﷺ said,

دَخَلَ رَسُولُ اللهِ ﷺ الْـمَسْجِدَ، وَحَبْلٌ مَمْدُودٌ بَيْنَ سَارِيَتَيْنِ. فَقَالَ: مَا هَذَا؟ قَالُوا لِزَيْنَبَ تُصَلِّي. فَإِذَا كَسِلَتْ أَوْ فَتَرَتْ أَمْسَكَتْ بِهِ. فَقَالَ: حُلُّوهُ. ثُمَّ قَالَ: لِيُصَلِّ أَحَدُكُمْ نَشَاطَهُ. فَإِذَا كَسِلَ أَوْ فَتَرَ، فَلْيَقْعُدْ.

Allah's Messenger ﷺ once entered the mosque and discovered a rope tied between two pillars. He asked, 'What is this?' and the Companions ﷺ replied, 'This is used by Zaynab when she prays; whenever she gets tired or fatigued, she holds onto

[146] Ibid., Bk.: *al-Nikāḥ* [The Marriage], Ch.: "The Encouragement to Marry," 5:1949 §4776; •Muslim in *al-Ṣaḥīḥ:* Bk.: *al-Nikāḥ* [Marriage], Ch.: "The Recommendation of Marriage for Those who are Able," 2:1020 §1401.

[147] Ibid., Bk.: *Jazāʾ al-ṣayd* [The Penalty for Hunting During Hajj], Ch.: "Concerning the One Who Vows to Walk to the Kaʿba," 2:659 §1766; •Muslim in *al-Ṣaḥīḥ:* Bk.: *al-Nadhr* [Vows], Ch.: Concerning the One Who Vows to Walk to the Kaʿba," 3:1263 1642.

[148] Ibid.

it.' The Prophet ﷺ said, 'Untie it.' Then he said, 'You should pray for as long as you have the energy, but once you become drowsy or fatigued you should sit down.'[149]

Reported by Muslim and the wording is Aḥmad's.

2.10 Extremism Destroys Communities

Anas ﷺ reported that the Prophet ﷺ said,

إِنَّ هَذَا الدِّينَ مَتِينٌ، فَأَوْغِلُوا فِيهِ بِرِفْقٍ.

Indeed, this religion is powerful, so advance to it with gentleness.[150]

Reported by Aḥmad and al-Ḍiyāʾ al-Maqdisī in *al-Mukhtāra*.

Similarly, there is the hadith of ʿAbd Allāh b. ʿAbbās ﷺ mentioned earlier:

إِيَّاكُمْ وَالْغُلُوَّ فِي الدِّينِ. فَإِنَّمَا أَهْلَكَ مَنْ كَانَ قَبْلَكُمُ الْغُلُوُّ فِي الدِّينِ.

Beware of going to extremes in the religion, for the only thing that destroyed those before you was extremism in the religion.[151]

Reported by Aḥmad, al-Nasāʾī, Ibn Mājah and Ibn al-Jārūd. Ibn Khuzayma, Ibn Ḥibbān and al-Ḥākim declared it authentic.

The takeaway from all of this is that the Muslim should not cause his self to resent the worship of Allah, for the one who burdens his riding animal more than it can bear will neither travel across a land

---

[149] Set forth by •Muslim in *al-Ṣaḥīḥ:* Bk.: *Ṣalāt al-musāfirīn* [The Travelers' Prayer], Ch.: "The Command for the One who is Drowsy while Praying, or Who Mixes up The Qurʾān or Remembrance, to Take Rest," 1:541 §784; •Aḥmad b. Ḥanbal in *al-Musnad*, 3:101.

[150] Set forth by •Aḥmad b. Ḥanbal, *al-Musnad*, 6:198; •al-Maqdisī, *al-Aḥādīth al-mukhtāra*, 6:120 §2115.

[151] Set forth by •al-Nasāʾī, *al-Sunan*, 5:268 §3058; •Ibn Mājah, *al-Sunan*, 2:1008 §3029; •Ibn Ḥibbān, *al-Ṣaḥīḥ*, 9:183–184 §3871; •Abū Yaʿlā, *al-Musnad*, 4:316 §2427; •al-Ṭabarānī, *al-Muʿjam al-kabīr*, 12:156 §12747; •al-Bayhaqī, *al-Sunan al-kubrā*, 5:127.

nor preserve its strength.

The exalted Messenger ﷺ taught that when someone experiences drowsiness while praying, he should take rest and discontinue his prayer. ʿĀʾisha ﷺ reported that the Prophet ﷺ said,

إِذَا نَعَسَ أَحَدُكُمْ فِي صَلَاتِهِ فَلْيَرْقُدْ، حَتَّى يَذْهَبَ عَنْهُ النَّوْمُ؛ فَإِنَّ أَحَدَكُمْ إِذَا صَلَّى وَهُوَ نَاعِسٌ، لَا يَدْرِي لَعَلَّهُ يَذْهَبُ يَسْتَغْفِرُ فَيَسُبَّ نَفْسَهُ.

> When one of you experiences drowsiness while praying, he should lie down until he is no longer sleepy. If someone prays when he is drowsy, he may not know whether he is asking for forgiveness or cursing himself.[152]
>
> This hadith is narrated by Mālik.

Another manifestation of the tolerance, ease and moderation of Islam is the fact that the Prophet forbade extremism and excessiveness in statements or actions. According to ʿAbd Allāh b. Masʿūd ﷺ, Allah's Messenger ﷺ said thrice,

هَلَكَ الْـمُتَنَطِّعُونَ.

> The extremists have perished.[153]

According to this hadith, extremism is forbidden since it leads a Muslim to destruction.

Another manifestation of the tolerance, ease, moderation and mercy in Islam is the fact that it is possible for a Muslim to catch up if he misses something, so long as he does not miss it by neglecting a legal ruling or abandon it altogether. This is why we find numerous instances where the Prophet ﷺ would say, "Do it; there is no harm done."

---

[152] Set forth by •al-Bukhārī in *al-Ṣaḥīḥ:* Bk.: *al-Wuḍūʾ* [The Ablution], Ch.: "On Performing Ablution after Sleep," 1:87 §209; •Muslim in *al-Ṣaḥīḥ:* Bk.: *Ṣalāt al-musāfirīn* [The Travelers' Prayer], Ch.: "The Command for the One who is Drowsy while Praying, or Who Mixes up The Qurʾān or Remembrance, to Take Rest," 1:542 §786.

[153] Set forth by •Muslim in *al-Ṣaḥīḥ:* Bk.: *al-ʿIlm* [The Knowledge], Ch.: "The Extremists Have Perished," 4:2055 §2670.

According to ʿAbd Allāh b. ʿAmr b. al-ʿĀṣ ؓ:

إِنَّ رَسُولَ اللهِ ﷺ وَقَفَ فِي حَجَّةِ الْوَدَاعِ بِمِنًى لِلنَّاسِ يَسْأَلُونَهُ. فَجَاءَهُ رَجُلٌ، فَقَالَ: لَمْ أَشْعُرْ، فَحَلَقْتُ قَبْلَ أَنْ أَذْبَحَ. فَقَالَ: اذْبَحْ وَلَا حَرَجَ. فَجَاءَ آخَرُ، فَقَالَ: لَمْ أَشْعُرْ فَنَحَرْتُ قَبْلَ أَنْ أَرْمِيَ. قَالَ: ارْمِ وَلَا حَرَجَ. فَمَا سُئِلَ النَّبِيُّ ﷺ عَنْ شَيْءٍ قُدِّمَ وَلَا أُخِّرَ إِلَّا قَالَ: افْعَلْ وَلَا حَرَجَ.

Allah's Messenger ﷺ stood at Mina during the farewell pilgrimage as the people were asking him questions. A man came to him and said, "I inadvertently had my hair cut before I sacrificed." The Prophet ﷺ said, "Sacrifice; there is no harm done." Another man came and said, "I inadvertently sacrificed an animal before I cast the stones." The Prophet ﷺ said, "Cast them; there is no harm done." Everything that the Prophet ﷺ was asked about before or after its time, he replied, "Do it; there is no harm done."[154]

Agreed upon.

Saʿīd b. Jubayr ؓ said,

حَدَّثَنَا ابْنُ عَبَّاسٍ: أَنَّ رَسُولَ اللهِ ﷺ جَمَعَ بَيْنَ الصَّلَاةِ فِي سَفْرَةٍ سَافَرَهَا فِي غَزْوَةِ تَبُوكَ، فَجَمَعَ بَيْنَ الظُّهْرِ وَالْعَصْرِ وَالْمَغْرِبِ وَالْعِشَاءِ. قَالَ سَعِيدٌ: فَقُلْتُ لِابْنِ عَبَّاسٍ: مَا حَمَلَهُ عَلَى ذَلِكَ؟ قَالَ: أَرَادَ أَنْ لَا يُحْرِجَ أُمَّتَهُ.

Ibn ʿAbbās ؓ related to us that Allah's Messenger ﷺ would join the prayers when he was on a journey, and that during the battle of Tabuk he combined between Ẓuhr and ʿAṣr and Maghrib and ʿIshāʾ. Saʿīd said, "I said to Ibn ʿAbbās, 'What motivated him to do that? He replied, 'He did not want to

---

154 Set forth by •al-Bukhārī in *al-Ṣaḥīḥ:* Bk.: *al-ʿIlm* [The Knowledge], Ch.: "Delivering Fatwas While Stationary upon an Animal," 1:43 §83; •Muslim in *al-Ṣaḥīḥ:* Bk.: *al-Ḥajj* [The Hajj], Ch.: "Regarding the One Who Shaves His Head before Sacrificing or Sacrifices before Casting Stones," 2:948 §1306.

make things difficult for his *Umma*.'[155]

Reported by Muslim.

2.11 Recommendation of Lenience and Tolerance

Another manifestation of Islam's tolerance and moderation is the fact that the Prophet ﷺ forbade his noble Companions from engaging in perpetual fasts. This was out of his mercy toward them. They saw that the Prophet ﷺ would fast perpetually without breaking his fast, but he informed them that he was not like them, and that Allah provides him with food and drink. This has been mass-transmitted from the Prophet ﷺ and is mentioned in the collections of al-Bukhārī and Muslim from the hadith of Abū Hurayra, Ibn ʿUmar, ʿĀʾisha, Anas and Abū Saʿīd ﷺ.

Abū Hurayra ﷺ reported,

قَالَ رَسُولُ اللهِ ﷺ: إِيَّاكُمْ وَالْوِصَالَ! قَالُوا: فَإِنَّكَ تُوَاصِلُ، يَا رَسُولَ اللهِ! قَالَ: إِنَّكُمْ لَسْتُمْ فِي ذَلِكَ مِثْلِي. إِنِّي أَبِيتُ يُطْعِمُنِي رَبِّي وَيَسْقِينِي، فَاكْلَفُوا مِنَ الْأَعْمَالِ مَا تُطِيقُونَ.

Allah's Messenger ﷺ said, 'Beware of perpetual fasting!' The Companions said, 'But you engage in perpetual fasts, O Allah's Messenger!' He said, 'Indeed, I am not like you all. I spend the night and my Lord provides me with food and drink. Take upon yourself the actions that you can bear.'[156]

Agreed upon.

Another manifestation of Islam's tolerance, ease and mercy for the servants is the fact that the Prophet ﷺ encouraged us to be lenient when buying and selling and settling accounts, and in every other interaction we have with others. Jābir b. ʿAbd Allāh ﷺ reported that

---

[155] Set forth by •Muslim in *al-Ṣaḥīḥ:* Bk.: *Ṣalāt al-musāfirīn* [The Travelers' Prayer], Ch.: "On Combining between Two Prayers while Resident," 1:489 §705.

[156] Set forth by •al-Bukhārī in *al-Ṣaḥīḥ:* Bk.: *al-Ṣawm* [The Fasting], Ch.: "On Perpetual Fasts," 2:694 §1865; •Muslim in *al-Ṣaḥīḥ:* Bk.: *al-Ṣiyām* [The Fasting], Ch.: "The Prohibition of Engaging in a Perpetual Fast," 2:774 §1103.

Allah's Messenger ﷺ said,

رَحِمَ اللهُ رَجُلًا سَمْحًا إِذَا بَاعَ، وَإِذَا اشْتَرَى، وَإِذَا اقْتَضَى.

May Allah have mercy upon the man who is lenient when he buys, sells and settles accounts.[157]

Reported by al-Bukhārī.

Abū Hurayra ؓ related,

أَنَّ رَجُلًا تَقَاضَى رَسُولَ اللهِ ﷺ، فَأَغْلَظَ لَهُ. فَهَمَّ بِهِ أَصْحَابُهُ، فَقَالَ: دَعُوهُ فَإِنَّ لِصَاحِبِ الْحَقِّ مَقَالًا. وَاشْتَرُوا لَهُ بَعِيرًا فَأَعْطُوهُ إِيَّاهُ. وَقَالُوا: لَا نَجِدُ إِلَّا أَفْضَلَ مِنْ سِنِّهِ. قَالَ: اشْتَرُوهُ فَأَعْطُوهُ إِيَّاهُ. فَإِنَّ خَيْرَكُمْ أَحْسَنُكُمْ قَضَاءً.

A man asked Allah's Messenger ﷺ to settle his debt and began to speak coarsely to him. His Companions went for him and Allah's Messenger ﷺ said, 'Leave him alone; the one with a right is allowed to speak. Buy him a camel and give it to him.' The Companions ؓ said, 'O Allah's Messenger! We can only find one that is better than the age that this one warrants.' He said, 'Buy it and give it to him. The best of you is he who is most generous in settlement.'[158]

Agreed upon.

Allah's Messenger ﷺ also explained to us the Afterworldly virtues of being lenient to the one who is in dire straits. Abū al-Yasar ؓ reported that Allah's Messenger ﷺ said,

مَنْ أَنْظَرَ مُعْسِرًا أَوْ وَضَعَ عَنْهُ أَظَلَّهُ اللهُ فِي ظِلِّهِ.

[157] Ibid., Bk.: *al-Istiqrāḍ* [The Loans], Ch.: "Easyness in Sale and Purchase," 2:730 §1970.

[158] Ibid., Bk.: *al-Istiqrāḍ* [The Loans], Ch.: "Seeking Loans for Camels," 2:842 §2260; •Muslim in *al-Ṣaḥīḥ:* Bk.: *al-Musāqāt* [The Sharecropping], Ch.: "On the One Whose Property is Damaged and Receives Something Better than It," 3:1225 §1601.

Whoever gives more time to the debtor in dire straits or forgoes his debt, Allah shall shade him in His Shade.[159]

Reported by Muslim.

2.12 Allah's Pleasure Lies in Helping and Forgiving Behaviour

Abū Qatāda ﵁ reported that Allah's Messenger ﷺ said,

مَنْ سَرَّهُ أَنْ يُنْجِيَهُ اللهُ مِنْ كُرَبِ يَوْمِ الْقِيَامَةِ، فَلْيُنَفِّسْ عَنْ مُعْسِرٍ أَوْ يَضَعْ عَنْهُ.

Whoever would be pleased that Allah grants him safety from a difficulty on the Day of Resurrection, let him relieve the difficulty of someone in dire straits, or let him forgo his debt.[160]

Reported by Muslim.

Abū Hurayra ﵁ reported that Allah's Messenger ﷺ said,

إِنَّ رَجُلًا لَمْ يَعْمَلْ خَيْرًا قَطُّ وَكَانَ يُدَايِنُ النَّاسَ. فَيَقُولُ لِرَسُولِهِ: خُذْ مَا تَيَسَّرَ وَاتْرُكْ مَا عَسُرَ، وَتَجَاوَزْ لَعَلَّ اللهَ تَعَالَى أَنْ يَتَجَاوَزَ عَنَّا. فَلَمَّا هَلَكَ، قَالَ اللهُ لَهُ: هَلْ عَمِلْتَ خَيْرًا قَطُّ؟ قَالَ: لَا، إِلَّا أَنَّهُ كَانَ لِي غُلَامٌ، وَكُنْتُ أُدَايِنُ النَّاسَ، فَإِذَا بَعَثْتُهُ لِيَتَقَاضَى، قُلْتُ لَهُ: خُذْ مَا تَيَسَّرَ وَاتْرُكْ مَا عَسُرَ، وَتَجَاوَزْ لَعَلَّ اللهَ يَتَجَاوَزُ عَنَّا. قَالَ اللهُ تَعَالَى: قَدْ تَجَاوَزْتُ عَنْكَ.

There was a man who was extremely lax in performing good deeds and he used to loan money to people. [When he would loan money out] he would say to his secretary, "Take [in repayment of a loan] that which is easy and leave that which is difficult and overlook it, for perhaps God Most High will overlook us [our faults]." When that man perished, God

---

159 Set forth by •Muslim in *al-Ṣaḥīḥ:* Bk.: *al-Zuhd* [Renunciation], Ch.: "The Long Hadith of Jābir and the Story of Abū al-Yasar," 4:2302 §3006.

160 Ibid., Bk.: *al-Musāqāt* [The Sharecropping], Ch.: "On Giving Reprieve to the Debtor," 3:1196 §1563.

Most High said to him, "Did you ever do any good deeds?" The man replied, "No, but I did have a young servant and I used to loan money to people, so when I would send him to collect the money owed, I would say to him, 'Take that which is easy and leave that which is difficult and overlook it, for perhaps God Most High will overlook us'." God then said, "I have overlooked your faults."[161]

Reported by Aḥmad and this is the wording of al-Nasāʾī.

2.13 Everything is Permissible unless Expressly Prohibited

Allah ﷻ has blessed the Umma with great favour and bounty, originally declaring everything permissible and *ḥalāl*. Only those things that are expressly declared *ḥarām* in the Holy Qurʾān or Sunna are forbidden. This principle has been termed as *al-ibāḥa al-aṣliyya*. The Holy Qurʾān has revealed:

﴿هُوَ ٱلَّذِى خَلَقَ لَكُم مَّا فِى ٱلْأَرْضِ جَمِيعًا﴾

﴾*He is the One Who created for you all that is in the earth.*﴿[162]

Allah ﷻ has created everything for the benefit of humankind.[163] However, the law of prohibition restrains this phenomenon concerning the things Shariah has forbidden. This principle of permissibility encompasses all the animals, birds, plants and human acts except those declared forbidden in Islam. Interpreting this verse, al-Nasafī and al-Zamakhsharī write:

﴿خَلَقَ لَكُم﴾ عَلَى أَنَّ الْأَشْيَاءَ الَّتِيْ يَصِحُّ أَنْ يُنْتَفَعَ بِهَا، وَلَمْ تَجْرِ مَجْرَى الْمَحْظُوْرَاتِ فِي الْعَقْلِ، خُلِقَتْ فِي الْأَصْلِ مُبَاحَةً مُطْلَقًا. لِكُلِّ أَحَدٍ أَنْ

---

[161] Set forth by •Aḥmad b. Ḥanbal in *al-Musnad*, 2:361 §8715; •al-Nasāʾī in *al-Sunan:* Bk.: *al-Buyūʿ* [The Sales], Ch.: "On Dealing with Others Well and Being Kind in Seeking Repayment of Loans," 7:381 §3696; •Ibn Ḥibbān in *al-Ṣaḥīḥ*, 11:422 §5403; •al-Ḥākim in *al-Mustadrak*, 2:33 §2223.

[162] Qurʾān 2:29.

[163] Al-Ṭabarī, *Jāmiʿ al-bayān fī tafsīr al-Qurʾān*, 1:149.

يَّتَنَاوَلَـهَا وَيَسْتَنْفِعَ بِهَا.

> The phrase *khalaqa lakum* ﴿*He created for you all*﴾ implies the things that are profited to the maximum and do not harm wisdom (mental faculties) any way. All such things are originally permissible and everyone can use and benefit from them.[164]

Another verse of the Holy Qur'ān explicitly elaborates:

﴿قُلْ مَنْ حَرَّمَ زِينَةَ ٱللَّهِ ٱلَّتِىٓ أَخْرَجَ لِعِبَادِهِۦ وَٱلطَّيِّبَٰتِ مِنَ ٱلرِّزْقِ﴾

> ﴿*Say: Who has forbidden the adornment (and beautification) of Allah that He has produced for His servants and (who has also forbidden) the pure and clean food?*﴾[165]

Here Allah ﷻ has enjoined His Beloved Prophet ﷺ to forbid people nudity and indecency and declare lawful the embellishment and decent embroidery on dresses and whatever has been made permissible in foods and beverages.[166]

Interpreting this verse, Abū al-Sa'ūd writes:

وَفِيْهِ دَلِيْلٌ عَلَى أَنَّ الْأَصْلَ فِي الْـمَطَاعِمِ وَالْـمَلَابِسِ وَأَنْوَاعِ التَّجَمُّلَاتِ الْإِبَاحَةُ.

> Here is a proof that originally all foods, dresses and diverse ways of ornamentation are permissible.[167]

In the preceding verse (7:31), Almighty Allah states:

﴿ وَٱشْرَبُواْ وَلَا تُسْرِفُوٓاْ إِنَّهُۥ لَا يُحِبُّ ٱلْمُسْرِفِينَ﴾

---

[164] Al-Nasafī, *Madārik al-tanzīl*, 1:35; •Al-Zamakhsharī, *al-Kashshāf 'an ḥaqā'iq ghawāmiḍ al-tanzīl*, 1:152.

[165] Qur'ān 7:32.

[166] Al-Ṭabarī, *Jāmi' al-bayān fī tafsīr al-Qur'ān*, 8:163.

[167] Abū al-Sa'ūd, *Irshād al-'aql al-salīm ilā mazāyā al-Qur'ān al-karīm*, 3:224.

﴾*And eat and drink, but do not spend extravagantly because certainly He does not like the extravagant.*﴿[168]

Al-Ṭabarī has stated that *lā tusrifū* ﴾*do not spend extravagantly*﴿ also means 'do not declare anything forbidden unless I have declared it *ḥarām* in My Book or on the tongue of My Beloved Prophet ﷺ.'[169]

The examples to prove the validation of benefit principle are many where Allah ﷻ has clearly mentioned the forbidden things. However, He has not issued any injunctions to declare things that are permissible because they include ﴾*all that is created for you in the earth*﴿.

When it comes to the relations forbidden for marriage, described in detail in verse 4:23, He has clearly revealed the permissible relations in the very next verse:

﴿وَأُحِلَّ لَكُم مَّا وَرَآءَ ذَٰلِكُمْ﴾

﴾*And (all women) other than these are made lawful for you.*﴿[170]

He has categorically mentioned the detailed list of forbidden relations for wedlock and clearly stated that every other relation is fair for the contract of marriage.

In like manner, Allah has described the forbidden animals in the Holy Qur'ān, but has not mentioned the permissible foods anywhere. He said:

﴿حُرِّمَتْ عَلَيْكُمُ ٱلْمَيْتَةُ وَٱلدَّمُ وَلَحْمُ ٱلْخِنزِيرِ وَمَآ أُهِلَّ لِغَيْرِ ٱللَّهِ بِهِۦ
وَٱلْمُنْخَنِقَةُ وَٱلْمَوْقُوذَةُ وَٱلْمُتَرَدِّيَةُ وَٱلنَّطِيحَةُ وَمَآ أَكَلَ ٱلسَّبُعُ إِلَّا مَا
ذَكَّيْتُمْ وَمَا ذُبِحَ عَلَى ٱلنُّصُبِ وَأَن تَسْتَقْسِمُوا۟ بِٱلْأَزْلَٰمِ ۚ ذَٰلِكُمْ فِسْقٌ﴾

﴾*Forbidden to you is carrion (the animal that dies and is not slaughtered according to Islamic law) and (the discharged) blood and pork and that (animal) on which the name of someone other than Allah has been invoked whilst*

---

168 Qur'ān 7:31.

169 Al-Ṭabarī, *Jāmiʿ al-bayān fī tafsīr al-Qur'ān*, 8:159.

170 Qur'ān 4:24.

slaughtering and (the animal) that dies by strangling or by a violent blow (not by any sharp instrument) or by falling from a height or the one that has been gored to death or which has been ripped apart and gnawed by a wild beast, save the one which you slaughter (before it dies), and (that animal too is forbidden) which has been slaughtered on idolatrous altars (dedicated to false gods). And this (is also unlawful) that you learn your fortune through divining (with arrows or divide shares by such means). All these works are sins.﴾[171]

﴿قَدْ فَصَّلَ لَكُم مَّا حَرَّمَ عَلَيْكُمْ﴾

﴿*He has spelled out to you in detail (all) those things which He has forbidden to you.*﴾[172]

This explains why Allah ﷻ has forbidden asking many questions. A question may elicit reply amounting to the commandment of forbiddance of the thing questioned. Allah ﷻ has said:

﴿يَٰٓأَيُّهَا ٱلَّذِينَ ءَامَنُوا۟ لَا تَسْـَٔلُوا۟ عَنْ أَشْيَآءَ إِن تُبْدَ لَكُمْ تَسُؤْكُمْ وَإِن تَسْـَٔلُوا۟ عَنْهَا حِينَ يُنَزَّلُ ٱلْقُرْءَانُ تُبْدَ لَكُمْ عَفَا ٱللَّهُ عَنْهَا ۗ وَٱللَّهُ غَفُورٌ حَلِيمٌ﴾

﴿*O believers! Do not ask about things (on which the Qur'ān is quiet,) for if they are disclosed to you, they may put you in strain (and you will be repelled by them). But if you enquire about them whilst the Qur'ān is being sent down, they will be disclosed to you (i.e., fixated through revealing the commandments, but this will put an end to your choice of discretion, binding you to only one command). Allah has (so far) overlooked (these matters and questions), and Allah is Most Forgiving, Most Forbearing.*﴾[173]

---

[171] Ibid., 5:3.

[172] Ibid., 6:119.

[173] Ibid., 5:101.

This verse signifies that if a clear command has not yet been revealed about a matter, people should not ask about it because Allah ﷻ may reveal its forbiddance in reply to the question, restricting the choice. It alludes to the original permissibility of that thing before it is questioned about.

The pagan Arabs had forbidden themselves the meat or milk of certain animals of their own accord. Allah ﷻ categorically condemned it, challenging who vested them with the authority to declare this forbidden and that permissible. Allah ﷻ said:

﴿وَلَا تَقُولُوا۟ لِمَا تَصِفُ أَلْسِنَتُكُمُ ٱلْكَذِبَ هَٰذَا حَلَٰلٌ وَهَٰذَا حَرَامٌ لِّتَفْتَرُوا۟ عَلَى ٱللَّهِ ٱلْكَذِبَ ۚ إِنَّ ٱلَّذِينَ يَفْتَرُونَ عَلَى ٱللَّهِ ٱلْكَذِبَ لَا يُفْلِحُونَ﴾

﴿And do not tell a lie which your tongues utter: 'This is lawful and that is forbidden,' thus fabricating a lie against Allah. Indeed, those who fabricate lies against Allah will (never) be delivered.﴾[174]

Elsewhere Allah ﷻ condemns their subjective preferences:

﴿قُلْ أَرَءَيْتُم مَّآ أَنزَلَ ٱللَّهُ لَكُم مِّن رِّزْقٍ فَجَعَلْتُم مِّنْهُ حَرَامًا وَحَلَٰلًا قُلْ ءَآللَّهُ أَذِنَ لَكُمْ ۖ أَمْ عَلَى ٱللَّهِ تَفْتَرُونَ﴾

﴿Say: 'Give your view: Allah sent down for you (pure and clean) provision, but you declared some of those (things) unlawful and (others) lawful.' Say: 'Did Allah accord you (its) permission? Or are you fabricating a lie against Allah?'﴾[175]

Both these verses prove that all things are permissible in origin unless declared forbidden by Allah or His Prophet ﷺ. No human has the authority to declare anything forbidden.

The Prophet of Mercy ﷺ also stated this principle of permissibility in many traditions. Salmān ؓ has narrated:

---

[174] Ibid., 16:116.

[175] Ibid., 10:59.

سُئِلَ رَسُولُ اللهِ ﷺ عَنِ السَّمْنِ وَالْـجُبْنِ وَالْفِرَاءِ. فَقَالَ: الْـحَلَالُ مَا أَحَلَّ اللهُ فِي كِتَابِهِ، وَالْـحَرَامُ مَا حَرَّمَ اللهُ فِي كِتَابِهِ، وَمَا سَكَتَ عَنْهُ فَهُوَ مِـمَّـا عَفَا عَنْهُ.

Once Allah's Messenger ﷺ was asked about ghee, cheese and furry clothes. He replied, 'Permissible is what Allah has declared permissible in His Book and forbidden is what Allah has declared forbidden in His Book; and the things about which He has remained silent are forgiven.'[176]

Reported by al-Tirmidhī and Ibn Mājah.

According to Saʿd b. Abī al-Waqqāṣ ﵁, the Prophet of Mercy ﷺ said:

إِنَّ أَعْظَمَ الْـمُسْلِمِينَ جُرْمًا مَنْ سَأَلَ عَنْ شَيْءٍ لَـمْ يُحَرَّمْ، فَحُرِّمَ مِنْ أَجْلِ مَسْأَلَتِهِ.

The Muslim with the greatest sin is the one who asks about something that has not been forbidden, but then it was forbidden because he asked about it.[177]

Reported by al-Bukhārī and Muslim.

This saying of the Holy Prophet ﷺ clearly establishes the fact that the categorical commandment of Allah ﷻ or His Prophet ﷺ is an unavoidable pre-requisite for declaring something forbidden. If something has not been decreed forbidden, that act or thing will be considered permissible in Shariah.

---

[176] Set forth by •al-Tirmidhī in *al-Sunan: Bk.: al-Libās* [The Dresses], Ch.: "What is said about furry clothes?" 4:220 §1726; and Ibn Mājah in *al-Sunan:* Bk.: *al-Aṭʿima* [The Foods], Ch.: "Eating of ghee and cheese," 2:1117 §3367.

[177] Set forth by •al-Bukhārī in *al-Ṣaḥīḥ:* Bk.: *al-Iʿtiṣām bi al-Kitāb wa al-Sunna* [Holding Fast to the Book and the Sunna], Ch.: "What is disliked of asking too many questions and burdening oneself with that which does not concern one," 6:2658 §6859; and Muslim in *al-Ṣaḥīḥ:* Bk.: *al-Faḍāʾil* [The Virtues and Merits], Ch.: "The Prophet's veneration and leaving aside the questions which are not required," 4:1831 §2358.

Explaining this hadith, Ibn Ḥajar al-ʿAsqalānī writes:

إِنَّ السُّؤَالَ عَنِ الشَّيْءِ بِحَيْثُ يَصِيْرُ سَبَبًا لِتَحْرِيْمِ شَيْءٍ مُبَاحٍ، هُوَ أَعْظَمُ الْـجُرْمِ لِأَنَّهُ صَارَ سَبَبًا لِتَضْيِيْقِ الْأَمْرِ عَلَى جَمِيْعِ الْـمُكَلَّفِيْنَ؛ فَالْقَتْلُ – مَثَلًا – كَبِيْرَةٌ وَلَكِنَّ مَضَرَّتَهُ رَاجِعَةٌ إِلَى الْـمَقْتُوْلِ وَحْدَهُ، أَوْ إِلَى مَنْ هُوَ مِنْهُ بِسَبِيْلٍ بِخِلَافِ صُوْرَةِ الْـمَسْأَلَةِ، فَضَرَرُهَا عَامٌّ لِلْجَمِيْعِ. ... وَفِي الْـحَدِيْثِ أَنَّ الْأَصْلَ فِي الْأَشْيَاءِ الْإِبَاحَةُ حَتَّى يَرِدَ الشَّرْعُ بِخِلَافِ ذَلِكَ.

If a question effects prohibition of a thing, questioning becomes a major sin as it brings about the stricture of law and constrains all Muslims to forbiddance of a permissible thing. Killing someone is a major sin but its harm is only limited to the person murdered. Contrarily, the harm of enticing prohibition of a thing through raising a question affects the entire Muslim community. ... And the hadith narrates that, originally, things are permissible until some commandment is found that annuls the permissibility.[178]

Allah ﷻ and His Beloved Prophet ﷺ expanded the sphere of *ḥilla* (permissibility) and constricted the ambit of prohibition and forbiddance (*ḥurma*) for the welfare of mankind. Following is the famous legal maxim that vividly depicts the unanimous viewpoint of imams in the books of Islamic jurisprudence:

اَلْأَصْلُ فِي الْأَشْيَاءِ إِبَاحَةٌ.

The original rule for everything is permissibility (unless a legal evidence prohibits it).[179]

In this way, practising Islamic teachings and injunctions has been made easy through the humanitarian principle of *al-ibāḥa al-aṣliyya*.

---

[178] Ibn Ḥajar al-ʿAsqalānī, *Fatḥ al-bārī*, 13:268.

[179] Cited by •al-Sarakhsī in *al-Mabṣūṭ*, 24:77; and al-Suyūṭī in *al-Ashbāh wa al-naẓāʾir*, p. 60.

2.14 Legal Dispensations under Pressing Needs

The boundless mercy of the Holy Prophet ﷺ covers the dire human needs and sanctions many exemptions from forbiddance. These dispensations vary from permission of certain food items to concessions in some farming and commercial practices. We can eat fish and locust, liver and spleen, and can practise contracts, such as *ʿarāyā* [to give away one or two palm trees for someone to sell], and farming and commerce, such as sharecropping, sales on credit [*nasiya*], the right of returning goods [*khiyār al-majlis*], advance payments [*salam*], preemption [*shufʿa*] and so forth.

While proclaiming the forbidden foods, Allah ﷻ has conceded dispensations as well when life is under threat:

﴿إِنَّمَا حَرَّمَ عَلَيْكُمُ ٱلْمَيْتَةَ وَٱلدَّمَ وَلَحْمَ ٱلْخِنزِيرِ وَمَآ أُهِلَّ بِهِۦ لِغَيْرِ ٱللَّهِ ۖ
فَمَنِ ٱضْطُرَّ غَيْرَ بَاغٍ وَلَا عَادٍ فَلَآ إِثْمَ عَلَيْهِ ۚ إِنَّ ٱللَّهَ غَفُورٌ رَّحِيمٌ﴾

﴿He has made unlawful for you only the dead animals and blood and the flesh of swine and the animal over which, whilst sacrificing, the name of someone other than Allah has been invoked. But he who is forced by necessity and is neither disobedient nor transgressing will not incur any sin on himself (if he eats that much which is required to survive). Allah is, indeed, Most Forgiving, Ever-Merciful.﴾[180]

Here Allah ﷻ has allowed to eat the forbidden foods to save one's life. It means that Islam does not question such acts as are committed in a state of dire need.

Protection and safeguard of human life is incumbent upon the individual himself. Islam has declared several food items unlawful due to various reasons:

﴿حُرِّمَتْ عَلَيْكُمُ ٱلْمَيْتَةُ وَٱلدَّمُ وَلَحْمُ ٱلْخِنزِيرِ وَمَآ أُهِلَّ لِغَيْرِ ٱللَّهِ بِهِۦ
وَٱلْمُنْخَنِقَةُ وَٱلْمَوْقُوذَةُ وَٱلْمُتَرَدِّيَةُ وَٱلنَّطِيحَةُ وَمَآ أَكَلَ ٱلسَّبُعُ إِلَّا مَا
ذَكَّيْتُمْ وَمَا ذُبِحَ عَلَى ٱلنُّصُبِ﴾

---

[180] Qurʾān 2:173.

﴾*Forbidden to you is carrion (the animal that dies and is not slaughtered according to Islamic law) and (the discharged) blood and pork and that (animal) on which the name of someone other than Allah has been invoked whilst slaughtering and (the animal) that dies by strangling or by a violent blow (not by any sharp instrument) or by falling from a height or the one that has been gored to death or which has been ripped apart and gnawed by a wild beast, save the one which you slaughter (before it dies), and (that animal too is forbidden) which has been slaughtered on idolatrous altars (dedicated to false gods).*﴿[181]

Islamic law may even award punishment to a believer on consuming certain unlawful items. Contrarily, Islam decrees to eat or drink these illicit objects when it becomes necessary to save life under survival conditions:

﴿فَمَنِ ٱضۡطُرَّ فِي مَخۡمَصَةٍ غَيۡرَ مُتَجَانِفٖ لِّإِثۡمٖ فَإِنَّ ٱللَّهَ غَفُورٞ رَّحِيمٞ﴾

﴾*Then if someone gets into a survival situation (and is forced by) ravenous hunger (and intense thirst i.e., driven by dire necessity, provided) he is not prone to sinning (i.e., eats what is forbidden without being wilfully inclined to sin), then Allah is indeed Most Forgiving, Ever-Merciful.*﴿[182]

When a clear law has explained what is lawful and unlawful in food, it is wrong for humans to proclaim anything lawful that is scripturally forbidden.

Allah has revealed in *sūra al-Anʿām* (6:119):

﴿وَمَا لَكُمۡ أَلَّا تَأۡكُلُواْ مِمَّا ذُكِرَ ٱسۡمُ ٱللَّهِ عَلَيۡهِ وَقَدۡ فَصَّلَ لَكُم مَّا
حَرَّمَ عَلَيۡكُمۡ إِلَّا مَا ٱضۡطُرِرۡتُمۡ إِلَيۡهِ﴾

﴾*And what is the matter with you that you do not eat of that (meat) over which the Name of Allah has been pronounced (at the time of slaughter? You regard these lawful animals*

[181] Ibid., 5:3.

[182] Ibid.

as unlawful without any reason), whilst He has spelled out to you in detail (all) those things which He has forbidden to you except when (under the unavoidable circumstances) you are forced (to eat the bare necessity just as a life-saving measure. So do not declare more things forbidden on your own anymore).﴾

See the following verse of *sūra al-Anʿām* (6:145):

﴿قُل لَّآ أَجِدُ فِي مَآ أُوحِيَ إِلَيَّ مُحَرَّمًا عَلَىٰ طَاعِمٖ يَطۡعَمُهُۥٓ إِلَّآ أَن يَكُونَ
مَيۡتَةً أَوۡ دَمٗا مَّسۡفُوحًا أَوۡ لَحۡمَ خِنزِيرٖ فَإِنَّهُۥ رِجۡسٌ أَوۡ فِسۡقًا أُهِلَّ لِغَيۡرِ ٱللَّهِ
بِهِۦۚ فَمَنِ ٱضۡطُرَّ غَيۡرَ بَاغٖ وَلَا عَادٖ فَإِنَّ رَبَّكَ غَفُورٞ رَّحِيمٞ﴾

﴿*Say: 'I do not find in that Revelation which has been sent to me anything forbidden to anyone who eats (such things) as he takes in food except carrion, or flowing blood, or the flesh of swine, for it is filthy and impious, or the sinfully-slaughtered animal on which some name other than Allah's Name has been invoked at the time of slaughter. But he who becomes helpless (due to hunger), and is neither disobeying nor transgressing, then surely your Lord is Most Forgiving, Ever-Merciful.'*﴾

On another occasion, the Holy Qurʾān has proclaimed:

﴿إِنَّمَا حَرَّمَ عَلَيۡكُمُ ٱلۡمَيۡتَةَ وَٱلدَّمَ وَلَحۡمَ ٱلۡخِنزِيرِ وَمَآ أُهِلَّ لِغَيۡرِ ٱللَّهِ بِهِۦۖ
فَمَنِ ٱضۡطُرَّ غَيۡرَ بَاغٖ وَلَا عَادٖ فَإِنَّ ٱللَّهَ غَفُورٞ رَّحِيمٞ﴾

﴿*He has only forbidden you carrion, blood, the flesh of swine and (the animal) on which the name of other than Allah is invoked at the time of slaughter. But he who is faced with a survival condition (forced by necessity), neither defying (Allah's injunctions seeking taste of lust), nor transgressing (the limit of necessity), then Allah is surely Most Forgiving, Ever-Merciful.*﴾[183]

---

[183] Ibid., 16:115.

These verses of the Holy Qurʾān have unambiguously described the forbidden things. Alongside forbiddance, Allah ﷻ has also conferred exception to the rule on those who face some danger to their life. This signifies the right to life. Since human life has to be saved at all costs, the law of forbiddance is held in abeyance under survival conditions. Islam does not allow the believers to kill themselves with their own hands, i.e., through following the injunctions of Islam strictly without caring for necessities of life. For example, ablution is necessary before offering the ritual prayer, but if one does not find water or cannot perform ablution, he is allowed dry ablution—*tayammum*—to rub face and hands with pure dust. The Holy Qurʾān states:

﴿وَإِن كُنتُم مَّرْضَىٰٓ أَوْ عَلَىٰ سَفَرٍ أَوْ جَآءَ أَحَدٌ مِّنكُم مِّنَ ٱلْغَآئِطِ
أَوْ لَـٰمَسْتُمُ ٱلنِّسَآءَ فَلَمْ تَجِدُوا۟ مَآءً فَتَيَمَّمُوا۟ صَعِيدًا طَيِّبًا فَٱمْسَحُوا۟
بِوُجُوهِكُمْ وَأَيْدِيكُمْ﴾

﴿And if you are sick, or on a journey, or return from a call of nature, or make sexual contact with (your) women and then fail to find water, then clean yourselves by using pure soil. So wipe your faces and hands.﴾[184]

The philosophy of *tayammum* has been described in the following verse:

﴿مَا يُرِيدُ ٱللَّهُ لِيَجْعَلَ عَلَيْكُم مِّنْ حَرَجٍ وَلَـٰكِن يُرِيدُ لِيُطَهِّرَكُمْ وَلِيُتِمَّ
نِعْمَتَهُۥ عَلَيْكُمْ لَعَلَّكُمْ تَشْكُرُونَ﴾

﴿Allah does not want to make things hard for you, but He wants to purify you, and complete the bestowal of His favour upon you so that you may become grateful.﴾[185]

This is the philosophy of ease and exception in Islam. We find numerous examples of dispensation practised in the Prophet's life and in the Caliphate period as well.

Islam has prohibited men from wearing silk. However, the Holy

[184] Ibid., 4:43.

[185] Ibid., 5:6.

Prophet ﷺ allowed two of his Companions to don silk. They are ʿAbd al-Raḥmān b. ʿAwf and al-Zubayr ؓ. He awarded them this exception on medical grounds. According to Anas ؓ:

أَنَّ عَبْدَ الرَّحْمَنِ بْنَ عَوْفٍ وَالزُّبَيْرَ شَكَوَا إِلَى النَّبِيِّ ﷺ يَعْنِي الْقَمْلَ، فَأَرْخَصَ لَهُمَا فِي الْحَرِيرِ، فَرَأَيْتُهُ عَلَيْهِمَا فِي غَزَاةٍ.

ʿAbd al-Raḥmān b. ʿAwf and al-Zubayr ؓ complained to the Prophet ﷺ about lice, and he allowed them to wear silk. I saw them wearing it during an expedition.[186]

Reported by al-Bukhārī.

Abū Wāqid al-Laythī ؓ narrated:

قُلْتُ: يَا رَسُولَ اللهِ! إِنَّا بِأَرْضٍ تُصِيبُنَا بِهَا مَخْمَصَةٌ، فَمَا يَحِلُّ لَنَا مِنَ الْمَيْتَةِ؟ قَالَ: إِذَا لَمْ تَصْطَبِحُوا وَلَمْ تَغْتَبِقُوا وَلَمْ تَحْتَفِئُوا بَقْلًا، فَشَأْنُكُمْ بِهَا.

I said, 'O Messenger of Allah! We live in a land where famine often strikes us. Therefore, we do not have any option to avoid dead meat.' The Prophet ﷺ replied, 'When you do not find food for lunch and dinner, nor have any produce to eat, then eat from it.'[187]

Only Aḥmad collected this narration and its chain meets the criteria of the two *Ṣaḥīḥs*.

These Qurʾānic verses and Prophetic traditions have established that Islam wants to save human life in every situation and under all circumstances. If one cannot save life except by making use of forbidden things, one is allowed to take them as much as is required for survival. If some obligatory acts of worship strait-lace the performance of the rituals, Shariah allows relaxation in performing the obligatory acts of worship to protect life. For example, if

---

186 Set forth by •al-Bukhārī in *al-Ṣaḥīḥ*: Bk.: *al-Jihād wa al-siyar* [Jihad and Military Expeditions], Ch.: "Silk during war," 3:169 §2763.

187 Set forth by •Aḥmad b. Ḥanbal in *al-Musnad*, 5:218 §§21948, 21951; and al-Bayhaqī in *al-Sunan al-kubrā*, 9:356.

someone fears loss of life due to enemy assault in the state of offering ritual prayer, he is allowed to break the prayer to safeguard his life. If someone's life is threatened due to extreme hunger or thirst while fasting, he can break his fast. A woman who fears abortion due to unbearable condition while fasting has the permission to break her fast. If someone fails to find the safe way to Mecca to perform pilgrimage, he can defer this duty to perform Hajj. Islam has sanctioned these and many other dispensations to ease the believers to protect their lives from impending dangers.

These are a few examples of some extreme necessities where Islam allows exception to the rule for the safety of human life. The authorities on Islamic jurisprudence have formulated the following principles pertaining to the conditions of necessity:

اَلضَّرُوْرَاتُ تُبِيْحُ الْمَحْظُوْرَاتِ.

Necessities legalize exception to prohibitions.[188]

اَلْأَمْرُ إِذَا ضَاقَ اتَّسَعَ.

When a matter constricts, it dilates and expands.[189]

2.15 SUMMARY

In sum, the manifestations of ease and tolerance in Islam are manifold and include every foundation and subsidiary branch of the religion. Another manifestation of the ease and tolerance of Islam is the fact that worship is made easy. It is difficult to present the individual proofs for all the examples of ease in our religion, but let us look at the ease found in the main issues. When it comes to ritual purification [*ṭahāra*], the Lawgiver has allowed us to purify ourselves with seawater and other types of water, just as He has allowed dry ablution for the one who cannot find water, or who finds it difficult to use. Likewise, He has allowed us to wipe over leather socks due to cold weather and the

188 Cited by •al-Sarakhsī in *al-Mabṣūṭ*, 10:154; and al-Shāṭibī in *al-Muwāfaqāt*, 4:145–146.

189 Cited by •al-Nawawī in *al-Majmūʿ*, 1:576 & 8:16, 204; and al-Suyūṭī in *al-Ashbāh wa al-naẓāʾir*, p. 83.

like. Moreover, the Lawgiver has informed us that the believer is not considered impure, even if he is in a state requiring major ritual purity [*junub*] and so on and so forth.

2.15.1 Obligatory Prayer

When it comes to prayer, the Lawgiver has allowed us to join and shorten them when travelling. He has allowed us to pray our supererogatory prayers on a riding animal, no matter what direction it turns. The Lawgiver has not made the ritual prayer conditional upon its performance in a particular place—it is allowed anywhere—and He has not made it incumbent on women to pray during menses.

2.15.2 Obligatory Fasting

When it comes to fasting, the Lawgiver has allowed us to break our fast during journeys, and has allowed us to break it while being resident if we are unable to fast due to sickness and the like. Likewise, it is allowed to eat, drink and have intimate relations during the nights of Ramaḍān.

2.15.3 Obligatory Charity [Zakat]

When it comes to Zakat, the Lawgiver has only made it incumbent upon those who possesses the minimum required amount to pay [*niṣāb*] and it has been in their possession for a year. Not only that, but the actual percentage of money that is paid as Zakat is small, and it is not due on items that are used.

2.15.4 Performance of Hajj

When it comes to the Hajj, the Lawgiver has not made it compulsory upon the one who is able, provided the way is secure. He has allowed certain actions to be done before or after their proper time on the day of sacrifice, and nothing of the Prophet's actions on that day was made obligatory except for the standing. Likewise, the one upon whom there is an expiation is given the choice of performing a sacrifice, fasting or feeding the poor.

2.15.5 Tenets of Faith

When it comes to the tenets of faith [*ʿaqīda*], the texts of the Shariah are vividly clear. There is no obscurity, complication or inexplicability. The rulings of the Sacred Law are applied according to their outward purport and no one is given a burden heavier than he or she can bear. There is no extremism in the religion, and simple mistakes, forgetfulness and coercion are forgiven. In our doctrine, the basis for things is that of permissibility [*ibāḥa*], and the forbidden things are relatively few in comparison to the great number of things that are allowed.

2.15.6 Acts of Worship

When it comes to acts of worship, it is recommended to follow the legal dispensations just as it is recommended to follow the strictures of the law. Legal dispensations include shortening prayers during travel, breaking the fast during sickness or journey, performing the dry ablution when water is either absent or difficult to use, reciting the Qurʾān in one of the seven modes of recitation, being brief in one's prayer and not lengthening it, and praying while seated for the one who is unable to stand and so on.

2.15.7 Manner of Invitation [*Daʿwa*]

When it comes to invitation and calling others, the calling is to be done with wisdom and goodly preaching and the caller should listen to the views of others. The caller should not isolate himself or herself or charge the Muslims with disbelief or blameworthy innovations and so on.

2.15.8 *Muʿāmalāt* [Interactions]

When it comes to interactions [*muʿāmalāt*], we are encouraged to be lenient in buying and selling. Both the buyer and the seller should have the option of return. It is urged to forgive the debtor who is in dire straits and it is prohibited to unjustly consume the wealth of orphans and so on.

2.15.9 Marriage

When it comes to marriage, it is allowed for the potential groom to look at the potential bride with the intention of betrothing her. In addition, Islam recommends setting a low dowry price and making marriage easy. It is made incumbent for the husband to financially maintain his wife and it has legislated divorce and annulment.

2.15.10 Family Relations

When it comes to personal relations, Islam prescribes familial piety, kindness to seniors and inheritance. It demands that the roads are given their rights. It allows for people to interact with women during their menses and informs us that their actions are permissible and that they do not defile the home, beddings or food.

2.15.11 International Relations

When it comes to international relations, Islam's tolerance and ease manifests in times of peace and war. It enjoins kind treatment to the prisoners of war and forbids finishing the wounded off. It prescribes kind treatment to the People of the Scripture and the inhabitants of conquered lands and commands that we bury their dead.

2.15.12 Sins and Punishments

Other examples include: cancellation of the punishment of death for the person if the victim's heirs agree to accept blood-money; prayer in any location; the sufficiency of repentance and remorse; the legality of dry ablution when water is absent or difficult to use; removal of the punishment in the grave for one who does not safeguard himself from urine dropping on his clothing or skin (it being sufficient to wash the affected location with water); the removal of sin from one who errs or forgets or is coerced; the dispensation for husband and close male relatives to mix with menstruating women; and many other things that were considered unlawful in the previous communities.

And finally, when it comes to the self and the psyche, Islam has allowed the good things and forbidden the vile things. All of these are bounties from Allah ﷻ and indicate the immense tolerance and mercy of Islam.

اَلْبَابُ الثَّالِثُ

كَوْنُ اَلْقُرْآنِ رَحْمَةً وَشِفَاءً

Chapter Three

The Holy Qur'ān as Mercy and Cure

AL-RAḤMĀN [MOST COMPASSIONATE] AND AL-RAḤĪM [EVER-Merciful] are the beautiful names of Almighty Allah which He manifested in the first verse of the Holy Qur'ān. His Last Prophet Muhammad ﷺ is also a mercy for all the worlds. Moreover, the last book of Almighty Allah which was revealed to the Messenger of Mercy ﷺ is also mercy and blessing. The Holy Qur'ān is Almighty Allah's prestigious gift to mankind and a generous manifestation of His Beautiful Names—al-Raḥmān [Most Compassionate] and al-Raḥīm [Ever-Merciful]. The Qur'ān is truly a blessing from our Lord. Almighty Allah stated this attribute of the Holy Qur'ān in many places:

﴿وَمَآ أَنزَلۡنَا عَلَيۡكَ ٱلۡكِتَٰبَ إِلَّا لِتُبَيِّنَ لَهُمُ ٱلَّذِي ٱخۡتَلَفُواْ فِيهِ وَهُدٗى
وَرَحۡمَةٗ لِّقَوۡمٖ يُؤۡمِنُونَ﴾

﴾*And We have not revealed to you the Book except that you may explain clearly to them those (matters) in which they differ; and (also that this Book) is guidance and mercy for the people that have embraced faith.*﴿[190]

﴿وَإِنَّهُۥ لَهُدٗى وَرَحۡمَةٞ لِّلۡمُؤۡمِنِينَ﴾

﴾*And verily, it is guidance and mercy for the believers.*﴿[191]

﴿تِلۡكَ ءَايَٰتُ ٱلۡكِتَٰبِ ٱلۡحَكِيمِ ٢ هُدٗى وَرَحۡمَةٗ لِّلۡمُحۡسِنِينَ﴾

﴾*These are Verses of the Book of Wisdom, Guidance and mercy for the pious.*﴿[192]

---

[190] Ibid., 16:64.

[191] Ibid., 27:77.

[192] Ibid., 31:2–3.

﴿رَحْمَةً مِّن رَّبِّكَ ۚ إِنَّهُۥ هُوَ ٱلسَّمِيعُ ٱلْعَلِيمُ﴾

﴾(It) is mercy from your Lord. Verily, He is All-Hearing, All-Knowing.﴿[193]

﴿هَٰذَا بَصَٰٓئِرُ لِلنَّاسِ وَهُدًى وَرَحْمَةٌ لِّقَوْمٍ يُوقِنُونَ﴾

﴾This (Qurʾān) contains proofs, which provide vision and lessons of warning to the people, and is guidance and mercy for those who believe with certitude.﴿[194]

Not only a blessing and mercy, but the Holy Qurʾān is also a cause of mercy:

﴿وَهَٰذَا كِتَٰبٌ أَنزَلْنَٰهُ مُبَارَكٌ فَٱتَّبِعُوهُ وَٱتَّقُوا۟ لَعَلَّكُمْ تُرْحَمُونَ﴾

﴾And this (Qurʾān) is a Book which We have revealed full of blessings. So (now) follow it and fear (Allah) persistently so that you are shown mercy.﴿[195]

﴿وَإِذَا قُرِئَ ٱلْقُرْءَانُ فَٱسْتَمِعُوا۟ لَهُۥ وَأَنصِتُوا۟ لَعَلَّكُمْ تُرْحَمُونَ﴾

﴾And when the Qurʾān is recited, listen to it attentively, and observe silence so that mercy may be bestowed upon you.﴿[196]

In some places Almighty Allah stated that the Holy Qurʾān is cure for both soul and body. The Holy Qurʾān has remedies to illness, not only impurity within our heart and weakness of *īmān* but it can cure real diseases. Almighty Allah stated:

﴿يَٰٓأَيُّهَا ٱلنَّاسُ قَدْ جَآءَتْكُم مَّوْعِظَةٌ مِّن رَّبِّكُمْ وَشِفَآءٌ لِّمَا فِى ٱلصُّدُورِ
وَهُدًى وَرَحْمَةٌ لِّلْمُؤْمِنِينَ﴾

---

193 Ibid., 44:6.

194 Ibid., 45:20.

195 Ibid., 16:64.

196 Ibid., 6:155.

﴾*O mankind! Surely, there has come to you an admonition from your Lord, and a cure for all those (diseases) which are (hidden) in the breasts. And it is guidance and mercy (too) for those who are blessed with faith.*﴿[197]

﴿وَنُنَزِّلُ مِنَ ٱلْقُرْءَانِ مَا هُوَ شِفَآءٌ وَرَحْمَةٌ لِّلْمُؤْمِنِينَ﴾

﴾*And We are sending down in the Qur'ān what is healing and mercy for the believers.*﴿[198]

﴿وَلَوْ جَعَلْنَٰهُ قُرْءَانًا أَعْجَمِيًّا لَّقَالُوا۟ لَوْلَا فُصِّلَتْ ءَايَٰتُهُۥٓ ۖ ءَا۬عْجَمِىٌّ وَعَرَبِىٌّ ۗ
قُلْ هُوَ لِلَّذِينَ ءَامَنُوا۟ هُدًى وَشِفَآءٌ ۖ وَٱلَّذِينَ لَا يُؤْمِنُونَ فِىٓ ءَاذَانِهِمْ وَقْرٌ وَهُوَ
عَلَيْهِمْ عَمًى ۚ أُو۟لَٰٓئِكَ يُنَادَوْنَ مِن مَّكَانٍۭ بَعِيدٍ﴾

﴾*And if We had revealed this (Book) as a Qur'ān in a non-Arabic language, they would certainly have said: 'Why have its Verses not been expounded expressly? Is the Book non-Arabic and the Prophet an Arab?' (So, O Esteemed Beloved, We have revealed the Qur'ān also in your language.) Say: 'That (Qur'ān) is guidance as well as healing for the believers, but those who do not believe, their ears are heavy with deafness, and that is blindness (as well) in their case, (as if) they are like men called from afar.'*﴿[199]

This is one of the miraculous attributes of the Holy Qur'ān that it provides all kinds of blessings, mercy and cures. There are numerous hadiths that elaborate this peculiar aspect of the Holy Qur'ān.

Here are some of these hadith reports.

1. According to ʿĀ'isha ﵂,

إِنَّ النَّبِيَّ ﷺ كَانَ يَنْفُثُ عَلَى نَفْسِهِ فِي الْـمَرَضِ الَّذِي مَاتَ فِيْهِ بِالْـمُعَوِّذَاتِ،

---

[197] Ibid., 10:57.

[198] Ibid., 17:82.

[199] Ibid., 41:44.

فَلَمَّا ثَقُلَ كُنْتُ أَنْفُثُ عَلَيْهِ بِهِنَّ وَأَمْسَحُ بِيَدِ نَفْسِهِ لِبَرَكَتِهَا.

فَسَأَلْتُ الزُّهْرِيَّ: كَيْفَ يَنْفُثُ؟ قَالَ: كَانَ يَنْفُثُ عَلَى يَدَيْهِ ثُمَّ يَمْسَحُ بِهِمَا وَجْهَهُ.

The Prophet ﷺ, after reciting the *muʿawwidhāt* (the Qurʾānic exorcist formulae), used to blow on himself in the illness from which he died. When the illness aggravated, I used to blow the same chapters of refuge on him and would wipe his (own) sacrosanct hand over him for blessing.

Maʿmar, the sub-narrator, asked Ibn Shihāb al-Zuhrī: 'How would he blow the exorcist formula?' He said: '(After reciting the chapters of refuge) the Prophet ﷺ used to blow on his hands, wiping the face with them.'[200]

Agreed upon.

2. According to ʿĀʾisha ﵂,

كَانَ رَسُولُ اللهِ ﷺ إِذَا مَرِضَ أَحَدٌ مِنْ أَهْلِهِ، نَفَثَ عَلَيْهِ بِالْـمُعَوِّذَاتِ. فَلَمَّا مَرِضَ مَرَضَهُ الَّذِي مَاتَ فِيهِ، جَعَلْتُ أَنْفُثُ عَلَيْهِ وَأَمْسَحُهُ بِيَدِ نَفْسِهِ لِأَنَّهَا كَانَتْ أَعْظَمَ بَرَكَةً مِنْ يَدِي.

When any of the members of the household of Allah's Messenger ﷺ fell ill, he would recite the *muʿawwidhāt* (the last two refuge chapters of the Qurʾān) and blow on him.

---

[200] Set forth by •al-Bukhārī in *al-Ṣaḥīḥ*: Bk.: *al-Ṭibb* [The Medicine], Ch.: "Using Incantations and the Refuge *Sūras* of the Qurʾān," 5:2165 §5403 & in Ch.: "A Woman Doing an Incantation for a Man," 5:2170 §5419. •Muslim in *al-Ṣaḥīḥ*: Bk.: *al-Salām* [The Well-being], Ch.: "Doing an Incantation for a Patient," 4:1723 §2192. •Aḥmad b. Ḥanbal in *al-Musnad*, 6:114 §24875, 24971, 26306. •Ibn Mājah in *al-Sunan*: Bk.: *al-Ṭibb* [The Medicine], Ch.: "What Should be Recited When One Goes to the Bed," 2:1275 §3875. •al-Nasāʾī in *al-Sunan al-Kubrā*, 4:255 §7086. •Mālik in *al-Muwaṭṭaʾ*, 2:942 §1687. •Ibn Ḥibbān in *al-Ṣaḥīḥ*, 7:230 §2963. •ʿAbd b. Ḥumayd in *al-Musnad*, 1:429 §1474.

When the disease that proved fatal visited him, I used to blow on him and rub his sacred hand over his body as his hand had greater healing power than my hand.[201]

Agreed upon by al-Bukhārī and Muslim.

3. According to ʿĀʾisha ﵂,

كَانَ رَسُوْلُ اللهِ ﷺ إِذَا أَوَى إِلَى فِرَاشِهِ نَفَثَ فِي كَفَّيْهِ: بِـ: ﴿قُلْ هُوَ ٱللَّهُ أَحَدٌ﴾ وَبِالْـمُعَوِّذَتَيْنِ جَمِيْعًا، ثُمَّ يَمْسَحُ بِهِمَـا وَجْهَهُ وَمَا بَلَغَتْ يَدَاهُ مِنْ جَسَدِهِ. قَالَتْ عَائِشَةُ: فَلَمَّـا اشْتَكَى كَانَ يَأْمُرُنِي أَنْ أَفْعَلَ ذَالِكَ بِهِ.

When the Messenger of Allah ﷺ went to bed, he blew on his hands after reciting the *Sūra al-Ikhlās* and the two *sūrās* of refuge (*Sūra al-Falaq* and *Sūra al-Nās*) and then he would wipe his face and his body with them as far as his hands could reach." ʿĀʾisha ﵂ added, "When the Prophet ﷺ was ill, he ordered me to do that (being unable to do it himself owing to debility).[202]

Reported by al-Bukhārī.

4. According to ʿUqba b. ʿĀmir ﵁,

بَيْنَا أَنَا أَسِيْرُ مَعَ رَسُولِ اللهِ ﷺ بَيْنَ الْـجُحْفَةِ وَالْأَبْوَاءِ إِذْ غَشِيَتْنَا رِيْحٌ وَظُلْمَةٌ شَدِيْدَةٌ، فَجَعَلَ رَسُولُ اللهِ ﷺ يَتَعَوَّذُ بِـ: ﴿قُلْ أَعُوذُ بِرَبِّ ٱلْفَلَقِ﴾

---

[201] Set forth by •al-Bukhārī in *al-Ṣaḥīḥ:* Bk.: *Faḍāʾil al-Qurʾān* [The Excellent Merits of the Qurʾān], Ch.: "The Excellent Merits of the *Muʿawwidhāt* (the Last Two Chapters of the Qurʾān)," 4:1916 §4728; •Muslim in *al-Ṣaḥīḥ:* Bk.: *al-Salām* [The Well-being], Ch.: "Doing an Incantation for a Patient with the *Muʿawwidhāt* (the Last Two Chapters of the Qurʾān) and Blowing," 4:1723 §2192. •Abū Dāwūd in *al-Sunan:* Bk.: *al-Ṭibb* [The Medicine], Ch.: "How to Perform the Incantation," 4:15 §3902. •Ibn Mājah in *al-Sunan:* Bk.: *al-Ṭibb* [The Medicine], Ch.: "Blowing in the Course of Performimg Incantation," 2:1166 §3529. •al-Nasāʾī in *al-Sunan al-Kubrā*, 6:250 §10847.

[202] Set forth by •al-Bukhārī in *al-Ṣaḥīḥ:* Bk.: *al-Ṭibb* [The Medicine], Ch.: "Blowing in the Course of Performimg Incantation," 5:2169 §5416. •Aḥmad b. Ḥanbal in *al-Musnad*, 6:154 §25249. •Ibn Ḥibbān in *al-Ṣaḥīḥ*, 12:352 §5543. •al-Ḥakīm al-Tirmidhī in *Nawādir al-Uṣūl*, 3:213.

وَ﴿قُلْ أَعُوذُ بِرَبِّ ٱلنَّاسِ﴾ وَيَقُولُ: يَا عُقْبَةُ، تَعَوَّذْ بِهِمَا فَمَا تَعَوَّذَ مُتَعَوِّذٌ بِمِثْلِهِمَا. قَالَ: وَسَمِعْتُهُ يَؤُمُّنَا بِهِمَا فِي الصَّلَاةِ.

While I was travelling with the Allah's Messenger ﷺ between al-Juḥfa and al-Abwāʾ, a windstorm and intense darkness enveloped us. Upon this Allah's Messenger ﷺ began to seek refuge with Allah, reciting: 'I seek refuge with the Lord of daybreak,' and 'I seek refuge with the Lord of (the whole of) mankind.' He enjoined me persistently: "ʿUqba, use them seeking refuge in Allah, for no one seeks refuge with anything comparable to these *sūrās* (though they are granted refuge).' I heard him reciting them when he led the people in prayer.[203]

Reported by Abū Dāwūd and al-Bayhaqī.

5. According to ʿAlī ؓ,

بَيْنَا رَسُولُ اللهِ ﷺ ذَاتَ لَيْلَةٍ يُصَلِّي فَوَضَعَ يَدَهُ عَلَى الْأَرْضِ فَلَدَغَتْهُ عَقْرَبٌ فَتَنَاوَلَهَا رَسُولُ اللهِ ﷺ بِنَعْلِهِ فَقَتَلَهَا فَلَمَّا انْصَرَفَ قَالَ: لَعَنَ اللهُ الْعَقْرَبَ. لَا تَدَعُ مُصَلِّيًا وَلَا غَيْرَهُ أَوْ نَبِيًّا وَلَا غَيْرَهُ إِلَّا لَدَغَتْهُمْ ثُمَّ دَعَا بِمِلْحٍ وَمَاءٍ فَجَعَلَهُ فِي إِنَاءٍ ثُمَّ جَعَلَ يَصُبُّهُ عَلَى إِصْبَعِهِ حَيْثُ لَدَغَتْهُ وَيَمْسَحُهَا وَيُعَوِّذُهَا بِالْمُعَوِّذَتَيْنِ.

وَفِي رِوَايَةٍ لِلطَّبَرَانِيِّ وَالْبَيْهَقِيِّ: رَوَاهُ ابْنُ فُضَيْلٍ عَنْ مُطَرِّفٍ: لَمْ يَذْكُرْ تَنَاوُلَهَا بِالْفِعْلِ قَالَ: ثُمَّ دَعَا بِمَاءٍ، وَمِلْحٍ وَجَعَلَ يَمْسَحُ عَلَيْهَا وَيَقْرَأُ: ﴿قُلْ هُوَ ٱللَّهُ أَحَدٌ﴾ وَ﴿قُلْ أَعُوذُ بِرَبِّ ٱلْفَلَقِ﴾ وَ﴿قُلْ أَعُوذُ بِرَبِّ ٱلنَّاسِ﴾.

---

[203] Set forth by •Abū Dāwūd in *al-Sunan:* Bk.: *al-Adhān* [The Call to Prayer], Ch.: "On the Two *Sūrās* of Refuge (*Sūra al-Falaq* and *Sūra al-Nās*)," 2:73 §1463. •al-Bayhaqī in *al-Sunan al-kubrā*, 2:294 §3856 & in *Shuʿab al-īmān*, 2:511, 517 §2563, 2573. •al-Mundharī in *al-Targhīb wa al-tarhīb*, 2:251 §2283.

One night, while the Messenger of Allah ﷺ was performing the ritual prayer, a scorpion stung him when he put his hand on ground. He struck it with his sandal and killed it and said after completing the prayer: 'Allah curse the scorpion! It does not spare the person engaged in the ritual prayer and the one not engaged in the ritual prayer, or the Prophet and other than the Prophet.' He then called for salt and water, put it into a vessel, and poured it over where the scorpion had stung. He rubbed it with his hand, seeking refuge with Allah by reciting the *muʿawwidhāt* (the last two chapters of the Qur'ān).[204]

Reported by Ibn Mājah in brief, Ibn Abī Shayba (the wording is his), al-Bayhaqī and al-Ṭabarānī. Its chain of transmission is fine.

According to al-Ṭabarānī and al-Bayhaqī, on the authority of Fuḍayl, on the authority of Muṭarrif and he has not mentioned the Prophet's killing the scorpion; (sufficing to state that) he called for water and salt and rubbed his finger with his hand and recited the Refuge *Sūrās* (that is, the last three chapters of the Qur'ān) over it.[205]

6. According to ʿAbd Allāh ؓ,

قَالَ رَسُولُ اللهِ ﷺ: عَلَيْكُمْ بِالشِّفَاءَيْنِ: الْقُرْآنِ وَالْعَسَلِ.

Allah's Messenger ﷺ said: 'You must use the two healers: the Qur'ān and honey.'[206]

---

[204] Set forth by •Ibn Mājah in *al-Sunan* on the authority of ʿĀ'isha ؓ, Bk.: *Iqāmat al-Ṣalāt wa al-Sunna fi-hā* [The Performance of the Ritual Prayer and the Sunna therein], Ch.: "What Has Come to us Concerning Killing the Scorpion and the Snake in the Course of Ritual Prayer," 1:395 §1246. •Ibn Abī Shayba in *al-Muṣannaf*, 5:44 §23553. •al-Daylamī in *al-Firdaws bi-ma'thūr al-khiṭāb*, 3:465 §5442.

[205] Set forth by •al-Bayhaqī in *Shuʿab al-īmān*, 2:518 §2575. •al-Ṭabarānī in *al-Muʿjam al-awsaṭ*, 6:91 §5890 & in *al-Muʿjam al-ṣaghīr*, 2:87 §830. •al-Daylamī in *al-Firdaws bi-ma'thūr al-khiṭāb*, 3:465 §5442. Accordning to al-Haythamī: "Its chain of transmission is excellent."

[206] Set forth by •al-Ḥākim in *al-Mustadrak*, 4:223 §7437. •Ibn Abī Shayba

Reported by al-Ḥākim, Ibn Abī Shayba, al-Ṭabarānī and al-Bayhaqī (the wording is his). According to al-Ḥākim: 'This is an authentic tradition in conformity with the stipulation of Muslim.'

7. According to ʿAbd Allāh b. Masʿūd ﵁,

فِي الْقُرْآنِ شِفَاءَانِ: الْقُرْآنِ وَالْعَسَلِ. اَلْقُرْآنُ شِفَاءٌ لِمَا فِي الصُّدُورِ وَالْعَسَلُ شِفَاءٌ مِنْ كُلِّ دَاءٍ.

The Qurʾān contains two healers: the Qurʾān (itself) and honey. The Qurʾān cures all the diseases of breast and honey remedies all other diseases.[207]

Reported by al-Bayhaqī.

8. According to Wāthila b. al-Asqaʿ ﵁,

إِنَّ رَجُلًا شَكَى إِلَى رَسُولِ اللهِ ﷺ وَجْعَ حَلْقِهِ قَالَ: عَلَيْكَ بِقِرَاءَةِ الْقُرْآنِ.

A person complained to Allah's Messenger ﷺ of his throat trouble. He said: 'Make the recitation of the Qurʾān incumbent upon you (whereupon the throat trouble will disappear).'[208]

Reported by al-Bayhaqī.

9. According to Ṭalḥa b. Maṣraf ﵁,

كَانَ يُقَالُ: إِنَّ الْمَرِيْضَ إِذَا قُرِئَ عِنْدَهُ الْقُرْآنُ وَجَدَ لَهُ خِفَّةً. فَدَخَلْتُ عَلَى خَيْثَمَةَ وَهُوَ مَرِيْضٌ، فَقُلْتُ: إِنِّي أَرَاكَ الْيَومَ صَالِحًا. قَالَ: إِنَّهُ قُرِئَ عِنْدِي الْقُرْآنُ.

They would say when the Qurʾān is recited near a patient, he feels better. When I went to Khaythama ﵁ to inquire after his well-being, I told him that I found him better.' He replied:

---

in *al-Muṣannaf*, 5:60 §23689 & in 6:126 §30019. •al-Ṭabarānī in *al-Muʿjam al-kabīr*, 9:222 §9076. •al-Bayhaqī in *Shuʿab al-īmān*, 2:519 §2581.

207 Set forth by •al-Bayhaqī in *al-Sunan al-kubrā*, 9:345.

208 Set forth by •al-Bayhaqī in *Shuʿab al-īmān*, 2:519 §2580.

'The Qur'ān has been recited near me (and this is due to the blessing of the Qur'ān).'[209]

Reported by al-Bayhaqī.

10. According to ʿAlī ﷺ,

خَمْسٌ يَذْهَبْنَ بِالنِّسْيَانِ وَيَزِدْنَ فِي الْحِفْظِ وَيُذْهِبْنَ الْبَلْغَمَ: السِّوَاكُ وَالصِّيَامُ وَقِرَاءَةُ الْقُرْآنِ وَالْعَسَلُ وَاللِّبَانُ.

There are five things that cure forgetfulness, improve memory and end mucus: tooth brush, fasting, the recitation of the Qur'ān, honey and milk.[210]

Reported by al-Daylamī.

---

209 Set forth by •al-Bayhaqī in *Shuʿab al-īmān*, 2:518 §2579.

210 Set forth by •al-Daylamī in *al-Firdaws bi-ma'thūr al-khiṭāb*, 2:197 §2980.

Part II

اَلْبَابُ الرَّابِعُ

إِنَّ رَحْمَةَ اللهِ تَعَالَى غَالِبَةٌ عَلَى غَضَبِهِ

CHAPTER FOUR

ON THE PRECEDENCE OF ALLAH'S MERCY OVER HIS WRATH

١/١. عَنْ أَبِي هُرَيْرَةَ رضي الله عنه عَنِ النَّبِيِّ ﷺ قَالَ: لَمَّا خَلَقَ اللهُ الْخَلْقَ كَتَبَ فِي كِتَابِهِ وَهُوَ يَكْتُبُ عَلَى نَفْسِهِ وَهُوَ وَضْعٌ عِنْدَهُ عَلَى الْعَرْشِ: إِنَّ رَحْمَتِي تَغْلِبُ غَضَبِي.

مُتَّفَقٌ عَلَيْهِ.

1/1. According to Abū Hurayra ﵁, the Prophet ﷺ said,

"When Allah created the Creation, He wrote in His Book—and inscribes for Himself—that is near the Throne: 'My mercy exceeds My wrath.'"

Agreed upon by al-Bukhārī and Muslim.

٢/٢. عَنْ أَبِي هُرَيْرَةَ رضي الله عنه عَنِ النَّبِيِّ ﷺ قَالَ: إِنَّ اللهَ لَمَّا قَضَى الْخَلْقَ كَتَبَ عِنْدَهُ فَوْقَ عَرْشِهِ: إِنَّ رَحْمَتِي سَبَقَتْ غَضَبِي.

رَوَاهُ الْبُخَارِيُّ وَالنَّسَائِيُّ.

2/2. According to Abū Hurayra ﵁, the Prophet ﷺ said,

"When Allah completed His creation, He wrote above His Throne: 'Indeed My mercy precedes My wrath.'"

---

[1] Set forth by •al-Bukhārī in *al-Ṣaḥīḥ*, Bk.: *al-Tawḥīd*, [Divine Unity], Ch.: "The words of Allah: ﴾*and Allah warns you against Himself*﴿," 6:2694 §6969; •Muslim in *al-Ṣaḥīḥ:* Bk.: *al-Tawba*, [The Repentance], Ch.: "The Vastness of Allah's Mercy and That His Mercy Precedes His Wrath," 4:2107 §2751; •al-Tirmidhī in *al-Sunan:* Bk.: *al-Daʿawāt*, [The Invocations], Ch.: "Allah Created One Hundred Mercies," 5:549 §3543; •Ibn Mājah in *al-Sunan:* Bk.: *al-Zuhd* [The Renunciation], Ch.: "What Is Hoped of Allāh's Mercy on the Day of Resurrection," 2:1435 §4295; •al-Nasāʾī in *al-Sunan al-kubrā*, 4:417 §7751.

[2] Set forth by •al-Bukhārī in *al-Ṣaḥīḥ:* Bk.: *al-Tawḥīd*, [Divine Unity], Ch.: "﴾*And His Throne Was on Water, and He is the Lord of the Mighty Throne*﴿," 6:2700 §6986; •al-Nasāʾī in *al-Sunan al-kubrā*, 4:418 §7757; •al-Ṭabarānī in *Musnad al-Shāmiyyīn*, 4:275 §3270.

Reported by al-Bukhārī and al-Nasāʾī.

٣/ ٣. عَنْ أَبِي هُرَيْرَةَ ﷺ عَنْ رَسُوْلِ اللهِ ﷺ قَالَ: إِنَّ اللهَ حِيْنَ خَلَقَ الْخَلْقَ كَتَبَ بِيَدِهِ عَلَى نَفْسِهِ إِنَّ رَحْمَتِي تَغْلِبُ غَضَبِي.

رَوَاهُ التِّرْمِذِيُّ وَالنَّسَائِيُّ وَابْنُ أَبِي شَيْبَةَ، وَقَالَ التِّرْمِذِيُّ: هَذَا حَدِيْثٌ حَسَنٌ صَحِيحٌ.

3/3. According to Abū Hurayra ﷺ, Allah's Messenger ﷺ said,

"When Allah created the Creation, He wrote with His own blessed Hand, making it incumbent upon Himself: 'Surely My mercy overtakes My wrath.'"

Reported by al-Tirmidhī, al-Nasāʾī and Ibn Abī Shayba. According to al-Tirmidhī, "This is a fine authentic tradition."

٤/ ٤. عَنْ أَبِي ذَرٍّ ﷺ عَنِ النَّبِيِّ ﷺ فِيمَا رَوَى عَنِ اللهِ تَبَارَكَ وَتَعَالَى أَنَّهُ قَالَ: يَا عِبَادِي، إِنِّي حَرَّمْتُ الظُّلْمَ عَلَى نَفْسِي وَجَعَلْتُهُ بَيْنَكُمْ مُحَرَّمًا فَلَا تَظَالَمُوْا. يَا عِبَادِي، كُلُّكُمْ ضَالٌّ إِلَّا مَنْ هَدَيْتُهُ فَاسْتَهْدُوْنِي أَهْدِكُمْ. يَا عِبَادِي، كُلُّكُمْ جَائِعٌ إِلَّا مَنْ أَطْعَمْتُهُ فَاسْتَطْعِمُوْنِي أُطْعِمْكُمْ. يَا عِبَادِي، كُلُّكُمْ عَارٍ إِلَّا مَنْ كَسَوْتُهُ فَاسْتَكْسُوْنِي أَكْسُكُمْ. يَا عِبَادِي، إِنَّكُمْ تُخْطِئُوْنَ بِاللَّيْلِ وَالنَّهَارِ وَأَنَا أَغْفِرُ الذُّنُوْبَ جَمِيْعًا فَاسْتَغْفِرُوْنِي أَغْفِرْ لَكُمْ. يَا عِبَادِي، إِنَّكُمْ لَنْ تَبْلُغُوْا ضَرِّي فَتَضُرُّوْنِي وَلَنْ تَبْلُغُوْا نَفْعِي فَتَنْفَعُوْنِي. يَا عِبَادِي، لَوْ أَنَّ أَوَّلَكُمْ وَآخِرَكُمْ وَإِنْسَكُمْ وَجِنَّكُمْ كَانُوْا عَلَى أَتْقَى قَلْبِ رَجُلٍ وَاحِدٍ مِنْكُمْ مَا زَادَ ذَلِكَ فِي مُلْكِي شَيْئًا. يَا عِبَادِي، لَوْ أَنَّ أَوَّلَكُمْ وَآخِرَكُمْ وَإِنْسَكُمْ وَجِنَّكُمْ

---

[3] Set forth by •Aḥmad b. Ḥanbal in *al-Musnad*, 2:433 §9595; •al-Tirmidhī in *al-Sunan:* Bk.: *al-Daʿwāt ʿan Rasūl Allāh* ﷺ [The Invocations from Allah's Messenger ﷺ], Ch.: "Allāh Created One Hundred Mercies," 5:549 §3543; •al-Nasāʾī in *al-Sunan al-kubrā*, 4:417 §7751; •Ibn Abī Shayba in *al-Muṣannaf*, 7:60 §34199.

كَانُوا عَلَى أَفْجَرِ قَلْبِ رَجُلٍ وَاحِدٍ مَا نَقَصَ ذَلِكَ مِنْ مُلْكِي شَيْئًا. يَا عِبَادِي، لَوْ أَنَّ أَوَّلَكُمْ وَآخِرَكُمْ وَإِنْسَكُمْ وَجِنَّكُمْ قَامُوا فِي صَعِيدٍ وَاحِدٍ فَسَأَلُونِي فَأَعْطَيْتُ كُلَّ إِنْسَانٍ مَسْأَلَتَهُ مَا نَقَصَ ذَلِكَ مِمَّا عِنْدِي إِلَّا كَمَا يَنْقُصُ الْـمِخْيَطُ إِذَا أُدْخِلَ الْبَحْرَ. يَا عِبَادِي، إِنَّمَا هِيَ أَعْمَالُكُمْ أُحْصِيهَا لَكُمْ ثُمَّ أُوَفِّيكُمْ إِيَّاهَا. فَمَنْ وَجَدَ خَيْرًا فَلْيَحْمَدِ اللهَ وَمَنْ وَجَدَ غَيْرَ ذَلِكَ فَلَا يَلُومَنَّ إِلَّا نَفْسَهُ.

رَوَاهُ مُسْلِمٌ وَالتِّرْمِذِيُّ وَابْنُ أَبِي شَيْبَةَ، وَقَالَ التِّرْمِذِيُّ : هَذَا حَدِيثٌ حَسَنٌ.

4/4. According to Abū Dharr ⬥, the Prophet ⬥ narrated from Allah, the Blessed and Exalted,

"O My servants! I have forbidden oppression for Myself and have made it forbidden for you, so do not oppress one another. O My servants! All of you are astray except those whom I have guided, so seek guidance from Me and I shall guide you. O My servants! All of you are hungry except those whom I have fed, so seek nourishment from Me and I shall feed you. O My servants! All of you are naked except those whom I have clothed, so seek clothing from Me and I shall clothe you. O My servants! You sin by night and by day, and I forgive all sins, so seek forgiveness from Me and I shall forgive you. O My servants! You will never attain to harming so as to harm Me, and you will never attain to benefitting so as to benefit Me. O My servants, were the first of you and the last of you, the human of you and the jinn of you, to be as pious as the most pious heart of any one man of you, that would not increase My kingdom a bit. O My servants, were the

---

4 Set forth by •Muslim in al-Ṣaḥīḥ: Bk.: al-Birr wa al-ṣila wa al-ādāb [Piety, Familial Integration and Manners], Ch.: "The Prohibition of Oppression," 4:1944 §2577; •al-Tirmidhī in al-Sunan: Bk.: Ṣifat al-qiyāma wa al-raqāʾiq wa al-waraʿ ʿan Rasūl Allāh ⬥ [Description of the Resurrection, Heart Softeners and the Scrupulousness of Allāh's Messenger ⬥], 4:656 §2495; •Ibn Abī Shayba in al-Muṣannaf, 6:72 §29557; •ʿAbd al-Aʿlā b. Mashar in Nuskhat Abī Mashar, 1:23 §1.

first of you and the last of you, the human of you and the jinn of you, to be as corrupt as the most corrupt heart of any one man of you, that would not decrease My kingdom a bit. O My servants! Were the first of you and the last of you, the human of you and the jinn of you, to stand on a single plain and ask of Me, and were I to grant everyone what he asked, that would not decrease what I have, any more than a needle decreases the sea if put into it [and then taken out]. O My servants, it is but your deeds that I count for you and then recompense you for, so let him who finds good praise Allah, and let him who finds other than that blame no one but himself."

Reported by Muslim, al-Tirmidhī and Ibn Abī Shayba. According to al-Tirmidhī, "This is a fine tradition."

٥/ ٥. عَنْ أَبِـي هُرَيْرَةَ ﵁ قَالَ: سَمِعْتُ النَّبِيَّ ﷺ قَالَ: إِنَّ عَبْدًا أَصَابَ ذَنْبًا وَرُبَّمَا قَالَ: أَذْنَبَ ذَنْبًا فَقَالَ: رَبِّ أَذْنَبْتُ وَرُبَّمَا قَالَ: أَصَبْتُ فَاغْفِرْ لِي. فَقَالَ رَبُّهُ: أَعَلِمَ عَبْدِي أَنَّ لَهُ رَبًّا يَغْفِرُ الذَّنْبَ وَيَأْخُذُ بِهِ؟ غَفَرْتُ لِعَبْدِي. ثُمَّ مَكَثَ مَا شَاءَ اللهُ ثُمَّ أَصَابَ ذَنْبًا أَوْ أَذْنَبَ ذَنْبًا فَقَالَ: رَبِّ، أَذْنَبْتُ أَوْ أَصَبْتُ آخَرَ فَاغْفِرْهُ. فَقَالَ: أَعَلِمَ عَبْدِي أَنَّ لَهُ رَبًّا يَغْفِرُ الذَّنْبَ وَيَأْخُذُ بِهِ؟ غَفَرْتُ لِعَبْدِي. ثُمَّ مَكَثَ مَا شَاءَ اللهُ ثُمَّ أَذْنَبَ ذَنْبًا وَرُبَّمَا قَالَ: أَصَابَ ذَنْبًا قَالَ: قَالَ: رَبِّ، أَصَبْتُ أَوْ قَالَ: أَذْنَبْتُ آخَرَ فَاغْفِرْهُ لِي. فَقَالَ: أَعَلِمَ عَبْدِي أَنَّ لَهُ رَبًّا يَغْفِرُ الذَّنْبَ وَيَأْخُذُ بِهِ غَفَرْتُ لِعَبْدِي ثَـلَاثًا فَلْيَعْمَلْ مَا شَاءَ.

رَوَاهُ الْبُخَارِيُّ وَأَحْمَدُ.

5/5. According to Abū Hurayra ﵁,

"I heard the Prophet ﷺ say, 'A servant committed a sin and said, "O my Lord! I have committed a sin" or he said, "I have erred," "so

[5] Set forth by •al-Bukhārī in *al-Ṣaḥīḥ:* Bk.: *al-Tawḥīd* [Divine Unity], Ch.: "The Words of Allāh, Most High: ﴾*They want to replace the speech of Allāh*﴿, 6:2725 §7068; •Aḥmad b. Ḥanbal in *al-Musnad*, 2:405 §9245; •al-Ḥākim in *al-Mustadrak*, 4:270 §7608 (who said, "This is a rigorously authentic narration that fulfills the conditions of al-Bukhārī and Muslim."); •al-Bayhaqī in *al-Sunan al-kubrā*, 10:188 §20553, •*al-Arbaʿūn al-ṣughrā*, 1:30 §9.

forgive me." His Lord said, "Does My servant know that he has a Lord who forgives sins and seizes on that account? I forgive him." Then he refrained from sin until Allah willed. After some time, the man committed another sin and said, "O my Lord! I have committed a sin, (or I have erred,) so forgive me." His Lord said, "Does My servant know that he has a Lord who forgives sins and seizes on that account? I forgive him." He again abstained until Allah willed. After some time, the man committed yet another sin and said, "O my Lord! I have committed a sin, (or I have erred,) so forgive me." His Lord said, "Does My servant know that he has a Lord who forgives sins and seizes on that account? I have forgiven My servant the third time as well. So let him do what he likes.'"

Reported by al-Bukhārī and Aḥmad.

٦/٦. عَنْ أَبِـي هُرَيْرَةَ ﵁ عَنِ النَّبِيِّ فِيْمَا يَحْكِي عَنْ رَبِّهِ ﷻ قَالَ: أَذْنَبَ عَبْدٌ ذَنْبًا، فَقَالَ: اللَّهُمَّ، اغْفِرْ لِي ذَنْبِـي. فَقَالَ تَـبَارَكَ وَتَعَالَى: أَذْنَبَ عَبْدِي ذَنْبًا فَعَلِمَ أَنَّ لَهُ رَبًّا يَغْفِرُ الذَّنْبَ وَيَأْخُذُ بِالذَّنْبِ. ثُمَّ عَادَ فَأَذْنَبَ فَقَالَ: أَيْ رَبِّ اغْفِرْ لِي ذَنْبِـي. فَقَالَ تَـبَارَكَ وَتَعَالَى: عَبْدِي أَذْنَبَ ذَنْبًا فَعَلِمَ أَنَّ لَهُ رَبًّا يَغْفِرُ الذَّنْبَ وَيَأْخُذُ بِالذَّنْبِ. ثُمَّ، عَادَ فَأَذْنَبَ فَقَالَ: أَيْ رَبِّ اغْفِرْ لِي ذَنْبِـي. فَقَالَ تَـبَارَكَ وَتَعَالَى: أَذْنَبَ عَبْدِي ذَنْبًا فَعَلِمَ أَنَّ لَهُ رَبًّا يَغْفِرُ الذَّنْبَ وَيَأْخُذُ بِالذَّنْبِ. اعْمَلْ مَا شِئْتَ فَقَدْ غَفَرْتُ لَكَ. قَالَ عَبْدُ الْأَعْلَى: لَا أَدْرِي أَقَالَ فِي الثَّالِثَةِ أَوْ الرَّابِعَةِ: اعْمَلْ مَا شِئْتَ.

رَوَاهُ مُسْلِمٌ وَأَحْمَدُ وَابْنُ حِبَّانَ.

6/6. According to Abū Hurayra ﵁, the Prophet ﷺ narrated from Allah, "A servant committed a sin and said, 'O Allah, forgive me my sin.'

[6] Set forth by •Muslim in *al-Ṣaḥīḥ:* Bk.: *al-Tawba* [The Repentance], Ch.: "The Acceptance of Repenting from Sins," 4:2112 §2758; •Aḥmad b. Ḥanbal in *al-Musnad*, 2:492 §10384; •Ibn Ḥibbān in *al-Ṣaḥīḥ*, 2:392 §625; •Abū Yaʿlā in *al-Musnad*, 11:408 §6534; •al-Ḥākim in *al-Mustadrak*, 4:270 §7608 (who said, "This is an authentic tradition conforming to the stipulation of the two Shaykhs [i.e., al-Bukhārī and Muslim])

Allah ﷻ said, 'My servant committed a sin and knew that he had a Lord who forgives sins and also calls him to account for sinning.' (So He forgives him.) That servant then committed another sin and said, 'O Allah, forgive me my sin.' Allah ﷻ said, 'My servant committed a sin and knew that he had a Lord who forgives sins and also calls him to account for sinning.' (So He forgives him.) That servant then committed yet another sin and said, 'O Allah, forgive me my sin.' Allah ﷻ said, 'My servant committed a sin and knew that he had a Lord who forgives sins and also calls him to account for sinning. (O My servant,) do as you like, for I have forgiven you'." ʿAbd al-Aʿlā [one of the narrators] added, "I do not know if the statement 'do as you like' was after the third or fourth time."

Reported by Muslim, Aḥmad and Ibn Ḥibbān.

٧/ ٧. عَنْ أَبِي هُرَيْرَةَ ؓ عَنْ رَسُوْلِ اللهِ ﷺ قَالَ: إِنَّ رَجُلَيْنِ مِمَّنْ دَخَلَ النَّارَ اشْتَدَّ صِيَاحُهُمَا. فَقَالَ الرَّبُّ ﷻ: أَخْرِجُوْهُمَا. فَلَمَّا أُخْرِجَا قَالَ لَهُمَا: لِأَيِّ شَيْءٍ اشْتَدَّ صِيَاحُكُمَا؟ قَالَا: فَعَلْنَا ذَلِكَ لِتَرْحَمَنَا. قَالَ: إِنَّ رَحْمَتِي لَكُمَا أَنْ تَنْطَلِقَا فَتُلْقِيَا أَنْفُسَكُمَا حَيْثُ كُنْتُمَا مِنَ النَّارِ. فَيَنْطَلِقَانِ فَيُلْقِي أَحَدُهُمَا نَفْسَهُ فَيَجْعَلُهَا عَلَيْهِ بَرْدًا وَسَلَامًا. وَيَقُوْمُ الْآخَرُ فَلَا يُلْقِي نَفْسَهُ. فَيَقُوْلُ لَهُ الرَّبُّ ﷻ: مَا مَنَعَكَ أَنْ تُلْقِيَ نَفْسَكَ كَمَا أَلْقَى صَاحِبُكَ؟ فَيَقُوْلُ: يَا رَبِّ، إِنِّي لَأَرْجُوْ أَنْ لَا تُعِيْدَنِي فِيْهَا بَعْدَ مَا أَخْرَجْتَنِي. فَيَقُوْلُ لَهُ الرَّبُّ: لَكَ رَجَاؤُكَ. فَيَدْخُلَانِ جَمِيْعًا الْجَنَّةَ بِرَحْمَةِ اللهِ.

رَوَاهُ التِّرْمِذِيُّ وَابْنُ الْمُبَارَكِ.

7/7. According to Abū Hurayra ؓ, Allah's Messenger ﷺ said,

"The two of the men who would enter the Hellfire would severely scream therein. The Lord would say, 'Take them out.' When taken out, Allah would ask them, 'Why were your screams so severe?' They

[7] Set forth by •al-Tirmidhī in *al-Sunan:* Bk.: *Ṣifat jahannam ʿan Rasūl Allāh* ﷺ [The Description of *Jahannam* as Told by Allāh's Messenger ﷺ], 4:714 §2599; •Ibn al-Mubārak in *al-Musnad*, 1:68 §111.

would say, 'We did that so You would have mercy upon us.' Allah would say, 'My mercy for you both is that you return to your places in the Hellfire and cast yourselves therein.' Both of them would leave and the first man would cast himself back into the Hellfire and He [Allah] would make it a coolness and safety for him. The other one would hesitate and would not cast himself back into the Hellfire. The Lord would ask him, 'What prevents you from casting yourself back into Hellfire as your companion did?' The man would say, 'O my Lord! I hope that You do not cause me to return to it after having taken me out.' The Lord would say to him, 'Your hope shall be fulfilled,' and then both men would enter Paradise out of Allah's mercy."

Reported by al-Tirmidhī and Ibn al-Mubārak.

٨/ ٨. عَنْ أَبِـي ذَرٍّ ﵁ قَالَ: قَالَ رَسُوْلُ اللهِ ﷺ: يَقُوْلُ اللهُ تَعَالَى: يَا عِبَادِي، كُلُّكُمْ ضَالٌّ إِلَّا مَنْ هَدَيْتُهُ فَسَلُونِي الْـهُدَى أَهْدِكُمْ. وَكُلُّكُمْ فَقِيْرٌ إِلَّا مَنْ أَغْنَيْتُ فَسَلُوْنِي أَرْزُقْكُمْ. وَكُلُّكُمْ مُذْنِبٌ إِلَّا مَنْ عَافَيْتُ فَمَنْ عَلِمَ مِنْكُمْ أَنِّي ذُوْ قُدْرَةٍ عَلَى الْـمَغْفِرَةِ فَاسْتَغْفَرَنِي غَفَرْتُ لَهُ وَلَا أُبَالِي. وَلَوْ أَنَّ أَوَّلَكُمْ وَآخِرَكُمْ وَحَيَّكُمْ وَمَيِّتَكُمْ وَرَطْبَكُمْ وَيَابِسَكُمُ اجْتَمَعُوْا عَلَى أَتْقَى قَلْبِ عَبْدٍ مِنْ عِبَادِي مَا زَادَ ذَلِكَ فِي مُلْكِي جَنَاحَ بَعُوْضَةٍ. وَلَوْ أَنَّ أَوَّلَكُمْ وَآخِرَكُمْ وَحَيَّكُمْ وَمَيِّتَكُمْ وَرَطْبَكُمْ وَيَابِسَكُمُ اجْتَمَعُوْا عَلَى أَشْقَى قَلْبِ عَبْدٍ مِنْ عِبَادِي، مَا نَقَصَ ذَلِكَ مِنْ مُلْكِي جَنَاحَ بَعُوْضَةٍ. وَلَوْ أَنَّ أَوَّلَكُمْ وَآخِرَكُمْ وَحَيَّكُمْ وَمَيِّتَكُمْ وَرَطْبَكُمْ وَيَابِسَكُمْ اجْتَمَعُوْا فِي صَعِيْدٍ وَاحِدٍ فَسَأَلَ كُلُّ إِنْسَانٍ مِنْكُمْ مَا بَلَغَتْ أُمْنِيَّتُهُ فَأَعْطَيْتُ كُلَّ سَائِلٍ مِنْكُمْ مَا سَأَلَ مَا نَقَصَ ذَلِكَ مِنْ مُلْكِي إِلَّا كَمَا لَوْ أَنَّ أَحَدَكُمْ مَرَّ بِالْبَحْرِ فَغَمَسَ فِيْهِ إِبْرَةً ثُمَّ رَفَعَهَا إِلَيْهِ. ذَلِكَ بِأَنِّي جَوَّادٌ مَاجِدٌ أَفْعَلُ مَا أُرِيْدُ. عَطَائِي كَلَامٌ وَعَذَابِـي كَلَامٌ. إِنَّمَا أَمْرِي لِشَيْءٍ إِذَا أَرَدْتُهُ أَنْ أَقُوْلَ لَهُ كُنْ، فَيَكُوْنُ.

رَوَاهُ أَحْمَدُ وَالتِّرْمِذِيُّ وَابْنُ مَاجَه، وَقَالَ التِّرْمِذِيُّ: هَذَا حَدِيْثٌ حَسَنٌ.

8/8. According to Abū Dharr ﵁, Allah's Messenger ﷺ said,

"Allah ﷻ said, 'O My servants! All of you are astray except those whom I have guided, so seek guidance from Me. I shall guide you. (O My servants!) All of you are impoverished except those whom I have enriched, so seek provision from Me and I shall provide for you. (O My servants!) All of you are sinful except those whom I have pardoned, so those of you who know that I am able to forgive should seek My forgiveness and I shall forgive him and I will not care. (O My servants,) were the first of you and the last of you, the living of you and the deceased of you, and the moist of you and the dry of you to be as pious as the most pious heart of any servant among My servants, that would not increase My kingdom the weight of a gnat's wing. And were the first of you and the last of you, the living of you and the deceased of you, and the moist of you and the dry of you to be as wretched as the most wretched heart of any servant among My servants, that would not decrease My kingdom the weight of a gnat's wing. And were the first of you and the last of you, the living of you and the deceased of you, and the moist of you and the dry of you to stand on a single plain and ask of Me, and were I to grant everyone what he asked, that would not decrease what I have any more than the sea is decreased if one of you passes by it and puts a needle into it and pulls it out. That is because I am the Magnanimous and the Majestic and I do as I want. My giving is but speech and My punishment is but speech. Whenever I want something all I say to it, "Be" and it becomes.'"

Reported by Aḥmad, al-Tirmidhī and Ibn Mājah. According to al-Tirmidhī, "This is a fine tradition."

٩/٩. عَنْ أَنَسِ بْنِ مَالِكٍ ﵁ قَالَ: سَمِعْتُ رَسُوْلَ اللهِ ﷺ يَقُوْلُ: قَالَ اللهُ تَبَارَكَ وَتَعَالَى: يَا ابْنَ آدَمَ، إِنَّكَ مَا دَعَوْتَنِي وَرَجَوْتَنِي غَفَرْتُ لَكَ عَلَى مَا كَانَ فِيْكَ وَلَا

[8] Set forth by •Aḥmad b. Ḥanbal in *al-Musnad*, 5:154 §21405; •al-Tirmidhī in *al-Sunan:* Bk.: *Ṣifat al-qiyāma wa al-raqā'iq wa al-wara' 'an Rasūl Allāh* ﷺ [The Description of the Resurrection, Heart Softeners and the Scrupulousness of Allāh's Messenger ﷺ], 4:656 §2495; •Ibn Mājah in *al-Sunan:* Bk.: *al-Zuhd* [The Asceticism], Ch.: "Repentance," 2:1422 §4257.

أُبَالِي. يَا ابْنَ آدَمَ، لَوْ بَلَغَتْ ذُنُوبُكَ عَنَانَ السَّمَاءِ ثُمَّ اسْتَغْفَرْتَنِي غَفَرْتُ لَكَ وَلَا أُبَالِي. يَا ابْنَ آدَمَ، إِنَّكَ لَوْ أَتَيْتَنِي بِقُرَابِ الْأَرْضِ خَطَايَا ثُمَّ لَقِيتَنِي لَا تُشْرِكُ بِي شَيْئًا، لَأَتَيْتُكَ بِقُرَابِهَا مَغْفِرَةً.

رَوَاهُ التِّرْمِذِيُّ وَالطَّبَرَانِيُّ وَأَبُو نُعَيْمٍ، وَقَالَ التِّرْمِذِيُّ: هَذَا حَدِيثٌ حَسَنٌ.

9/9. According to Anas b. Mālik ﷺ,

"I heard Allah's Messenger ﷺ say, 'Allah ﷻ says, "O son of Ādam! As long as you call upon Me and have hope in Me, I shall forgive you your sins; what sins are there in you, I will not care. O son of Ādam! If your sins reached the furthest expanse of the skies, but you sought My forgiveness, I would forgive you and I would not care. O son of Ādam! If you came to Me with the earth's weight in sins but met Me having not associated any partner along with Me, I would come to you with the earth's weight in forgiveness."'"

Reported by al-Tirmidhī, al-Ṭabarānī and Abū Nuʿaym. According to al-Tirmidhī, "This is a fine tradition."

١٠/ ١٠. عَنْ حُذَيْفَةَ ﷺ قَالَ: إِنِّي سَمِعْتُ رَسُولَ اللهِ ﷺ يَقُولُ: إِنَّ مَعَ الدَّجَّالِ إِذَا خَرَجَ مَاءً وَنَارًا. فَأَمَّا الَّذِي يَرَى النَّاسُ أَنَّهَا النَّارُ فَمَاءٌ بَارِدٌ وَأَمَّا الَّذِي يَرَى النَّاسُ أَنَّهُ مَاءٌ بَارِدٌ فَنَارٌ تُحْرِقُ. فَمَنْ أَدْرَكَ مِنْكُمْ فَلْيَقَعْ فِي الَّذِي يَرَى أَنَّهَا نَارٌ فَإِنَّهُ عَذْبٌ بَارِدٌ. قَالَ حُذَيْفَةُ: وَسَمِعْتُهُ يَقُولُ: إِنَّ رَجُلًا كَانَ فِيمَنْ كَانَ قَبْلَكُمْ أَتَاهُ الْمَلَكُ لِيَقْبِضَ رُوحَهُ. فَقِيلَ لَهُ: هَلْ عَمِلْتَ مِنْ خَيْرٍ؟ قَالَ: مَا أَعْلَمُ. قِيلَ لَهُ: انْظُرْ. قَالَ: مَا أَعْلَمُ شَيْئًا غَيْرَ أَنِّي كُنْتُ أُبَايِعُ النَّاسَ فِي الدُّنْيَا وَأُجَازِيهِمْ. فَأُنْظِرُ الْمُوسِرَ وَأَتَجَاوَزُ عَنِ الْمُعْسِرِ. فَأَدْخَلَهُ اللهُ الْجَنَّةَ. فَقَالَ: وَسَمِعْتُهُ يَقُولُ: إِنَّ رَجُلًا حَضَرَهُ الْمَوْتُ.

---

[9] Set forth by •al-Tirmidhī in *al-Sunan:* Bk.: *al-Daʿawāt ʿan Rasūl Allāh* ﷺ, [Invocation from Allāh's Messenger ﷺ], Ch.: "The Virtue of Repentance and Seeking Forgiveness," 5:548 §3540; •al-Ṭabarānī in *al-Muʿjam al-awsaṭ*, 4:315 §4305; •Abū Nuʿaym in *Ḥilyat al-Awliyāʾ*, 2:231.

فَلَمَّا يَئِسَ مِنَ الْحَيَاةِ، أَوْصَى أَهْلَهُ: إِذَا أَنَا مُتُّ فَاجْمَعُوْا لِي حَطَبًا كَثِيْرًا وَأَوْقِدُوْا فِيْهِ نَارًا حَتَّى إِذَا أَكَلَتْ لَحْمِي وَخَلَصَتْ إِلَى عَظْمِي فَامْتُحِشَتْ فَخُذُوْهَا فَاطْحَنُوْهَا ثُمَّ انْظُرُوْا يَوْمًا رَاحًا فَاذْرُوْهُ فِي الْيَمِّ. فَفَعَلُوْا. فَجَمَعَهُ اللهُ، فَقَالَ لَهُ: لِمَ فَعَلْتَ ذَلِكَ؟ قَالَ: مِنْ خَشْيَتِكَ. فَغَفَرَ اللهُ لَهُ. قَالَ عُقْبَةُ بْنُ عَمْرٍو: وَأَنَا سَمِعْتُهُ يَقُوْلُ ذَاكَ وَكَانَ نَبَّاشًا.

رَوَاهُ الْبُخَارِيُّ.

10/10. According to Ḥudhayfa ﵁,

"I heard Allah's Messenger ﷺ say, 'When the Anti-Christ appears, he will have fire and water with him. What the people will consider as fire will be cold water, and what the people will consider as cold water will be fire that will burn. If any of you encounters him, he should fall in that which will appear to him as fire, for it will be fresh cold water in reality.' I also heard the Prophet ﷺ say, 'There was a man from bygone people to whom the Angel of Death visited in order to seize his soul. He was asked [after his soul was seized], "Did you ever perform good deeds?" He replied, "I do not know." He was then asked to think about it more, after which he replied, "I do not know; however, I used to trade with people in the world and deal leniently with them. I would give respite to those of straitened means and forgive the debts of those in dire straits." Because of this, Allah allowed him to enter Paradise.' I also heard the Prophet ﷺ say, 'Once there was a man in his death throes who, after losing all hope of surviving, ordered his family, saying, "When I die, gather for me a large heap of wood and kindle a fire under it. When it consumes my flesh and bones, take them and crush them into a fine powder, and then wait for a windy day and cast them over the sea." And thus they did. When Allah recomposed him, He asked, "Why did you do that?" The man replied, "It was for fear of You." So for that, Allah forgave him.'" ʿUqba b. ʿĀmir ﵁ added,

---

10 Set forth by •al-Bukhārī in *al-Ṣaḥīḥ:* Bk.: *al-Anbiyāʾ* [The Prophets ﷺ], Ch.: "What Has Been Mentioned About the Children of Israel," 3:1272 §3266, and in Bk.: *al-Buyūʿ* [Trade], Ch.: "Giving Time to Someone who is Able to Pay His Debt," 2:731 §1971.

"I heard him [the Prophet ﷺ] say that this man was a grave-digger."

Reproted by al-Bukhārī.

١١/١١. عَنْ أَبِي سَعِيدٍ رضي الله عنه عَنِ النَّبِيِّ ﷺ أَنَّ رَجُلًا كَانَ قَبْلَكُمْ رَغَسَهُ اللهُ مَالًا. فَقَالَ لِبَنِيهِ لَمَّا حُضِرَ: أَيَّ أَبٍ كُنْتُ لَكُمْ؟ قَالُوْا: خَيْرَ أَبٍ. قَالَ: فَإِنِّي لَمْ أَعْمَلْ خَيْرًا قَطُّ. فَإِذَا مُتُّ فَأَحْرِقُوْنِي ثُمَّ اسْحَقُوْنِي ثُمَّ ذَرُّوْنِي فِي يَوْمٍ عَاصِفٍ. فَفَعَلُوْا فَجَمَعَهُ اللهُ تعالى فَقَالَ: مَا حَمَلَكَ؟ قَالَ: مَخَافَتُكَ. فَتَلَقَّاهُ بِرَحْمَتِهِ.

رَوَاهُ الْبُخَارِيُّ وَأَحْمَدُ وَابْنُ حِبَّانَ.

11/11. According to Abū Saʿīd al-Khudrī رضي الله عنه, the Prophet ﷺ said,

"There was a man among the communities before you to whom Allah had provided abundant wealth. As he was on his deathbed, he called for his children and asked, 'What kind of father have I been toward you?' They replied, 'You have been the best father.' He said, 'I have never done any good deeds, so when I die, burn my corpse and crush its remains and then scatter it on a windy day.' They did as he had asked and when Allah recomposed him, He asked, 'What motivated you to do that?' The man replied, 'You fear.' Allah then cloaked him in His mercy."

Reported by al-Bukhārī, Aḥmad and Ibn Ḥibbān.

١٢/١٢. عَنْ حُذَيْفَةَ رضي الله عنه قَالَ: سَمِعْتُ النَّبِيَّ ﷺ يَقُوْلُ: إِنَّ رَجُلًا حَضَرَهُ الْمَوْتُ. لَمَّا أَيِسَ مِنَ الْحَيَاةِ، أَوْصَى أَهْلَهُ: إِذَا مُتُّ فَاجْمَعُوْا لِي حَطَبًا كَثِيْرًا ثُمَّ أَوْرُوْا نَارًا حَتَّى إِذَا أَكَلَتْ لَحْمِي وَخَلَصَتْ إِلَى عَظْمِي فَخُذُوْهَا فَاطْحَنُوْهَا فَذَرُّوْنِي فِي الْيَمِّ فِي يَوْمٍ

---

[11] Set forth by •al-Bukhārī in *al-Ṣaḥīḥ:* Bk.: *al-Anbiyā'* [The Prophets عليهم السلام], Ch.: "The Narration of the Cave," 3:1282 §3291, and in Bk.: *al-Riqāq* [Heart Softeners], Ch.: "Fearing Allāh," 5:2378 §6116; •Aḥmad b. Ḥanbal in *al-Musnad*, 3:69 §§11682,11753; •Ibn Ḥibbān in *al-Ṣaḥīḥ*, 2:417 §649; •Abū Yaʿlā in *al-Musnad*, 2:314 §1047; •al-Ṭabarānī in *al-Muʿjam al-kabīr*, 19:423 §1026.

حَارٍّ أَوْ رَاحٍ. فَجَمَعَهُ اللهُ فَقَالَ: لِمَ فَعَلْتَ؟ قَالَ: خَشْيَتَكَ. فَغَفَرَ لَهُ.

رَوَاهُ الْبُخَارِيُّ وَالْبَزَّارُ.

12/12. According to Ḥudhayfa ,

"I heard the Prophet say, 'There was a man who, when in the throes of death and without hope of survival, called for his family and ordered them, "After I die, gather for me a large heap of wood and kindle a fire under it. When it consumes my flesh and bones, take them and crush them into a fine powder and then wait for a hot or windy day and cast them over the sea." When Allah recomposed and raised him, He asked, "Why did you do that?" The man replied, "It was merely for Your fear." So Allah forgave him.'"

Reported by al-Bukhārī and al-Bazzār.

١٣/ ١٣. عَنْ أَبِي هُرَيْرَةَ أَنَّ رَسُوْلَ اللهِ قَالَ: قَالَ رَجُلٌ لَمْ يَعْمَلْ خَيْرًا قَطُّ. فَإِذَا مَاتَ فَحَرِّقُوْهُ وَاذْرُوْا نِصْفَهُ فِي الْبَرِّ وَنِصْفَهُ فِي الْبَحْرِ، فَوَاللهِ، لَئِنْ قَدَرَ اللهُ عَلَيْهِ لَيُعَذِّبَنَّهُ عَذَابًا لَا يُعَذِّبُهُ أَحَدًا مِنَ الْعَالَمِيْنَ، فَأَمَرَ اللهُ الْبَحْرَ فَجَمَعَ مَا فِيْهِ وَأَمَرَ الْبَرَّ فَجَمَعَ مَا فِيْهِ، ثُمَّ قَالَ: لِمَ فَعَلْتَ؟ قَالَ: مِنْ خَشْيَتِكَ وَأَنْتَ أَعْلَمُ، فَغَفَرَ لَهُ.

مُتَّفَقٌ عَلَيْهِ.

13/13. According to Abū Hurayra , the Allah's Messenger said,

---

[12] Set forth by •al-Bukhārī in *al-Ṣaḥīḥ:* Bk.: *al-Anbiyā'* [The Prophets], Ch.: "The Narration of the Cave," 3:1283 §3292; •al-Bazzār in *al-Musnad*, 7:244 §2822; •al-Bayhaqī in *Shuʿab al-īmān*, 5:430 §7160; and cited by •Ibn Ḥajar in *Fatḥ al-Bārī*, 6:522 §3294; •al-ʿAynī in *ʿUmdat al-qārī*, 16:62 §9743; •Ibn Kathīr in *Tafsīr al-Qur'ān al-Aẓīm*, 3:583.

[13] Set forth by •al-Bukhārī in *al-Ṣaḥīḥ:* Bk.: *al-Tawḥīd* [Divine Oneness], Ch.: "The Words of Allāh, Most High: ﴾*They want to replace the speech of Allāh*﴿," 6:2725 §7067; •Muslim in *al-Ṣaḥīḥ:* Bk.: *al-Tawba* [The Repentance], Ch.: "The Vastness of Allah's Mercy and That His Mercy Precedes His Anger," 4:2109 §2756; •Mālik in *al-Muwaṭṭa'*, 1:240 §570.

"There was a man who did not perform any good deeds and upon his deathbed, he ordered his family to take his body and burn it and scatter half of its ash in the earth and the other half in the sea. He swore by Allah, if Allah gets hold of him, He would punish him with a punishment that none of the creation has received. [So his family members did the same.] After this, Allah commanded the sea and the earth to gather the scattered dust particles of his ash and then Allah asked him, 'Why did you do that?' The man replied, 'It was out of Your fear, and You know best.' So Allah forgave him."

Agreed upon by al-Bukhārī and Muslim.

١٤/ ١٤. عَنْ أَبِـي هُرَيْرَةَ ﵁ عَنِ النَّبِيِّ ﷺ قَالَ: أَسْرَفَ رَجُلٌ عَلَى نَفْسِهِ. فَلَـمَّا حَضَرَهُ الْـمَوْتُ أَوْصَى بَنِيْهِ فَقَالَ: إِذَا أَنَا مُتُّ فَأَحْرِقُوْنِي ثُمَّ اسْحَقُوْنِي ثُمَّ اذْرُوْنِي فِي الرِّيحِ فِي الْبَحْرِ، فَوَاللهِ، لَئِنْ قَدَرَ عَلَيَّ رَبِّي لَيُعَذِّبُنِي عَذَابًا مَا عَذَّبَهُ بِهِ أَحَدًا. قَالَ: فَفَعَلُوْا ذَلِكَ بِهِ. فَقَالَ لِلْأَرْضِ: أَدِّي مَا أَخَذْتِ. فَإِذَا هُوَ قَائِمٌ. فَقَالَ لَهُ: مَا حَمَلَكَ عَلَى مَا صَنَعْتَ؟ فَقَالَ: خَشْيَتُكَ، يَا رَبِّ، أَوْ قَالَ: مَخَافَتُكَ. فَغَفَرَ لَهُ بِذَلِكَ.

رَوَاهُ مُسْلِمٌ وَأَحْمَدُ وَابْنُ مَاجَه وَعَبْدُ الرَّزَّاقِ.

14/14. According to Abū Hurayra ﵁, the Prophet ﷺ said,

"There was once a man who transgressed against his own soul [spent a sinful life], and when he was in death throes he ordered his children, 'After I die, burn my corpse and turn it into a powder and then scatter my remains in the wind in the sea, for I swear by Allah, if my Lord gets hold of me, He will punish me in such a way that no one has suffered before.' And so his children did as he ordered. Allah then instructed the earth, 'Return that which you took of his dust particles,' and suddenly the man was recomposed. Allah asked him,

[14] Set forth by •Muslim in *al-Ṣaḥīḥ:* Bk.: *al-Tawba* [The Repentance], Ch.: "The Vastness of Allah's Mercy and That His Mercy Precedes His Wrath," 4:2110 §2756; •Aḥmad b. Ḥanbal in *al-Musnad*, 2:269 §7635; •Ibn Mājah in *al-Sunan:* Bk.: *al-Zuhd* [The Renunciation], Ch.: "Repentance," 2:1421 §4255; •ʿAbd al-Razzāq in *al-Muṣannaf*, 11:283 §20548.

'What motivated you to do what you did?' The man replied, 'It was for fear of You, O Lord,' or he said, 'It was out of fearfulness for You.' So for that Allah forgave him."

Reported by Muslim, Aḥmad, Ibn Mājah and ʿAbd al-Razzāq.

١٥/ ١٥. عَنْ أَبِي هُرَيْرَةَ رضي الله عنه أَنَّ رَسُوْلَ اللهِ ﷺ قَالَ: لَوْ يَعْلَمُ الْمُؤْمِنُ مَا عِنْدَ اللهِ مِنَ الْعُقُوْبَةِ مَا طَمِعَ بِجَنَّتِهِ أَحَدٌ وَلَوْ يَعْلَمُ الْكَافِرُ مَا عِنْدَ اللهِ مِنَ الرَّحْمَةِ مَا قَنَطَ مِنْ جَنَّتِهِ أَحَدٌ.

رَوَاهُ مُسْلِمٌ وَأَحْمَدُ وَالتِّرْمِذِيُّ.

15/15. According to Abū Hurayra (may Allah be pleased with him), Allah's Messenger ﷺ said,

"If the believers truly knew Allah's punishment, no one would hope of attaining to His Paradise, and if the disbelievers truly knew Allah's mercy, no one would despair of attaining to His Paradise."

Reported by Muslim, Aḥmad and al-Tirmidhī.

[15] Set forth by •Muslim in *al-Ṣaḥīḥ:* Bk.: *al-Tawba* [The Repentance], Ch.: "The Vastness of Allah's Mercy and That His Mercy Precedes His Wrath," 4:2109 §2755; •Aḥmad b. Ḥanbal in *al-Musnad*, 2:334 §8396; •al-Tirmidhī in *al-Sunan:* Bk.: *al-Daʿawāt ʿan Rasūl Allāh* ﷺ [Invocations from Allāh's Messenger ﷺ], Ch.: "Allāh Created One Hundred Mercies," 5:549 §3542; •Abū Yaʿlā in *al-Musnad*, 11:392 §6507; •al-Daylamī in *Musnad al-firdaws*, 3:349 §5056; •al-Qurashī in *Ḥusn al-ẓann billāh*, 1:29 §19.

اَلْبَابُ الخَامِسُ

إِنَّ لِلَّهِ تَعَالَى مِائَةَ رَحْمَةٍ وَأَنَّهُ ذَخَرَ تِسْعَةً وَتِسْعِيْنَ مِنْهَا لِيَوْمِ الْقِيَامَةِ

CHAPTER FIVE

ON THE ONE HUNDRED PARTS OF ALLAH'S MERCY, AND THAT NINETY-NINE OF THEM ARE RESERVED FOR THE DAY OF RESURRECTION

١٦ / ١. عَنْ أَبِـي هُرَيْرَةَ ﵁ قَالَ: سَمِعْتُ رَسُوْلَ اللهِ ﷺ يَقُوْلُ: جَعَلَ اللهُ الرَّحْمَةَ مِائَةَ جُزْءٍ. فَأَمْسَكَ عِنْدَهُ تِسْعَةً وَتِسْعِيْنَ جُزْءًا، وَأَنْزَلَ فِي الْأَرْضِ جُزْءًا وَاحِدًا. فَمِنْ ذَلِكَ الْـجُزْءِ يَتَرَاحَمُ الْـخَلْقُ حَتَّى تَرْفَعَ الْـفَرَسُ حَافِرَهَا عَنْ وَلَدِهَا خَشْيَةَ أَنْ تُصِيْبَهُ.

مُتَّفَقٌ عَلَيْهِ.

16/1. According to Abū Hurayra ﵁,

"I heard Allah's Messenger ﷺ say, 'Allah created mercy in one hundred parts; He retained ninety-nine parts and sent one part to the earth. Due to this one part, the creation show mercy to one another, so much that the mare lifts up its hoof from its young colt lest she harm it.'"

Agreed upon by al-Bukhārī and Muslim.

١٧ / ٢. عَنْ أَبِـي هُرَيْرَةَ ﵁ عَنِ النَّبِيِّ ﷺ قَالَ: إِنَّ للهِ مِائَةَ رَحْمَةٍ. أَنْزَلَ مِنْهَا رَحْمَةً وَاحِدَةً بَيْنَ الْـجِنِّ وَالْإِنْسِ وَالْبَهَائِمِ وَالْـهَوَامِّ. فَبِهَا يَتَعَاطَفُوْنَ وَبِهَا يَتَرَاحَمُوْنَ وَبِهَا تَعْطِفُ الْوَحْشُ عَلَى وَلَدِهَا. وَأَخَّرَ اللهُ تِسْعًا وَتِسْعِيْنَ رَحْمَةً يَرْحَمُ بِهَا عِبَادَهُ يَوْمَ الْقِيَامَةِ.

رَوَاهُ مُسْلِمٌ وَالتِّرْمِذِيُّ وَابْنُ مَاجَه.

---

[16] Set forth by •al-Bukhārī in *al-Ṣaḥīḥ:* Bk.: *al-Adab* [Good Manners], Ch.: "Allāh Made Mercy One Hundred Parts," 5:2236 §5654; •Muslim in *al-Ṣaḥīḥ:* Bk.: *al-Tawba* [The Repentance], Ch.: "The Vastness of Allāh's Mercy and That His Mercy Precedes His Wrath," 4:2108 §2752; •al-Dārimī in *al-Sunan*, 2:413 §2785; •Ibn Ḥibbān in *al-Ṣaḥīḥ*, 14:16 §6148; •al-Ṭabarānī in *al-Muʿjam al-awsaṭ*, 1:297 §991; •al-Bayhaqī in *Shuʿab al-īmān*, 7:457 §10975.

17/2. According to Abū Hurayra ﵁, the Prophet ﷺ said,

"Allah has one hundred parts of mercy. Of these, He sent one part that is shared between humankind and jinn and animals and insects. Because of this one part shared between them, they show mutual affection and mercy, and due to it, the wild beast shows mercy to her young. Allah has reserved the remaining ninety-nine parts of mercy which He will have upon His servants on the Day of Resurrection."

Reported by Muslim, al-Tirmidhī and Ibn Mājah.

١٨/ ٣. عَنْ جُنْدُبٍ ﵁ قَالَ: جَاءَ أَعْرَابِيٌّ فَأَنَاخَ رَاحِلَتَهُ ثُمَّ عَقَلَهَا، ثُمَّ صَلَّى خَلْفَ رَسُوْلِ اللهِ ﷺ. فَلَـمَّا صَلَّى رَسُوْلُ اللهِ ﷺ، أَتَى رَاحِلَتَهُ فَأَطْلَقَ عِقَالَهَا، ثُمَّ رَكِبَهَا، ثُمَّ نَادَى: اللَّهُمَّ، ارْحَمْنِي وَمُحَمَّدًا وَلَا تُشْرِكْ فِي رَحْمَتِنَا أَحَدًا. فَقَالَ رَسُوْلُ اللهِ ﷺ: أَتَقُوْلُوْنَ هَذَا أَضَلُّ أَمْ بَعِيْرُهُ؟ أَلَـمْ تَسْمَعُوْا مَا قَالَ؟ قَالُوْا: بَلَى. قَالَ: لَقَدْ حَظَرْتَ. رَحْمَةُ اللهِ وَاسِعَةٌ. إِنَّ اللهَ خَلَقَ مِائَةَ رَحْمَةٍ فَأَنْزَلَ اللهُ رَحْمَةً وَاحِدَةً، يَتَعَاطَفُ بِهَا الْـخَلَائِقُ جِنُّهَا وَإِنْسُهَا وَبَهَائِمُهَا، وَعِنْدَهُ تِسْعٌ وَتِسْعُوْنَ. أَتَقُوْلُوْنَ: هُوَ أَضَلُّ أَمْ بَعِيْرُهُ؟.

رَوَاهُ أَحْمَدُ وَأَبُوْ دَاوُدَ وَالْـحَاكِمُ، وَقَالَ الْـحَاكِمُ: هَذَا حَدِيْثٌ صَحِيْحُ الْإِسْنَادِ. وَقَالَ الْـهَيْثَمِيُّ: رَوَاهُ أَبُوْ دَاوُدَ بِاخْتِصَارٍ، وَرَوَاهُ أَحْمَدُ وَالطَّبَرَانِيُّ وَرَجَالُ أَحْمَدَ رِجَالُ الصَّحِيْحِ غَيْرُ أَبِي عَبْدِ اللهِ الْـجُشَمِيِّ وَلَـمْ يُضَعِّفْهُ أَحَدٌ.

---

[17] Set forth by •Muslim in *al-Ṣaḥīḥ:* Bk.: *al-Tawba* [Repentance], Ch.: "The Vastness of Allah's Mercy and That His Mercy Precedes His Wrath," 4:2108 §2752; •Aḥmad b. Ḥanbal in *al-Musnad*, 2:434 §9607; •al-Tirmidhī in *al-Sunan:* Bk.: *al-Daʿawāt ʿan Rasūl Allāh* ﷺ [Invocations from Allāh's Messenger ﷺ], Ch.: "Allāh Created One Hundred Mercies," 5:549 §3541; •Ibn Mājah in *al-Sunan:* Bk.: *al-Zuhd* [The Renunciation], Ch.: "Hope for Allāh's Mercy on the Day of Resurrection," 2:1435 §4293; •Ibn Ḥibbān in *al-Ṣaḥīḥ*, 14:15 §6147; •Ibn al-Mubārak in *al-Musnad*, 1:20 §35; •Abū Yaʿlā in *al-Musnad*, 11:328 §6445.

18/3. According to Jundub ☙,

"There was once a Bedouin who hobbled his camel and fastened its nose ring and then went to pray behind Allah's Messenger ﷺ. After Allah's Messenger ﷺ completed the prayer, the man went to his camel and untied it, mounted it, and called out, 'O Allah, have mercy upon me and Muḥammad and allow no one to share with us in that mercy!' Hearing this, Allah's Messenger ﷺ asked (his Companions ☙), 'Who would you say is the most deviant, this man, or his camel? Did you not hear what he said?' The Companions ☙ submitted, 'Yes (we have heard, O Messenger of Allah).' The Prophet ﷺ said, 'You have constricted Allah's vast mercy. Indeed, Allah created one hundred parts of mercy; He sent down one part by which the Creation—jinn and humankind and animals—show mutual affection toward each other, and has reserved the remaining ninety-nine parts. What do you say now, who is the most deviant, this man (who is unaware of the vastness of Allah's mercy), or his camel (that is under his command)?'"

> Reported by Aḥmad, Abū Dāwūd and al-Ḥākim. According to al-Ḥākim, "The chains of this tradition are authentic." According to al-Haythamī, "Abū Dāwūd reported its abridged form, and Aḥmad and al-Ṭabarānī narrated it. Aḥmad's sources are authentic, except for Abū ʿAbd Allāh al-Jushamī, but no one declared him weak."

١٩ / ٤. عَنْ سَلْمَانَ ﷺ عَنِ النَّبِيِّ ﷺ قَالَ: إِنَّ اللهَ ﷻ خَلَقَ مِائَةَ رَحْمَةٍ. فَمِنْهَا رَحْمَةٌ يَتَرَاحَمُ بِهَا الْخَلْقُ. فَبِهَا تَعْطِفُ الْوُحُوشُ عَلَى أَوْلَادِهَا. وَأَخَّرَ تِسْعَةً وَتِسْعِينَ إِلَى يَوْمِ الْقِيَامَةِ.

رَوَاهُ أَحْمَدُ وَالطَّبَرَانِيُّ وَالْبَيْهَقِيُّ.

---

[18] Set forth by •Aḥmad b. Ḥanbal in *al-Musnad*, 4:312 §18821; •Abū Dāwūd in *al-Sunan*: Bk.: *al-Adab* [Good Manners], Ch.: "Whom the Ruling of Backbiting Does Not Concern," 4:271 §4885; •al-Ruwayānī in *al-Musnad*, 2:140 §957; •al-Ḥākim in *al-Mustadrak*, 1:124 §187, and 4:276 §7630; •al-Ṭabarānī in *al-Muʿjam al-kabīr*, 2:161 §1667; •al-Haythamī in *Majmaʿ al-zawāʾid*, 10:213.

19/4. According to Salmān ﵁, the Prophet ﷺ said,

"Indeed, Allah ﷻ created one hundred parts of mercy. Because of one part, there is mercy shown between the Creation, and due to it, the wild beasts show affection to their young. Allah has reserved the remaining ninety-nine parts of mercy which He has deferred until the Day of Resurrection."

Reported by Aḥmad, al-Ṭabarānī and al-Bayhaqī.

٢٠/ ٥. عَنِ ابْنِ عَبَّاسٍ ﵄ قَالَ: قَالَ رَسُوْلُ اللهِ ﷺ: إِنَّ اللهَ ﷻ خَلَقَ مِائَةَ رَحْمَةٍ، رَحْمَةٌ مِنْهَا قَسَمَهَا بَيْنَ الْـخَلَائِقِ، وَتِسْعَةٌ وَتِسْعُوْنَ إِلَى يَوْمِ الْقِيَامَةِ.

رَوَاهُ الطَّبَرَانِيُّ وَالْـهَيْثَمِيُّ وَقَالَ: رَوَاهُ الطَّبَرَانِيُّ وَالْبَزَّارُ وَإِسْنَادُهُمَا حَسَنٌ.

20/5. According to Ibn ʿAbbās ﵄, Allah's Messenger ﷺ said,

"Indeed, Allah ﷻ created one hundred parts of mercy. Of them, one part has been distributed among the Creation, and the remaining ninety-nine are reserved until the Day of Resurrection."

Reported by al-Ṭabarānī and al-Haythamī. According to al-Haythamī, "Al-Ṭabarānī and al-Bazzār reported with a fine chain."

٢١/ ٦. عَنْ مُحَمَّدِ بْنِ سِيْرِيْنَ وَخِلَاسٍ كِلَاهُمَا عَنْ أَبِي هُرَيْرَةَ ﵁ عَنِ النَّبِيِّ ﷺ قَالَ: إِنَّ للهِ ﷻ مِائَةَ رَحْمَةٍ. قَسَمَ مِنْهَا رَحْمَةً بَيْنَ أَهْلِ الدُّنْيَا فَوَسِعَتْهُمْ إِلَى آجَالِـهِمْ، وَأَخَّرَ تِسْعَةً وَتِسْعِيْنَ لِأَوْلِيَائِهِ، وَإِنَّ اللهَ تَعَالَى قَابِضٌ تِلْكَ الرَّحْمَةَ الَّتِي قَسَمَهَا بَيْنَ أَهْلِ الدُّنْيَا إِلَى تِسْعٍ وَتِسْعِيْنَ فَكَمَّلَهَا مِائَةَ رَحْمَةٍ لِأَوْلِيَائِهِ يَوْمَ الْقِيَامَةِ.

رَوَاهُ أَحْمَدُ وَالْـحَاكِمُ وَاللَّفْظُ لَهُ، وَقَالَ الْـحَاكِمُ: هَذَا حَدِيْثٌ صَحِيْحٌ

---

19 Set forth by •Aḥmad b. Ḥanbal in *al-Musnad*, 5:439 §23771; •al-Ṭabarānī in *al-Muʿjam al-kabīr*, 6:250 §6126; •al-Bayhaqī in *Shuʿab al-īmān*, 2:15 §1038.

20 Set forth by •al-Ṭabarānī in *al-Muʿjam al-kabīr*, 11:374 §12047, and al-Haythamī in *Majmaʿ al-zawāʾid*, 10:214,385.

عَلَى شَرْطِ الشَّيْخَيْنِ. وَقَالَ الْـهَيْثَمِيُّ: وَعَنْ أَبِـي هُرَيْرَةَ ﵁ عَنِ النَّبِيِّ ﷺ قَالَ مِثْلَ ذَلِكَ رَوَاهُ وَالَّذِي قَبْلَهُ، أَحْمَدُ وَرِجَالُ الْـجَمِيْعِ رِجَالُ الصَّحِيْحِ. وَقَالَ الأَلْبَانِيُّ: هَذِهِ أَسَانِيْدُ صَحِيْحَةٌ مَوْصُوْلَةٌ عَنْ أَبِـي هُرَيْرَةَ ﵁.

21/6. According to Muḥammad b. Sīrīn and Khilās on the authority of Abū Hurayra ﵁, the Prophet ﷺ said,

"To Allah belong one hundred parts of mercy. He distributed one part of mercy among the denizens of the world, and it suffices them until their death. He reserved the remaining ninety-nine parts for His friends [*awliyā*ʾ]; and certainly Allah Most High shall take the one part of mercy that he divided among the inhabitants of the world and add it to the ninety-nine parts, completing thereby one hundred parts reserved for His friends [*awliyā*ʾ] on the Day of Resurrection."

> Reported by Aḥmad and al-Ḥākim (and this wording is his)." According to al-Ḥākim, "This is an authentic tradition conforming to the stipulations of the two Shaykhs [al-Bukhārī and Muslim]." According to al-Haythamī, "Abū Hurayra ﵁ reported a similar tradition from the Prophet ﷺ set forth by Aḥmad, and its sources are authentic." According to al-Albānī, "These are authentic chains of transmission contiguous to Abū Hurayra ﵁."

٢٢/ ٧. عَنْ مُعَاوِيَةَ بْنِ حَيْدَةَ ﵁ عَنِ النَّبِيِّ ﷺ، قَالَ: إِنَّ اللهَ تَعَالَى خَلَقَ مِائَةَ رَحْمَةٍ، فَرَحْمَةٌ بَيْنَ خَلْقِهِ يَتَرَاحَمُوْنَ بِهَا، وَادَّخَرَ لِأَوْلِيَائِهِ تِسْعَةً وَتِسْعِيْنَ.

رَوَاهُ الطَّبَرَانِيُّ وَتَمَّامٌ الرَّازِيُّ.

22/7. According to Muʿāwiya b. Ḥayda ﵁, the Prophet ﷺ said,

---

[21] Set forth by •Aḥmad b. Ḥanbal in *al-Musnad*, 2:514 §10681; •al-Ḥākim in *al-Mustadrak*, 1:123 §185; •al-Haythamī in *Majmaʿ al-zawāʾid*, 10:385; •al-Albānī in *Silsilat al-aḥādīth al-ṣaḥīḥa*, 4:176 §1634.

[22] Set forth by •al-Ṭabarānī in *al-Muʿjam al-kabīr*, 19:417 §1006; •Tamām al-Rāzī in *al-Fawāʾid*, 1:248 §606; •Ibn ʿAsākir in *Tārīkh Dimashq*, 8:259; •al-Haythamī in *Majmaʿ al-zawāʾid*, 10:385.

"Indeed, Allah Most High created one hundred parts of mercy. There is one part of mercy by which the Creation shows mercy to one another, and the remaining ninety-nine parts He has stored for his friends (for intercession)."

Reported by al-Ṭabarānī and Tammām al-Rāzī.

٢٣/ ٨. عَنِ الْـحَسَنِ قَالَ: بَلَغَنِي أَنَّ رَسُوْلَ اللهِ ﷺ قَالَ: للهِ سبحانه وتعالى مِائَةُ رَحْمَةٍ، وَإِنَّهُ قَسَمَ رَحْمَةً وَاحِدَةً بَيْنَ أَهْلِ الْأَرْضِ فَوَسِعَتْهُمْ إِلَى آجَالِـهِمْ، وَذَخَرَ تِسْعَةً وَتِسْعِيْنَ رَحْمَةً لِأَوْلِيَائِهِ. وَاللهُ سبحانه وتعالى قَابِضٌ تِلْكَ الرَّحْمَةَ الَّتِي قَسَمَهَا بَيْنَ أَهْلِ الْأَرْضِ إِلَى التِّسْعَةِ وَالتِّسْعِيْنَ فَيُكَمِّلُهَا مِائَةَ رَحْمَةٍ لِأَوْلِيَائِهِ يَوْمَ الْقِيَامَةِ.

رَوَاهُ أَحْمَدُ وَالْـحَاكِمُ. وَقَالَ الْـحَاكِمُ: هَذَا حَدِيْثٌ صَحِيْحٌ عَلَى شَرْطِ الشَّيْخَيْنِ. وَقَالَ الْـهَيْثَمِيُّ: وَعَنْ أَبِـي هُرَيْرَةَ رضي الله عنه عَنِ النَّبِيِّ ﷺ قَالَ مِثْلَ ذَلِكَ رَوَاهُ وَالَّذِي قَبْلَهُ أَحْمَدُ وَرِجَالُ الْـجَمِيْعِ رِجَالُ الصَّحِيْحِ وَرُوِيَ عَنْ خِلَاسٍ وَعَنْ مُحَمَّدِ بْنِ سِيْرِيْنَ قَالَ مِثْلَهُ وَرِجَالُهُ رِجَالُ الصَّحِيْحِ. وَقَالَ الْأَلْبَانِيُّ: هُوَ مُرْسَلٌ صَحِيْحُ الْإِسْنَادِ.

23/8. According to al-Ḥasan رضي الله عنه,

"It has reached me that Allah's Messenger ﷺ said, 'Allah has one hundred parts of mercy. He distributed one part of that mercy among the populace of the world and it suffices them until their deaths. He reserved the remaining ninety-nine parts for His friends and certainly Allah Most High shall take the one part of mercy that He distributed among the inhabitants of the world and add it to the ninety-nine parts, completing thereby one hundred parts reserved for His friends on the Day of Resurrection (blessing them with exalted stations, eminent grades and the right to intercede).'"

---

[23] Set forth by •Aḥmad b. Ḥanbal in *al-Musnad*, 2:514 §10680; •al-Ḥākim in *al-Mustadrak*, 4:276 §7629; •al-Haythamī in *Majmaʿ al-zawāʾid*, 10:214,385; •al-Albānī in *Silsilat al-aḥādīth al-ṣaḥīḥa*, 4:176 §1634.

Reported by Aḥmad and al-Ḥākim. According to al-Ḥākim, "This is an authentic tradition conforming to the stipulations of the two Shaykhs [al-Bukhārī and Muslim]." According to al-Haythamī, "Abū Hurayra ﷺ reported a similar tradition from the Prophet ﷺ set forth by Aḥmad, and its sources are authentic." Reported by Khilās and Muḥammad b. Sīrīn, and its sources are authentic." According to al-Albānī, "This is a link-missing [*mursal*] tradition with an authentic chain of transmission."

٢٤/ ٩. عَنْ أَبِي هُرَيْرَةَ ﷺ أَنَّ رَسُوْلَ اللهِ ﷺ قَالَ: خَلَقَ اللهُ مِائَةَ رَحْمَةٍ فَوَضَعَ رَحْمَةً وَاحِدَةً بَيْنَ خَلْقِهِ يَتَرَاحَمُوْنَ بِهَا وَعِنْدَ اللهِ تِسْعٌ وَتِسْعُوْنَ رَحْمَةً.

رَوَاهُ أَحْمَدُ وَالتِّرْمِذِيُّ وَقَالَ: هَذَا حَدِيْثٌ حَسَنٌ صَحِيْحٌ.

24/9. According to Abū Hurayra ﷺ, Allah's Messenger ﷺ said,

"Allah created one hundred parts of mercy and placed one part among the Creation. By this part they show mercy to one another. The remaining ninety-nine parts are with Allah."

Reported by Aḥmad and al-Tirmidhī. According to al-Tirmidhī, "This is a fine authentic tradition."

٢٥/ ١٠. عَنْ عُبَادَةَ بْنِ الصَّامِتِ ﷺ قَالَ: قَالَ رَسُوْلُ اللهِ ﷺ: قَسَمَ رَبُّنَا رَحْمَتَهُ مِائَةَ جُزْءٍ. فَأَنْزَلَ مِنْهَا جُزْءًا فِي الْأَرْضِ فَهُوَ الَّذِي يَتَرَاحَمُ بِهِ النَّاسُ وَالطَّيْرُ وَالْبَهَائِمُ. وَبَقِيَتْ عِنْدَهُ مِائَةُ رَحْمَةٍ إِلَّا رَحْمَةً وَاحِدَةً لِعِبَادِهِ يَوْمَ الْقِيَامَةِ.

رَوَاهُ الْهَيْثَمِيُّ وَالْهِنْدِيُّ.

25/10. According to ʿUbāda b. al-Ṣāmit ﷺ, Allah's Messenger ﷺ said,

[24] Set forth by •Aḥmad b. Ḥanbal in *al-Musnad*, 2:484 §10285; •al-Tirmidhī in *al-Sunan:* Bk.: *al-Daʿawāt ʿan Rasūl Allāh* ﷺ [Invocations from Allāh's Messenger ﷺ], Ch.: "Allāh Created One Hundred Mercies," 5:549 §3541; •Ibn Kathīr in *Tafsīr al-Qurʾān al-ʿAẓīm*, 2:201.

[25] Cited by al-Haythamī in *Majmaʿ al-zawāʾid*, 10:385, and al-Hindī in *Kanz*

"Our Lord divided His mercy into one hundred parts. Of them, He sent down one part to the earth, and by that part, people, birds and other creatures show mercy to one another. The remaining ninety-nine parts are with Him and are reserved for His servants on the Day of Resurrection."

Reported by al-Haythamī and al-Hindī.

---

al-ʿummāl, 4:439 §10406.

اَلْبَابُ السَّادِسُ

إِنَّ اللهَ تَعَالَى يُدْخِلُ مِنْ أُمَّةِ حَبِيْبِهِ الْجَنَّةَ سَبْعِيْنَ أَلْفًا بِغَيْرِ حِسَابٍ وَمَعَ كُلِّ أَلْفٍ سَبْعُوْنَ أَلْفًا

Chapter Six

Of the Seventy Thousand People of the Prophet's *Umma* to whom Allah shall Grant Paradise without reckoning, Every Thousand amongst them shall take another Seventy Thousand

٢٦/ ١. عَنْ سَهْلِ بْنِ سَعْدٍ ﷺ قَالَ: قَالَ النَّبِيُّ ﷺ: لَيَدْخُلَنَّ الْـجَنَّةَ مِنْ أُمَّتِي سَبْعُوْنَ أَلْفًا أَوْ سَبْعُ مِائَةِ أَلْفٍ، شَكَّ فِي أَحَدِهِمَا، مُتَمَاسِكِيْنَ آخِذٌ بَعْضُهُمْ بِبَعْضٍ، حَتَّى يَدْخُلَ أَوَّلُهُمْ وَآخِرُهُمُ الْـجَنَّةَ. وَوُجُوْهُهُمْ عَلَى ضَوْءِ الْقَمَرِ لَيْلَةَ الْبَدْرِ.

مُتَّفَقٌ عَلَيْهِ.

26/1. According to Sahl b. Saʿd ﷺ, the Prophet ﷺ said,

"Certainly, seventy thousand (or seven hundred thousand [the narrator was unsure which of the two the Prophet ﷺ said]) from my *Umma* shall enter Paradise (without reckoning). They shall all hold on (by virtue of affinity) to each other until all of them, the first (the leading one) and the last of them, enter Paradise. Their faces will shine like the moon when it is full."

Agreed upon by al-Bukhārī and Muslim.

٢٧/ ٢. عَنْ أَبِي هُرَيْرَةَ ﷺ قَالَ: سَمِعْتُ رَسُوْلَ اللهِ ﷺ يَقُوْلُ: يَدْخُلُ الْـجَنَّةَ مِنْ أُمَّتِي زُمْرَةٌ هُمْ سَبْعُوْنَ أَلْفًا، تُضِيءُ وُجُوْهُهُمْ إِضَاءَةَ الْقَمَرِ لَيْلَةَ الْبَدْرِ، وَقَالَ أَبُو هُرَيْرَةَ ﷺ: فَقَامَ عُكَّاشَةُ بْنُ مِحْصَنٍ الْأَسَدِيُّ يَرْفَعُ نَمِرَةً عَلَيْهِ، فَقَالَ: يَا رَسُوْلَ اللهِ،

26 Set forth by •al-Bukhārī in *al-Ṣaḥīḥ:* Bk.: *al-Riqāq* [Heart Softeners], Ch.: "Seventy Thousand Shall Enter Paradise Without Reckoning," 5:2396 §6177, and in Bk.: *Badʾ al-khalq* [The Beginning of Creation], Ch.: "The Description of Paradise and That it is Created," 3:1186 §3075, and in Bk.: *al-Riqāq* [Heart Softeners], Ch.: "The Description of Paradise and Fire," 5:2399 §6187; •Muslim in *al-Ṣaḥīḥ:* Bk.: *al-Īmān* [The Faith], Ch.: "The Proof That Some Groups of Muslims Shall Enter Paradise without Reckoning of Punishment," 1:198 §219; •Aḥmad b. Ḥanbal in *al-Musnad*, 5:335 §22839; •Ibn Kathīr in *Tafsīr al-Qurʾān al-ʿAẓīm*, 1:394.

اُدْعُ اللهَ أَنْ يَّجْعَلَنِي مِنْهُمْ. قَالَ: اَللّٰهُمَّ اجْعَلْهُ مِنْهُمْ. ثُمَّ قَامَ رَجُلٌ مِنَ الْأَنْصَارِ، فَقَالَ:

يَا رَسُوْلَ اللهِ، اُدْعُ اللهَ أَنْ يَّجْعَلَنِي مِنْهُمْ. فَقَالَ: سَبَقَكَ بِهَا عُكَّاشَةُ.

مُتَّفَقٌ عَلَيْهِ.

27/2. According to Abū Hurayra ṣ,

"I heard Allah's Messenger ṣ say, 'Seventy thousand members of my Community will enter the Garden of Paradise and their faces will shine like the moon on the night of the full moon.' Upon hearing that, ʿUkāsha b. Miḥṣan al-Asadī stood up, lifting his woolen mantle, and said, 'O Messenger of Allah! Supplicate Allah to make me one of them.' The Prophet ṣ said, 'O Allah, make him one of them.' After that, a man from the Anṣār stood and said, 'O Messenger of Allah! Supplicate Allah to make me one of them, too.' The Prophet ṣ said, "ʿUkāsha beat you to it.'"

Agreed upon by al-Bukhārī and Muslim.

٢٨/٣. عَنِ ابْنِ عَبَّاسٍ ☙ قَالَ: قَالَ النَّبِيُّ ﷺ: عُرِضَتْ عَلَيَّ الْأُمَمُ، فَأَخَذَ النَّبِيُّ يَمُرُّ مَعَهُ الْأُمَّةُ، وَالنَّبِيُّ يَمُرُّ مَعَهُ النَّفَرُ، وَالنَّبِيُّ يَمُرُّ مَعَهُ الْعَشَرَةُ، وَالنَّبِيُّ يَمُرُّ مَعَهُ الْخَمْسَةُ، وَالنَّبِيُّ يَمُرُّ وَحْدَهُ. فَنَظَرْتُ فَإِذَا سَوَادٌ كَثِيْرٌ. قُلْتُ: يَا جِبْرِيْلُ ☙، هَؤُلَاءِ أُمَّتِي؟ قَالَ: لَا، وَلَكِنِ انْظُرْ إِلَى الْأُفُقِ. فَنَظَرْتُ فَإِذَا سَوَادٌ كَثِيْرٌ. قَالَ: هَؤُلَاءِ أُمَّتُكَ، وَهَؤُلَاءِ سَبْعُوْنَ أَلْفًا قُدَّامَهُمْ، لَا حِسَابَ عَلَيْهِمْ وَلَا عَذَابَ. قُلْتُ: وَلِمَ؟ قَالَ: كَانُوْا لَا يَكْتَوُوْنَ وَلَا يَسْتَرْقُوْنَ وَلَا يَتَطَيَّرُوْنَ وَعَلَى رَبِّهِمْ يَتَوَكَّلُوْنَ. فَقَامَ إِلَيْهِ عُكَّاشَةُ بْنُ

---

27 Set forth by •al-Bukhārī in al-Ṣaḥīḥ: Bk.: al-Riqāq [Heart Softeners], Ch.: "Seventy Thousand Shall Enter Paradise Without Reckoning," 5:2396 §6176, and in Bk.: al-Libās [Clothing], Ch.: "The Cloak and Over garment," 5:2189 §5474; •Muslim in al-Ṣaḥīḥ: Bk.: al-Īmān [The Faith], Ch.: "The Proof That Some Groups of Muslims Shall Enter Paradise without Reckoning or Punishment," 1:197 §216; •Aḥmad b. Ḥanbal in al-Musnad, 2:400 §9202; •Ibn Manda in al-Īmān, 2:892 §970 (with an authentic chain of transmission); •Ibn Kathīr in Tafsīr al-Qurʾān al-ʿAẓīm, 1:394.

مِحْصَنٍ، فَقَالَ: اُدْعُ اللهَ أَنْ يَجْعَلَنِي مِنْهُمْ. قَالَ: اَللَّهُمَّ، اجْعَلْهُ مِنْهُمْ. ثُمَّ قَامَ إِلَيْهِ رَجُلٌ

آخَرُ. قَالَ: اُدْعُ اللهَ أَنْ يَجْعَلَنِي مِنْهُمْ. قَالَ: سَبَقَكَ بِهَا عُكَّاشَةُ.

رَوَاهُ الْبُخَارِيُّ.

28/3. According to Ibn ʿAbbās 🙵, the Prophet 🙵 said,

"The bygone communities were displayed to me, and I beheld one
Prophet passing by with a throng, another Prophet passing by with a
small group, another Prophet passing by with only ten people, another
Prophet passing by with only five people, and another Prophet passing
by all alone. Then I looked, and lo and behold, I saw a large multitude
of people. I asked Jibrīl 🙵, 'Are these my *Umma*?' 'No,' he replied, 'but
look to the horizon.' When I looked (to the horizon), I suddenly saw
a large multitude of people. Jibrīl 🙵 said, 'They are your Community
and at their forefront there are seventy thousand who shall not be
subjected to any reckoning or punishment.' 'Why?' I asked. Jibrīl
replied, 'They did not treat themselves with cauterization [*kayʾ*], and
they did not seek incantation [*ruqya*] from others, and they did not see
omens in things, and they used to put their trust completely in their
Lord.' On hearing that, ʿUkāsha b. Miḥṣan stood up and said, 'O
Messenger of Allah! Ask Allah to make me one of them.' The Prophet
🙵 said, 'O Allah, make him one of them.' After that, another man
stood and said, '(O Messenger of Allah!) Ask Allah to make me one of
them, too.' The Prophet 🙵 said, "ʿUkāsha beat you to it.'"

Reported by al-Bukhārī.

٤ / ٢٩. عَنْ أَبِي هُرَيْرَةَ 🙵 أَنَّ النَّبِيَّ 🙵 قَالَ: يَدْخُلُ مِنْ أُمَّتِي الْجَنَّةَ سَبْعُونَ

أَلْفًا بِغَيْرِ حِسَابٍ. فَقَالَ رَجُلٌ: يَا رَسُولَ اللهِ، اُدْعُ اللهَ أَنْ يَجْعَلَنِي مِنْهُمْ. قَالَ: اَللَّهُمَّ،

اجْعَلْهُ مِنْهُمْ. ثُمَّ قَامَ آخَرُ، فَقَالَ: يَا رَسُولَ اللهِ، اُدْعُ اللهَ أَنْ يَجْعَلَنِي مِنْهُمْ. قَالَ: سَبَقَكَ

بِهَا عُكَّاشَةُ.

---

28 Set forth by •al-Bukhārī in *al-Ṣaḥīḥ*: Bk.: *al-Riqāq* [Heart Softeners], Ch.:
"Seventy Thousand Shall Enter Paradise Without Reckoning," 5:2396 §6175.

رَوَاهُ مُسْلِمٌ وَأَحْمَدُ.

29/4. According to Abū Hurayra ﷺ,

"The Prophet ﷺ said, 'Seventy thousand of my *Umma* shall enter Paradise without reckoning.' Upon hearing that, a man said, 'O Messenger of Allah! Ask Allah to make me one of them.' The Prophet ﷺ said, 'O Allah, make him one of them.' After that, another man stood and said, 'O Messenger of Allah! Ask Allah to make me one of them, too.' The Prophet ﷺ said, "ʿUkāsha beat you to it.'"

Reported by Muslim and Aḥmad.

٣٠/ ٥. عَنْ جَابِرِ بْنِ عَبْدِ اللهِ ﷺ (فِي رِوَايَةٍ طَوِيْلَةٍ) قَالَ: ثُمَّ يَنْجُو الْـمُؤْمِنُوْنَ، فَتَنْجُوْ أَوَّلُ زُمْرَةٍ، وُجُوْهُهُمْ كَالْقَمَرِ لَيْلَةَ الْبَدْرِ سبْعُوْنَ أَلْفًا لَا يُحَاسَبُوْنَ، ثُمَّ الَّذِيْنَ يَلُوْنَهُمْ كَأَضْوَإِ نَجْمٍ فِي السَّمَاءِ ثُمَّ كَذَلِكَ.

رَوَاهُ مُسْلِمٌ وَأَحْمَدُ.

30/5. According to (the detailed account of) Jābir b. ʿAbd Allāh ﷺ, the Prophet ﷺ said,

"Then the believers will attain salvation; the first group to attain salvation will be seventy thousand who will not face reckoning. They will have faces shining like the moon when it is full. And those who come after them will have faces shining like luminous stars, and so on."

---

[29] Set forth by •Muslim in *al-Ṣaḥīḥ:* Bk.: *al-Īmān* [The Faith], Ch.: "The Proof That Some Groups of Muslims Shall Enter Paradise without Reckoning or Punishment," 1:197 §216; •Aḥmad b. Ḥanbal in *al-Musnad*, 2:302 §8016; •Ibn Rāhawayh in *al-Musnad*, 1:143 §76; •Ibn Manda in *al-Īmān*, 2:894 §974.

[30] Set forth by •Muslim in *al-Ṣaḥīḥ:* Bk.: *al-Īmān* [The Faith], Ch.: "Those on the Lowest Level of Paradise," 1:177 §191; •Aḥmad b. Ḥanbal in *al-Musnad*, 3:345 §14721 (and the narration is fully connected to the Prophet ﷺ); •ʿAbd Allāh b. Aḥmad b. Ḥanbal in *al-Sunna*, 1:248 §457; •Ibn Manda in *al-Īmān*, 2:825 §851 (with an authentic chain of transmission); •Ibn Kathīr in *Tafsīr al-Qurʾān al-ʿAẓīm*, 1:394–395.

Reported by Muslim and Aḥmad.

٣١/ ٦. عَنْ أَبِـي هُرَيْرَةَ ؓ، عَنْ رَسُوْلِ اللهِ ﷺ أَنَّهُ قَالَ: سَأَلْتُ رَبِّي، فَوَعَدَنِي أَنْ يُدْخِلَ مِنْ أُمَّتِي سَبْعِيْنَ أَلْفًا عَلَى صُوْرَةِ الْقَمَرِ لَيْلَةَ الْبَدْرِ. فَاسْتَزَدْتُ فَزَادَنِي مَعَ كُلِّ أَلْفٍ سَبْعِيْنَ أَلْفًا. فَقُلْتُ: أَيْ رَبِّ، إِنْ لَـمْ يَكُنْ هَؤُلَاءِ مُهَاجِرِي أُمَّتِي؟ قَالَ: إِذَنْ أُكْمِلُهُمْ لَكَ مِنَ الْأَعْرَابِ.

رَوَاهُ أَحْمَدُ وَابْنُ مَنْدَهْ، وَإِسْنَادُهُ صَحِيْحٌ.

31/6. According to Abū Hurayra ؓ, Allah's Messenger ﷺ said,

"I asked my Lord and He promised me that He would place seventy thousand of my *Umma* in Paradise with faces shining like the moon when it is full. I then asked Him to increase their number and He granted me that, adding seventy thousand for every thousand of them. I then said, 'O my Lord, even if they are not from the migrants of my *Umma*?' He said, 'In that case, I shall complete them for you with the Bedouins.'"

Reported by Aḥmad and Ibn Mandah and it has an authentic chain of transmission.

٣٢/ ٧. عَنْ حُذَيْفَةَ بْنِ الْيَمَانِ ؓ قَالَ: غَابَ عَنَّا رَسُوْلُ اللهِ ﷺ يَوْمًا، فَلَمْ يَخْرُجْ حَتَّى ظَنَنَّا أَنَّهُ لَنْ يَخْرُجَ. فَلَـمَّا خَرَجَ سَجَدَ سَجْدَةً، فَظَنَنَّا أَنَّ نَفْسَهُ قَدْ قُبِضَتْ فِيْهَا. فَلَـمَّا رَفَعَ رَأْسَهُ، قَالَ: إِنَّ رَبِّي تَـبَارَكَ وَتَعَالَى اسْتَشَارَنِي فِي أُمَّتِي مَاذَا أَفْعَلُ بِهِمْ. فَقُلْتُ: مَا شِئْتَ، أَيْ رَبِّ، هُمْ خَلْقُكَ وَعِبَادُكَ. فَاسْتَشَارَنِي الثَّانِيَةَ، فَقُلْتُ لَهُ كَذٰلِكَ. فَقَالَ: لَا أُحْزِنُكَ فِي أُمَّتِكَ، يَا مُحَمَّدُ. وَبَشَّرَنِي أَنَّ أَوَّلَ مَنْ يَدْخُلُ الْـجَنَّةَ مِنْ أُمَّتِي سَبْعُوْنَ أَلْفًا

---

[31] Set forth by •Aḥmad b. Ḥanbal in *al-Musnad*, 2:359 §8707; •Ibn Manda in *al-Īmān*, 2:895 §976 (with a rigorously authentic chain of transmission similar to those of Muslim); •al-Haythamī in *Majmaʿ al-zawāʾid*, 10:404 (who said: "Its men are those of rigorously authentic chains of transmission."); and cited by •Ibn Ḥajar in *Fatḥ al-Bārī*, 11:410 (who said: "It has a good chain").

مَعَ كُلِّ أَلْفٍ سَبْعُوْنَ أَلْفًا لَيْسَ عَلَيْهِمْ حِسَابٌ.

رَوَاهُ أَحْمَدُ وَابْنُ كَثِيْرٍ وَالْـهَيْثَمِيُّ، وَقَالَ: إِسْنَادُهُ حَسَنٌ.

32/7. According to Ḥudhayfa b. al-Yamān رضي الله عنه,

"Once, the Prophet ﷺ was away from us for an entire day. He did not come out and we feared he would not come out. After he came out, he fell into prostration and remained prostrate for so long that we thought his soul was taken while in that position. Then he raised his head from prostration and said, 'My Lord conferred with me about my *Umma*, asking what He should do with them. I said, "Whatever You will, my Lord. They are Your creation and Your servants." He conferred with me a second time and I said just as I did the first time. Then He said, 'I will not cause you to be saddened on account of your *Umma*, O Muhammad.' Then He gave me the glad tidings that the first [group] to enter Paradise will be seventy thousand, and that with each one thousand of them there will be an additional seventy thousand—none of them will face reckoning.'"

Reported by Aḥmad, Ibn Kathīr and al-Haythamī who said, "It has a fine chain of transmission."

٣٣/ ٨. عَنْ أَبِـي أُمَامَةَ رضي الله عنه قَالَ: سَمِعْتُ رَسُوْلَ اللهِ ﷺ يَقُوْلُ: وَعَدَنِي رَبِّي أَنْ يُدْخِلَ الْـجَنَّةَ مِنْ أُمَّتِي سَبْعِيْنَ أَلْفًا، لَا حِسَابَ عَلَيْهِمْ وَلَا عَذَابَ مَعَ كُلِّ أَلْفٍ سَبْعُوْنَ أَلْفًا وَثَـلَاثُ حَثَيَاتٍ مِنْ حَثَيَاتِهِ.

رَوَاهُ أَحْمَدُ وَالتِّرْمِذِيُّ وَابْنُ مَاجَه وَابْنُ أَبِـي شَيْبَةَ وَابْنُ أَبِـي عَاصِمٍ وَابْنُ كَثِيْرٍ، وَقَالَ التِّرْمِذِيُّ: هَذَا حَدِيْثٌ حَسَنٌ.

33/8. According to Abū Umāma رضي الله عنه,

---

[32] Set forth by •Aḥmad b. Ḥanbal in *al-Musnad*, 5:393 §23336; •Ibn Kathīr in *Tafsīr al-Qur'ān al-ʿAẓīm*, 2:122; •al-Haythamī in *Majmaʿ al-zawā'id*, 10:68.

[33] Set forth by •al-Tirmidhī in *al-Sunan:* Bk.: *Ṣifat al-qiyāma wa al-raqā'iq wa al-waraʿ* [The Description of the Resurrection, Heart Softeners and

"I heard Allah's Messenger ﷺ say, 'My Lord promised me that He would place seventy thousand of my *Umma* in Paradise without reckoning or punishment, and that with every one thousand among them there would be an additional seventy thousand and three Handfuls (of the denizens of Hell).'"

> Reported by Aḥmad, al-Tirmidhī, Ibn Mājah, Ibn Abī Shayba, Ibn Abī ʿĀṣim and Ibn Kathīr. According to al-Tirmidhī, "This is a fine tradition."

٣٤/ ٩. عَنْ أَبِي أُمَامَةَ رضي الله عنه أَنَّ رَسُوْلَ اللهِ ﷺ قَالَ: إِنَّ اللهَ سبحانه وتعالى وَعَدَنِي أَنْ يُدْخِلَ مِنْ أُمَّتِي الْجَنَّةَ سَبْعِيْنَ أَلْفًا بِغَيْرِ حِسَابٍ، فَقَالَ يَزِيْدُ بْنُ الْأَخْنِ السُّلَمِيُّ: وَاللهِ، مَا أُوْلَئِكَ فِي أُمَّتِكَ إِلَّا كَالذُّبَابِ الْأَصْهَبِ فِي الذِّبَّانِ. فَقَالَ رَسُوْلُ اللهِ ﷺ: كَانَ رَبِّي سبحانه وتعالى قَدْ وَعَدَنِي سَبْعِيْنَ أَلْفًا مَعَ كُلِّ أَلْفٍ سَبْعُوْنَ أَلْفًا، وَزَادَنِي ثَلَاثَ حَثَيَاتٍ.

رَوَاهُ أَحْمَدُ وَالطَّبَرَانِيُّ وَابْنُ أَبِي عَاصِمٍ وَابْنُ كَثِيْرٍ. وَإِسْنَادُهُ قَوِيٌّ، وَرِجَالُهُ رِجَالُ الصَّحِيْحِ.

34/9. According to Abū Umāma رضي الله عنه, Allah's Messenger ﷺ said,

"Indeed, Allah promised me that He would admit seventy thousand

---

Scrupulousness], Ch.: "Intercession," 4:626 §2437; •Aḥmad b. Ḥanbal in *al-Musnad*, 5:268 §22303 (with an authentic chain of transmission); •Ibn Mājah in *al-Sunan:* Bk.: *al-Zuhd* [The Renunciation], Ch.: "The Description of Muhammad ﷺ," 2:1433 §4286; •Ibn Abī Shayba in *al-Muṣannaf*, 6:315 §31714; •Ibn Abī ʿĀṣim in *al-Sunna*, 1:260,261 §§588,589; •Ibn Kathīr in *Tafsīr al-Qurʾān al-ʿAẓīm*, 1:295; and cited by •Ibn Ḥajar in *al-Iṣāba*, 6:646 §9233 (with an an authentic chain of transmission);

[34] Set forth by •Aḥmad b. Ḥanbal in *al-Musnad*, 5:250 §22156; •al-Ṭabarānī in *al-Muʿjam al-kabīr*, 8:159 §7276; •Ibn Abī ʿĀṣim in *al-Sunna*, 1:261 §588 (al-Albānī said: "Its chain is rigorously authentic and its men are all reliable"); •Ibn Abī ʿĀṣim in *al-Āḥād wa al-mathānī*, 2:445 §1247; •al-Mundhirī in *al-Targhīb wa al-tarhīb*, 4:225 §5473; •Ibn Kathīr in *Tafsīr al-Qurʾān al-ʿAẓīm*, 1:395 (who said: "This is an authentic chain of transmission"); and cited by •Ibn Ḥajar in *al-Iṣāba fī tamyīz al-ṣaḥāba*, 6:646 §9233 (with an authentic chain of transmission).

of my *Umma* into Paradise without reckoning." Yazīd b. al-Akhun al-Sulamī submitted, "By Allah, their presence in your *Umma* will be comparable to a reddish fly among black flies [i.e., miniscule in number]." Allah's Messenger ﷺ said, "My Lord promised me seventy thousand, and an additional seventy thousand with every one thousand among them, and then He increased me three Handfuls. (He will take three Handfuls from Hell and admit them to Paradise befitting His Glory.)"

Reported by Aḥmad, al-Ṭabarānī, Ibn Abī ʿĀṣim and Ibn Kathīr. It has a firm chain of transmission and its sources are authentic.

٣٥/ ١٠ . عَنْ عُتْبَةَ بْنِ عَبْدٍ السُّلَمِيِّ رضي الله عنه قَالَ: قَالَ رَسُوْلُ اللهِ ﷺ: إِنَّ رَبِّي وَعَدَنِي أَنْ يُدْخِلَ مِنْ أُمَّتِي الْـجَنَّةَ سَبْعِيْنَ أَلْفًا بِغَيْرِ حِسَابٍ ثُمَّ يُتْبِعُ كُلَّ أَلْفٍ بِسَبْعِيْنَ أَلْفًا (وَفِي رِوَايَةِ الطَّبَرَانِيِّ قَالَ: ثُمَّ يَشْفَعُ كُلُّ أَلْفٍ لِسَبْعِيْنَ أَلْفاً)، ثُمَّ يَحْثِي بِكَفِّهِ ثَـلَاثَ حَثَيَاتٍ. فَكَبَّرَ عُمَرُ. فَقَالَ: إِنَّ السَّبْعِيْنَ أَلْفًا الْأُوَلَ يُشَفِّعُهُمُ اللهُ فِي آبَائِهِمْ وَأُمَّهَاتِهِمْ وَعَشَائِرِهِمْ، وَأَرْجُوْ أَنْ يَجْعَلَ أُمَّتِي أَدْنَى الْـحَثَوَاتِ الْأَوَاخِرِ.

رَوَاهُ ابْنُ حِبَّانَ وَالطَّبَرَانِيُّ وَابْنُ كَثِيْرٍ، وَقَالَ ابْنُ كَثِيْرٍ: قَالَ الْـحَافِظُ الضِّيَاءُ أَبُوعَبْدِ اللهِ الْـمَقْدِسِيُّ فِي كِتَابِهِ 'صِفَةِ الْجَنَّةِ': لَا أَعْلَمُ لِهَذَا الْإِسْنَادِ عِلَّةً.

35/10. According to ʿUtba b. ʿAbd al-Sulamī رضي الله عنه, Allah's Messenger ﷺ said,

"Indeed, my Lord has promised me that He will place seventy thousand of my *Umma* in Paradise without reckoning and then for every one thousand among them there shall follow seventy thousand more [and in al-Ṭabarānī's words, 'Then every one thousand among them will intercede on behalf of seventy thousand people']," then Allah will deliver three handfuls of people from the Hell. Upon seeing

[35] Set forth by •Ibn Ḥibbān in *al-Ṣaḥīḥ*, 16:232 §7247; •al-Ṭabarānī in *al-Muʿjam al-kabīr*, 17:127 §312, and in •*al-Muʿjam al-awsaṭ*, 1:127 §402; •Ibn Kathīr in *Tafsīr al-Qurʾān al-ʿAẓīm*, 1:395; •al-Haythamī in *Majmaʿ al-zawāʾid*, 10:409,414.

this, ʿUmar said, "Allah is the Greatest!" The Prophet ﷺ then said, "Allah shall permit the first seventy thousand to intercede on behalf of their fathers, mothers, and families, and I hope that He will make my *Umma* closest of those handfuls."

> Reported by Ibn Ḥibbān, al-Ṭabarānī and Ibn Kathīr. According to Ibn Kathīr, "Al-Ḥāfiẓ al-Ḍiyāʾ Abū ʿAbd Allāh al-Maqdisī said in *Ṣifat al-Janna* (The description of Paradise), 'I find no defect in this chain.'"

٣٦/ ١١. عَنْ أَبِـي هُرَيْرَةَ ؓ قَالَ: قَالَ رَسُوْلُ اللهِ ﷺ: سَأَلْتُ (أَيْ اللهَ تَـبَارَكَ وَتَعَالَى) الشَّفَاعَةَ لِأُمَّتِي. فَقَالَ: لَكَ سَبْعُوْنَ أَلْفًا يَدْخُلُوْنَ الْـجَنَّةَ بِغَيْرِ حِسَابٍ. قُلْتُ: زِدْنِي. قَالَ: لَكَ مَعَ كُلِّ أَلْفٍ سَبْعُوْنَ أَلْفًا، قُلْتُ: زِدْنِي. قَالَ: فَإِنَّ لَكَ هَكَذَا وَهَكَذَا. فَقَالَ أَبُو بَكْرٍ: حَسْبُنَا. فَقَالَ عُمَرُ: يَا أَبَا بَكْرٍ، دَعْ رَسُوْلَ اللهِ ﷺ. فَقَالَ أَبُو بَكْرٍ: يَا عُمَرُ، إِنَّمَا نَحْنُ حَفْنَةٌ مِنْ حَفَنَاتِ اللهِ.

رَوَاهُ ابْنُ أَبِـي شَيْبَةَ وَالْـهَنَّادُ وَالدَّيْلَمِيُّ.

36/11. According to Abū Hurayra ؓ, Allah's Messenger ﷺ said,

"I interceded [with Allah ﷻ] on behalf of my *Umma* and He said, 'You shall have seventy thousand who shall enter Paradise without reckoning.' I said, 'Increase for me.' He said, 'For every one thousand among them, you shall have an additional seventy thousand.' I said, 'Increase for me.' He said, 'You have such-and-such.'" Abū Bakr said, "That is enough for us." ʿUmar said, "O Abū Bakr! Let Allah's Messenger ﷺ alone (accomplish)!" Abū Bakr said, "O ʿUmar! We are but one handful of Allah's many handfuls."

> Reported by Ibn Abī Shayba, al-Hannād and al-Daylamī.

---

[36] Set forth by •Ibn Abī Shayba in *al-Muṣannaf*, 6:318 §31739; •Hannād b. al-Sirrī in *al-Zuhd*, 1:135 §178; •al-Daylamī in *Musnad al-firdaws*, 2:311 §3407.

اَلْبَابُ السَّابِعُ

إِنَّ اللّٰهَ تَعَالَى يُدْخِلُ الْجَنَّةَ سَبْعُوْنَ أَلْفًا وَمَعَ كُلِّ وَاحِدٍ سَبْعُوْنَ أَلْفًا بِغَيْرِ حِسَابٍ

CHAPTER SEVEN

ON THE SEVENTY THOUSAND PEOPLE OF THE PROPHET'S *UMMA* TO WHOM ALLAH SHALL GRANT PARADISE WITHOUT RECKONING, AND EVERY SINGLE PERSON AMONG THEM WILL BE GRANTED ADDITIONAL SEVENTY THOUSAND TO ENTER PARADISE WITH HIM WITHOUT RECKONING

٣٧/ ١. عَنْ أَبِي بَكْرٍ الصِّدِّيْقِ ﵁ قَالَ: قَالَ رَسُوْلُ اللهِ ﷺ: أُعْطِيْتُ سَبْعِيْنَ أَلْفًا يَدْخُلُوْنَ الْجَنَّةَ بِغَيْرِ حِسَابٍ. وُجُوْهُهُمْ كَالْقَمَرِ لَيْلَةَ الْبَدْرِ وَقُلُوْبُهُمْ عَلَى قَلْبِ رَجُلٍ وَاحِدٍ. فَاسْتَزَدْتُ رَبِّي، فَزَادَنِي مَعَ كُلِّ وَاحِدٍ سَبْعِيْنَ أَلْفًا. قَالَ أَبُوْ بَكْرٍ: فَرَأَيْتُ أَنَّ ذَالِكَ آتٍ عَلَى أَهْلِ الْقُرَى وَمُصِيْبٌ مِنْ حَافَّاتِ الْبَوَادِي.

رَوَاهُ أَحْمَدُ وَأَبُوْ يَعْلَى.

37/1. According to Abū Bakr al-Ṣiddīq ﵁, Allah's Messenger ﷺ said, "I was granted seventy thousand who shall enter Paradise without reckoning. Their faces will shine like the moon when it is full and their hearts will be like the heart of one person. I then asked my Lord for more, and He granted me an additional seventy thousand with every single person." Abū Bakr ﵁ said, "I think this shall be for the inhabitants of the villages and the bare-footed nomads."

Reported by Aḥmad and Abū Yaʿlā.

٣٨/ ٢. عَنْ عَبْدِ الرَّحْمَنِ بْنِ أَبِي بَكْرٍ ﵄ أَنَّ رَسُوْلَ اللهِ ﷺ قَالَ: إِنَّ رَبِّي أَعْطَانِي سَبْعِيْنَ أَلْفًا مِنْ أُمَّتِي يَدْخُلُوْنَ الْجَنَّةَ بِغَيْرِ حِسَابٍ. فَقَالَ عُمَرُ: يَا رَسُوْلَ اللهِ، فَهَلَّا اسْتَزَدْتَهُ؟ قَالَ: قَدْ اسْتَزَدْتُهُ فَأَعْطَانِي مَعَ كُلِّ رَجُلٍ سَبْعِيْنَ أَلْفًا. قَالَ عُمَرُ: فَهَلَّا اسْتَزَدْتَهُ؟ قَالَ: قَدْ اسْتَزَدْتُهُ فَأَعْطَانِي هَكَذَا.

رَوَاهُ أَحْمَدُ وَالْبَزَّارُ.

---

[37] Set forth by •Aḥmad b. Ḥanbal in *al-Musnad*, 1:6 §22; •Abū Yaʿlā in *al-Musnad*, 1:104 §112; •al-Haythamī in *Majmaʿ al-zawāʾid*, 10:410; •Ibn Kathīr in *Tafsīr al-Qurʾān al-ʿAẓīm*, 1:393.

38/2. According to ʿAbd al-Raḥmān b. Abī Bakr ﵄, Allah's Messenger ﷺ said,

"Indeed, my Lord granted me seventy thousand from my *Umma* who shall enter Paradise without reckoning." ʿUmar said, "O Messenger of Allah! Did you not seek an increase to their number?" The Prophet ﷺ replied, "I sought more from Him and He granted me seventy thousand for every single person among them [the latter]." ʿUmar asked again, "O Messenger of Allah! Did you not seek an increase to their number?" The Prophet ﷺ replied, "I sought more from Him and He granted me this much more."

Reported by Aḥmad and al-Bazzār.

٣٩/ ٣. عَنْ أَنَسٍ ﵁، عَنِ النَّبِيِّ ﷺ قَالَ: يَدْخُلُ الْـجَنَّةَ مِنْ أُمَّتِي سَبْعُوْنَ أَلْفًا. قَالُوْا: زِدْنَا، يَا رَسُوْلَ اللهِ. قَالَ: لِكُلِّ رَجُلٍ سَبْعُوْنَ أَلْفًا. قَالُوْا: زِدْنَا، يَا رَسُوْلَ اللهِ. وَكَانَ عَلَى كَثِيْبٍ، فَحَثَا بِيَدِهِ. قَالُوْا: زِدْنَا، يَا رَسُوْلَ اللهِ، فَقَالَ: هَذَا وَحَثَا بِيَدِهِ. قَالُوْا: يَا نَبِيَّ اللهِ، أَبْعَدَ اللهُ مَنْ دَخَلَ النَّارَ بَعْدَ هَذَا.

رَوَاهُ أَبُوْ يَعْلَى وَالْـمَقْدِسِيُّ وَابْنُ كَثِيْرٍ، وَإِسْنَادُهُ حَسَنٌ.

39/3. According to Anas ﵁, the Prophet ﷺ said,

"There shall be seventy thousand of my *Umma* who shall enter Paradise [i.e., without reckoning]." The Companions ﵃ said, "Increase us, O Messenger of Allah!" He said, "For every person among them there will be seventy thousand more." The Companions ﵃ then said (to the Prophet ﷺ), "Increase us, O Messenger of Allah!" Then, as he was standing on a hill, the Prophet ﷺ added his handful. The

[38] Set forth by •Aḥmad b. Ḥanbal in *al-Musnad*, 1:197 §1706; •al-Bazzār in *al-Musnad*, 6:234 §2268; •al-Haythamī in *Majmaʿ al-zawāʾid*, 10:410; •Ibn Kathīr in *Tafsīr al-Qurʾān al-ʿAẓīm*, 1:393.

[39] Set forth by •Abū Yaʿlā in *al-Musnad*, 6:417 §3783; •al-Maqdisī in *al-Aḥādīth al-mukhtāra*, 6:54 §2028; •Ibn Kathīr in *Tafsīr al-Qurʾān al-ʿAẓīm*, 1:395 (who said, "It is an authentic tradition with reliable sources) ʿAbd al-Qādir b. al-Sirrī. When asked about him, Ibn Maʿīn said, 'A pious man.'"); •al-Haythamī in *Majmaʿ al-zawāʾid*, 10:404 (who said: "Its chain is authentic.").

Companions said again, "Increase us, O Messenger of Allah!" The Prophet said, "[Like] this," and then he added his handful. The Companions said, "O Allah's Prophet! May Allah keep away these who enter the Fire ever after this!"

Reported by Abū Yaʿlā, al-Maqdisī and Ibn Kathīr. Its chain is fine.

٤٠/ ٤. عَنْ عَمْرِو بْنِ حَزْمٍ رضي الله عنه عَنِ النَّبِيِّ ﷺ إِنَّهُ تَغَيَّبَ عَنْهُمْ ثَـلَاثًا لَا يَخْرُجُ إِلَّا لِصَلَاةٍ مَكْتُوْبَةٍ. فَقِيْلَ لَهُ فِي ذَالِكَ. قَالَ: إِنَّ رَبِّي وَعَدَنِي أَنْ يَدْخُلَ مِنْ أُمَّتِي الْـجَنَّةَ سَبْعُوْنَ أَلْفًا لَا حِسَابَ عَلَيْهِمْ، وَإِنِّي سَأَلْتُ رَبِّي فِي هَذِهِ الثَّـلَاثَةِ الْأَيَّامِ الْـمَزِيْدَ، فَوَجَدْتُ رَبِّي وَاجِدًا، مَاجِدًا، كَرِيْمًا. فَأَعْطَانِي مَعَ كُلِّ وَاحِدٍ مِنَ السَّبْعِيْنَ أَلْفًا سَبْعِيْنَ أَلْفًا. قَالَ قُلْتُ: يَا رَبِّ، وَتَبْلُغُ أُمَّتِي هَذَا؟ قَالَ: أُكَمِّلُ لَكَ الْعَدَدَ مِنَ الْأَعْرَابِ.

رَوَاهُ الْبَيْهَقِيُّ.

40/4. According to ʿAmr b. Ḥazm, the Prophet stayed inside for three days and would only come out to pray the congregational prayer. When asked about the reason for this, the Prophet replied,

"Indeed, my Lord promised me that He would place seventy thousand of my *Umma* in Paradise without reckoning, so during these three days I asked my Lord for an increase, and I certainly found my Lord as a Bestower, Glorious [*Mājid*] and Generous [*Karīm*]. After that He granted me an additional seventy thousand for every individual among the seventy thousand. I said, 'O my Lord! Will my *Umma* attain such a large number? He [Allah] said, 'I will complete the number for you by the Bedouins.'"

Reported by al-Bayhaqī.

٤١/ ٥. عَنْ أَبِـي أُمَامَةَ رضي الله عنه أَنَّهُ سَمِعَ رَسُوْلَ اللهِ ﷺ يَقُوْلُ: لَيَدْخُلَنَّ الْـجَنَّةَ بِشَفَاعَةِ رَجُلٍ لَيْسَ بِنَبِيٍّ، مِثْلُ الْـحَيَّيْنِ أَوْ مِثْلُ أَحَدِ الْـحَيَّيْنِ: رَبِيْعَةَ وَمُضَرَ. فَقَالَ رَجُلٌ: يَا

---

40 Set forth by •al-Bayhaqī in *Shuʿab al-īmān*, 1:252 §268.

رَسُوْلَ اللهِ، أَوَمَا رَبِيْعَةُ مِنْ مُضَرَ؟ فَقَالَ: إِنَّمَا أَقُوْلُ مَا أُقَوَّلُ.

رَوَاهُ أَحْمَدُ وَالطَّبَرَانِيُّ. وَقَالَ الْـهَيْثَمِيُّ: رِجَالُ أَحْمَدَ وَأَحَدُ أَسَانِيْدِ الطَّبَرَانِيِّ رِجَالُهُمْ رِجَالُ الصَّحِيْحِ غَيْرَ عَبْدِ الرَّحْمٰنِ بْنِ مَيْسَرَةَ وَهُوَ ثِقَةٌ.

41/5. Abū Umāma ﷺ reported that he heard Allah's Messenger ﷺ say,

"A large group, similar in size to the two tribes of Rabīʿa and Muḍar, shall enter Paradise due to the intercession of a man who is not a Prophet." A man asked, "O Messenger of Allah! Is not Rabīʿa from Muḍar?" The Prophet ﷺ replied, "I only utter what I am inspired to say."

Reported by Aḥmad and al-Ṭabarānī. According to al-Haythamī, "Aḥmad's sources and sources in one of al-Ṭabarānī's chains are authentic, except for ʿAbd al-Raḥmān b. Maysara, who is reliable."

٦/٤٢. عَنْ عَبْدِ اللهِ بْنِ قَيْسٍ قَالَ: كُنْتُ عِنْدَ أَبِي بُرْدَةَ ذَاتَ لَيْلَةٍ، فَدَخَلَ عَلَيْنَا الْـحَارِثُ بْنُ أُقَيْشٍ. فَحَدَّثَنَا الْـحَارِثُ لَيْلَتَئِذٍ أَنَّ رَسُوْلَ اللهِ ﷺ قَالَ: إِنَّ مِنْ أُمَّتِي مَنْ يَدْخُلُ الْـجَنَّةَ بِشَفَاعَتِهِ أَكْثَرُ مِنْ مُضَرَ، وَإِنَّ مِنْ أُمَّتِي مَنْ يَعْظُمُ لِلنَّارِ حَتَّى يَكُوْنَ أَحَدَ زَوَايَاهَا.

رَوَاهُ أَحْمَدُ وَابْنُ مَاجه وَابْنُ أَبِي شَيْبَةَ وَأَبُو يَعْلَى وَالْـحَاكِمُ. وَقَالَ: هَذَا حَدِيْثٌ صَحِيْحُ الْإِسْنَادِ عَلَى شَرْطِ مُسْلِمٍ.

42/6. According to ʿAbd Allāh b. Qays,

---

[41] Set forth by •Aḥmad b. Ḥanbal in *al-Musnad*, 5:257 §22215; •al-Ṭabarānī in *al-Muʿjam al-kabīr*, 8:143 §7638, and in •*Musnad al-Shāmiyyīn*, 2:147 §1079; •al-Haythamī in *Majmaʿ al-zawāʾid*, 10:381; •Ibn Kathīr in *Tafsīr al-Qurʾān al-ʿAẓīm*, 4:248.

[42] Set forth by •Aḥmad b. Ḥanbal in *al-Musnad*, 5:312; •Ibn Mājah in *al-Sunan:* Bk.: *al-Zuhd* [The Renunciation], Ch.: "The Description of Hell," 2:1446 §4323; •Ibn Abī Shayba in *al-Muṣannaf*, 6:313 §31702; •Abū Yaʿlā in

"One night I was with Abū Burda when al-Ḥārith b. Uqaysh came in. That night, he narrated to us that Allah's Messenger ﷺ said, 'Indeed, there is a group of people larger than Muḍar tribe who shall enter Paradise due to the intercession of one person from my *Umma*, and indeed, there is a person from my *Umma* whose size shall be increased (due to sins) in the Hellfire until he is one of its corners.'"

> Reported by Aḥmad, Ibn Mājah, Ibn Abī Shayba, Abū Yaʿlā and al-Ḥākim. According to al-Ḥākim said, "Its chain is rigorously authentic conforming to the stipulation of Muslim."

---

al-Musnad, 3:154 §1581; •al-Ḥākim in *al-Mustadrak ʿalā al-Ṣaḥīḥayn*, 1:242 §238; •Ibn Abī ʿĀṣim in *al-Āḥād wa al-mathānī*, 2:294 §1056.

اَلْبَابُ الثَّامِنُ

مُضَاعَفَةُ اللهِ تَعَالَى رَحْمَتَهُ لِعِبَادِهِ فِي جَزَاءِ الْحَسَنَاتِ وَتَجَاوُزِهِ عَنِ الْخَوَاطِرِ وَالسَّيِّئَاتِ

Chapter Eight

On the Increase of Allah's Mercy to His Servants in the Reward They Receive for Good Deeds, and the Pardoning of Passing Thoughts and Sins

٤٣/ ١. عَنِ ابْنِ عَبَّاسٍ رضي الله عنهما عَنِ النَّبِيِّ ﷺ فِيمَا يَرْوِي عَنْ رَبِّهِ تعالى قَالَ: قَالَ: إِنَّ اللهَ كَتَبَ الْحَسَنَاتِ وَالسَّيِّئَاتِ ثُمَّ بَيَّنَ ذَلِكَ. فَمَنْ هَمَّ بِحَسَنَةٍ فَلَمْ يَعْمَلْهَا كَتَبَهَا اللهُ لَهُ عِنْدَهُ حَسَنَةً كَامِلَةً. فَإِنْ هُوَ هَمَّ بِهَا فَعَمِلَهَا كَتَبَهَا اللهُ لَهُ عِنْدَهُ عَشْرَ حَسَنَاتٍ إِلَى سَبْعِ مِائَةِ ضِعْفٍ إِلَى أَضْعَافٍ كَثِيرَةٍ. وَمَنْ هَمَّ بِسَيِّئَةٍ فَلَمْ يَعْمَلْهَا كَتَبَهَا اللهُ لَهُ عِنْدَهُ حَسَنَةً كَامِلَةً. فَإِنْ هُوَ هَمَّ بِهَا فَعَمِلَهَا كَتَبَهَا اللهُ لَهُ سَيِّئَةً وَاحِدَةً.

مُتَّفَقٌ عَلَيْهِ.

43/1. According to Ibn ʿAbbās رضي الله عنهما, the Prophet ﷺ narrated from his Lord. He said, "Allah تعالى decreed the good deeds and the bad deeds and explained them. So whoever intends to do a good deed but does not do it, Allah تعالى shall write for him a single complete good deed. If he intends to do a good deed and then does it, Allah تعالى shall write for him ten good deeds, up to seven hundred good deeds, or even multiplied beyond that. And whoever wants to do a bad deed but does not do it, Allah تعالى shall write for him a single good deed. If he intends to do a bad deed and then does it, Allah تعالى shall write for him only one bad deed."

Agreed upon by al-Bukhārī and Muslim.

٤٤/ ٢. عَنْ أَبِي هُرَيْرَةَ رضي الله عنه أَنَّ رَسُوْلَ اللهِ ﷺ قَالَ: يَقُوْلُ اللهُ: إِذَا أَرَادَ عَبْدِي أَنْ

---

43 Set forth by •al-Bukhārī in *al-Ṣaḥīḥ:* Bk.: *al-Riqāq* [Heart Softeners], Ch.: "Thinking to Do Something Good or Bad," 5:2380 §6126; •Muslim in *al-Ṣaḥīḥ:* Bk.: *al-Īmān* [The Faith], Ch.: "When a Person Plans to Do a Righteous Deed It Is Written Down But When He Plans to Do an Evil Deed It Is Not Written Down," 1:118 §131; •Aḥmad b. Ḥanbal in *al-Musnad*, 1:310 §2828; •Ibn Manda in *al-Īmān*, 1:494 §380; •al-Mundhirī in *al-Targhīb wa al-tarhīb*, 1:27 §21.

يَعْمَلَ سَيِّئَةً فَلَا تَكْتُبُوْهَا عَلَيْهِ حَتَّى يَعْمَلَهَا. فَإِنْ عَمِلَهَا فَاكْتُبُوهَا بِمِثْلِهَا وَإِنْ تَرَكَهَا مِنْ أَجْلِي فَاكْتُبُوْهَا لَهُ حَسَنَةً. وَإِذَا أَرَادَ أَنْ يَعْمَلَ حَسَنَةً فَلَمْ يَعْمَلْهَا فَاكْتُبُوهَا لَهُ حَسَنَةً. فَإِنْ عَمِلَهَا فَاكْتُبُوهَا لَهُ بِعَشْرِ أَمْثَالِهَا إِلَى سَبْعِ مِائَةِ ضِعْفٍ.

رَوَاهُ الْبُخَارِيُّ وَابْنُ حِبَّانَ.

44/2. According to Abū Hurayra ﷺ, Allah's Messenger ﷺ said,

"Allah says [to the angels], 'When My servant wants to commit an evil deed, do not write it until he performs it. If he then does it, then only write a single bad deed, and if he does not commit it for My sake, then write for him a single good deed. And when My servant wants to perform a good deed but does not do it, write down for him a single good deed. And if he performs it, then write down for him ten good deeds, up to seven hundred.'"

Reported by al-Bukhārī and Ibn Ḥibbān.

٤٥/ ٣. عَنْ أَبِي هُرَيْرَةَ ﷺ قَالَ: قَالَ رَسُوْلُ اللهِ ﷺ: قَالَ اللهُ ﷻ: إِذَا هَمَّ عَبْدِي بِسَيِّئَةٍ فَلَا تَكْتُبُوْهَا عَلَيْهِ فَإِنْ عَمِلَهَا فَاكْتُبُوْهَا سَيِّئَةً. وَإِذَا هَمَّ بِحَسَنَةٍ فَلَمْ يَعْمَلْهَا فَاكْتُبُوهَا حَسَنَةً. فَإِنْ عَمِلَهَا فَاكْتُبُوْهَا عَشْرًا.

رَوَاهُ مُسْلِمٌ وَالنَّسَائِيُّ وَعَبْدُ الرَّزَّاقِ.

45/3. According to Abū Hurayra ﷺ, Allah's Messenger ﷺ said,

44 Set forth by •al-Bukhārī in *al-Ṣaḥīḥ:* Bk.: *al-Tawḥīd* [Divine Unity], Ch.: "The Words of Allāh, Most High: ⟨*They want to replace the speech of Allāh*⟩, 6:2724 §7062; •Ibn Ḥibbān in *al-Ṣaḥīḥ*, 2:105 §382; •al-Bayhaqī in *Shuʿab al-īmān*, 1:300 §336; •al-Ṭabarānī in *Musnad al-Shāmiyyīn*, 1:87 §123; •al-Daylamī in *Musnad al-firdaws*, 5:246 §8087; •al-Qazwīnī in *al-Tadwīn*, 1:489; •Abū Nuʿaym in *Tārīkh Aṣbahān*, 2:74 §1130; •Ibn Rajab in *Jāmiʿ al-ʿulūm wa al-ḥikam*, 1:349.

45 Set forth by •Muslim in *al-Ṣaḥīḥ:* Bk.: *al-Īmān* [The Faith], Ch.: "When a Person Plans to Do a Righteous Deed It Is Written Down But When He Plans to Do an Evil Deed It Is Not Written Down," 1:117 §128; •Aḥmad b. Ḥanbal

"Allah says [to the angels], 'When My servant thinks of performing a bad deed, do not write it against him, and if he commits it, write it down as a single bad deed. And if he thinks to perform a good deed but does not do it, write down for him a single good deed. And if he does it, then write down for him ten good deeds.'"

Reported by Muslim, al-Nasāʾī and ʿAbd al-Razzāq.

٤٦/ ٤. عَنْ أَبِي هُرَيْرَةَ ﵁ عَنْ رَسُوْلِ اللهِ ﷺ قَالَ: قَالَ اللهُ تَعَالَى: إِذَا هَمَّ عَبْدِي بِحَسَنَةٍ وَلَمْ يَعْمَلْهَا كَتَبْتُهَا لَهُ حَسَنَةً. فَإِنْ عَمِلَهَا كَتَبْتُهَا عَشْرَ حَسَنَاتٍ إِلَى سَبْعِ مِائَةِ ضِعْفٍ. وَإِذَا هَمَّ بِسَيِّئَةٍ وَلَمْ يَعْمَلْهَا لَمْ أَكْتُبْهَا عَلَيْهِ. فَإِنْ عَمِلَهَا كَتَبْتُهَا سَيِّئَةً وَاحِدَةً.

رَوَاهُ مُسْلِمٌ.

46/4. According to Abū Hurayra ﵁, Allah's Messenger ﷺ said,

"Allah Most High says, 'When My servant thinks of doing a good deed but does not do it, I write for him a single good deed. And if he does it, I write for him ten to seven hundred good deeds. And if he thinks to do a bad deed but does not do it, I do not write it against him. And if he does it, I write for him a single bad deed.'"

Reported by Muslim.

٤٧/ ٥. عَنْ أَبِي هُرَيْرَةَ ﵁ عَنْ مُحَمَّدٍ رَسُوْلِ اللهِ ﷺ قَالَ: قَالَ اللهُ تَعَالَى: إِذَا تَحَدَّثَ عَبْدِي بِأَنْ يَعْمَلَ حَسَنَةً فَأَنَا أَكْتُبُهَا لَهُ حَسَنَةً مَا لَمْ يَعْمَلْ فَإِذَا عَمِلَهَا فَأَنَا أَكْتُبُهَا بِعَشْرِ أَمْثَالِهَا. وَإِذَا تَحَدَّثَ بِأَنْ يَعْمَلَ سَيِّئَةً فَأَنَا أَغْفِرُهَا لَهُ مَا لَمْ يَعْمَلْهَا. فَإِذَا عَمِلَهَا

---

in *al-Musnad*, 2:242 §7294; •al-Nasāʾī in *al-Sunan al-kubrā*, 6:344 §11181; •ʿAbd al-Razzāq in *al-Muṣannaf*, 11:287 §20557; •Ibn Manda in *al-Īmān*, 1:491 §375; •Abū Yaʿlā in *al-Musnad*, 11:171 §6282.

[46] Set forth by •Muslim in *al-Ṣaḥīḥ*: Bk.: *al-Īmān* [The Faith], Ch.: "When a Person Plans to Do a Righteous Deed It Is Written Down But When He Plans to Do an Evil Deed It Is Not Written Down," 1:117 §128; •al-Ḥākim in *al-Mustadrak*, 4:275 §7624 (who said: "This tradition has an authentic chain of transmission"); •Ibn Manda in *al-Īmān*, 1:493 §378; •al-Daylamī in *Musnad al-firdaws*, 3:173 §4463; •Zayn al-Dīn in *al-Ittiḥāfāt al-saniyya*, 1:18 §21.

فَأَنَا أَكْتُبُهَا لَهُ بِمِثْلِهَا وَقَالَ رَسُوْلُ اللهِ ﷺ: قَالَتِ الْـمَلَائِكَةُ: رَبِّ، ذَاكَ عَبْدُكَ يُرِيْدُ أَنْ يَعْمَلَ سَيِّئَةً وَهُوَ أَبْصَرُ بِهِ فَقَالَ: ارْقُبُوْهُ فَإِنْ عَمِلَهَا فَاكْتُبُوْهَا لَهُ بِمِثْلِهَا وَإِنْ تَرَكَهَا فَاكْتُبُوْهَا لَهُ حَسَنَةً إِنَّمَا تَرَكَهَا مِنْ جَرَّايَ. وَقَالَ رَسُوْلُ اللهِ ﷺ: إِذَا أَحْسَنَ أَحَدُكُمْ إِسْلَامَهُ فَكُلُّ حَسَنَةٍ يَعْمَلُهَا تُكْتَبُ بِعَشْرِ أَمْثَالِهَا إِلَى سَبْعِ مِائَةِ ضِعْفٍ وَكُلُّ سَيِّئَةٍ يَعْمَلُهَا تُكْتَبُ بِمِثْلِهَا حَتَّى يَلْقَى اللهَ.

رَوَاهُ مُسْلِمٌ وَأَحْمَدُ وَابْنُ حِبَّانَ.

47/5. According to Abū Hurayra ؓ, Muhammad, Allah's Messenger ﷺ said,

"Allah ﷻ says, 'When My servant speaks to himself about performing a good deed, I write a single good deed for him so long as he performs it, after which I write for him ten times its like in good deeds. And when he speaks to himself about performing a bad deed, I forgive it for him so long as he does not do it. If he performs the bad deed, I write it only as a single bad deed.' The angels say, 'O Lord, this slave of Yours desires to commit a bad deed.' Allah says—and He is most aware of His servant— 'Keep a watch on him; if he does it then only write it down as a single bad deed, and if he abandons it, write it as a good deed for him, for he abstains from it only out of My fear.' So Allah's Messenger ﷺ said, 'When one of you perfects his Islam, each deed he performs is rewarded ten to seven hundred times over, and every sin he commits is only written as one bad deed—and this is until he meets Allah'."

Reported by Muslim, Aḥmad and Ibn Ḥibbān.

---

[47] Set forth by •Muslim in *al-Ṣaḥīḥ:* Bk.: *al-Īmān* [The Faith], Ch.: "When a Person Plans to Do a Righteous Deed It Is Written Down But When He Plans to Do an Evil Deed It Is Not Written Down," 1:117 §129; •Aḥmad b. Ḥanbal in *al-Musnad*, 2:315 §8151; •Hammām b. Munabbih al-Ṣanʿānī in *al-Ṣaḥīfa*, 1:41 §53; •Abū ʿAwāna in *al-Musnad*, 1:81 §240; •Ibn Ḥibbān in *al-Ṣaḥīḥ*, 2:103 §379; •al-Bayhaqī in *Shuʿab al-īmān*, 5:389 §7045; •Abū Nuʿaym in *Musnad al-mustakhraj*, 1:198 §335; •Ibn Ḥazm in *al-Muḥallā*, 1:18.

٤٨/ ٦. عَنْ أَبِي ذَرٍّ ﵁ قَالَ: قَالَ رَسُوْلُ اللهِ ﷺ: يَقُوْلُ اللهُ ﷻ: مَنْ جَاءَ بِالْحَسَنَةِ فَلَهُ عَشْرُ أَمْثَالِهَا وَأَزِيْدُ. وَمَنْ جَاءَ بِالسَّيِّئَةِ فَجَزَاؤُهُ سَيِّئَةٌ مِثْلُهَا أَوْ أَغْفِرُ. وَمَنْ تَقَرَّبَ مِنِّي شِبْرًا تَقَرَّبْتُ مِنْهُ ذِرَاعًا. وَمَنْ تَقَرَّبَ مِنِّي ذِرَاعًا تَقَرَّبْتُ مِنْهُ بَاعًا. وَمَنْ أَتَانِي يَمْشِي أَتَيْتُهُ هَرْوَلَةً. وَمَنْ لَقِيَنِي بِقُرَابِ الْأَرْضِ خَطِيْئَةً لَا يُشْرِكُ بِي شَيْئًا، لَقِيْتُهُ بِمِثْلِهَا مَغْفِرَةً.

رَوَاهُ مُسْلِمٌ وَأَحْمَدُ وَابْنُ مَاجَه وَالْبَزَّارُ.

48/6. According to Abū Dharr ﵁, Allah's Messenger ﷺ said,

"Allah ﷻ says, 'Whoever comes with a good deed will receive ten times its like, and I will increase him with more. And whoever comes with a sin, then his recompense is for that one sin only, or I forgive him. Whoever draws near to Me by a hand span, I draw near to him by an arm's length; whoever draws near to Me by an arm's length, I draw near to him by a bow's length; whoever comes to Me walking, I come to him running; and whoever meets Me with sins that fill the earth, but meets Me without having associated any partners with Me, I will meet him with a similar amount of forgiveness.'"

Reported by Muslim, Aḥmad, Ibn Mājah and al-Bazzār.

---

48 Set forth by •Muslim in *al-Ṣaḥīḥ:* Bk.: *al-Dhikr wa al-duʿā wa al-tawba wa al-istighfār* [Remembrance, Invocation, Repentance, and Seeking Forgiveness], Ch.: "The Virtue of Remembrance, Invocation and Seeking Nearness to Allāh, Most High," 4:2068 §2687; •Aḥmad b. Ḥanbal in *al-Musnad*, 5:153 §21398; •Ibn Mājah in *al-Sunan:* Bk.: *al-Adab* [Good Manners], Ch.: "The Virtue of Deeds," 2:1255 §3821; •al-Bazzār in *al-Musnad*, 9:399 §3991; •Abū Nuʿaym in *Ḥilyat al-awliyā*ʾ, 5:56; •Ibn al-Mubārak in *al-Zuhd*, 1:366 §1035; •al-Nawawī in *Riyāḍ al-ṣāliḥīn*, 1:124 §124.

اَلْبَابُ التَّاسِعُ

نُزُوْلُهُ تعَالَى إِلَى سَمَاءِ الدُّنْيَا وَنِدَاؤُهُ لِلْعِبَادِ

Chapter Nine

On Allah's Descent to the Lower Heavens and His Calling Out to His Servants

٤٩/ ١. عَنْ أَبِي هُرَيْرَةَ ﵁ أَنَّ رَسُوْلَ اللهِ ﷺ قَالَ: يَتَنَزَّلُ رَبُّنَا تَبَارَكَ وَتَعَالَى كُلَّ لَيْلَةٍ إِلَى السَّمَاءِ الدُّنْيَا حِيْنَ يَبْقَى ثُلُثُ اللَّيْلِ الْآخِرُ. يَقُولُ: مَنْ يَدْعُونِي فَأَسْتَجِيبَ لَهُ؟ مَنْ يَسْأَلُنِي فَأُعْطِيَهُ؟ مَنْ يَسْتَغْفِرُنِي فَأَغْفِرَ لَهُ؟

رَوَاهُ الْبُخَارِيُّ.

49/1. According to Abū Hurayra ﵁, Allah's Messenger ﷺ said,

"Our Lord, the Blessed and Exalted, descends each night to the lower heaven, when a third of the night remains and calls out, 'Who calls upon Me that I may respond to him? Who asks of Me that I may give him? Who seeks My forgiveness that I may forgive him?'"

Reported by al-Bukhārī.

٥٠/ ٢. عَنْ أَبِي هُرَيْرَةَ ﵁ أَنَّ رَسُوْلَ اللهِ ﷺ قَالَ: يَنْزِلُ رَبُّنَا ﷻ كُلَّ لَيْلَةٍ إِلَى السَّمَاءِ الدُّنْيَا حِينَ يَبْقَى ثُلُثُ اللَّيْلِ الْآخِرُ. يَقُوْلُ: مَنْ يَدْعُوْنِي فَأَسْتَجِيبَ لَهُ؟ مَنْ يَسْأَلُنِي فَأُعْطِيَهُ؟ مَنْ يَسْتَغْفِرُنِي فَأَغْفِرَ لَهُ؟

رَوَاهُ الْبُخَارِيُّ وَأَبُوْ دَاوُدَ وَالتِّرْمِذِيُّ.

50/2. According to Abū Hurayra ﵁, Allah's Messenger ﷺ said,

---

49 Set forth by •al-Bukhārī in *al-Ṣaḥīḥ:* Bk.: *al-Daʿawāt* [Supplications], Ch.: "Supplicating at Midnight," 5:2330 §5962, and in Bk.: *al-Tawḥīd* [Divine Unity], Ch.: "The Words of Allāh, Most High: ﴾*They want to replace the speech of Allāh*﴿," 6:2723 §7056; and cited by •Ibn Ḥajar in *Fatḥ al-Bārī*, 11:129; •al-ʿAynī in *ʿUmdat al-qārī*, 7:199.

50 Set forth by •al-Bukhārī in *al-Ṣaḥīḥ:* Bk.: *al-Jumuʿa* [Friday], Ch.: "Supplication in Prayer During the Last Part of the Night," 1:384 §1094; •al-Tirmidhī in *al-Sunan:* Bk.: *al-Daʿawāt ʿan Rasūl Allāh* ﷺ [Invocations from Allāh's Messenger ﷺ], 5:526 §3498 (al-Tirmidhī said: "This is a fine

"Our Lord, the Exalted and Sublime, descends each night to the lower heaven, when the last third of the night remains and He says, 'Who calls upon Me that I may respond to him? Who asks of Me that I may give him? Who seeks My forgiveness that I may forgive him?'"

Reported by al-Bukhārī, Abū Dāwūd and al-Tirmidhī.

٥١ / ٣. عَنْ أَبِـي هُرَيْرَةَ ﷺ عَنْ رَسُوْلِ اللهِ ﷺ قَالَ: يَنْزِلُ اللهُ إِلَى السَّمَاءِ الدُّنْيَا كُلَّ لَيْلَةٍ حِينَ يَمْضِي ثُلُثُ اللَّيْلِ الْأَوَّلُ فَيَقُوْلُ: أَنَا الْـمَلِكُ. أَنَا الْـمَلِكُ. مَنْ ذَا الَّذِي يَدْعُوْنِي فَأَسْتَجِيْبَ لَهُ؟ مَنْ ذَا الَّذِي يَسْأَلُنِي فَأُعْطِيَهُ؟ مَنْ ذَا الَّذِي يَسْتَغْفِرُنِي فَأَغْفِرَ لَهُ؟ فَـلَا يَزَالُ كَذَلِكَ حَتَّى يُضِيءَ الْفَجْرُ.

رَوَاهُ مُسْلِمٌ وَأَحْمَدُ وَالتِّرْمِذِيُّ.

51/3. According to Abū Hurayra ﷺ, Allah's Messenger ﷺ said,

"When the first third of each night passes, Allah descends to the lower heaven and says, 'I am the King. I am the King. Who is it that calls upon Me that I may respond to him? Who is it that asks of Me that I may give him? Who is it that seeks My forgiveness that I may forgive him?' He keeps on calling in this way until the dawn breaks."

Reported by Muslim, Aḥmad and al-Tirmidhī.

٥٢ / ٤. عَنْ أَبِـي هُرَيْرَةَ ﷺ قَالَ: قَالَ رَسُولُ اللهِ ﷺ: إِذَا مَضَى شَطْرُ اللَّيْلِ أَوْ ثُلُثَاهُ

authentic tradition"); •Abū Dāwūd in *al-Sunan:* Bk.: *al-Sunna* [The Sunna], Ch.: "Replying to the Jahmites," 4:234 §4733; •al-Dārimī in *al-Sunan*, 1:413 §1479; •al-Rabīʿ in *al-Musnad*, 1:202 §501.

[51] Set forth by •Muslim in *al-Ṣaḥīḥ:* Bk.: *Ṣalāt al-musāfirīn wa qaṣruhā* [The Traveler's Prayer and Shortening It], Ch.: "The Encouragement to Supplicate at the Last Part of the Night and How Supplications Are Answered During This Time," 1:522 §758; •Aḥmad b. Ḥanbal in *al-Musnad*, 2:419 §9426; •al-Tirmidhī in *al-Sunan:* Bk.: *al-Ṣalāh* [The Prayer], Ch.: "The Lord's Descending to the Lowest Heaven Every Night ," 2:307 §446 (al-Tirmidhī said: "The narration of Abū Hurayra ﷺ is *ḥasan-ṣaḥīḥ*"); •al-Maqdisī in *al-Targhīb fī al-duʿāʾ*, 1:69 §30.

يَنْزِلُ اللهُ تَبَارَكَ وَتَعَالَى إِلَى السَّمَاءِ الدُّنْيَا فَيَقُولُ: هَلْ مِنْ سَائِلٍ يُعْطَى؟ هَلْ مِنْ دَاعٍ يُسْتَجَابُ لَهُ؟ هَلْ مِنْ مُسْتَغْفِرٍ يُغْفَرُ لَهُ؟ حَتَّى يَنْفَجِرَ الصُّبْحُ.

رَوَاهُ مُسْلِمٌ وَالنَّسَائِيُّ.

52/4. According to Abū Hurayra ﵁, Allah's Messenger ﷺ said,

"When the half or last third of the night passes—until the time of dawn—Allah ﷻ descends to the lower heaven and says, 'Is there anyone who asks that he may be given? Is their anyone who supplicates that he may be granted? Is there anyone who seeks forgiveness that he may be forgiven?'"

Reported by Muslim and al-Nasāʾī.

٥٣/ ٥. عَنْ أَبِي هُرَيْرَةَ ﵁ يَقُوْلُ: قَالَ رَسُوْلُ اللهِ ﷺ: يَنْزِلُ اللهُ فِي السَّمَاءِ الدُّنْيَا لِشَطْرِ اللَّيْلِ أَوْ لِثُلُثِ اللَّيْلِ الآخِرِ فَيَقُوْلُ: مَنْ يَدْعُوْنِي فَأَسْتَجِيْبَ لَهُ؟ أَوْ يَسْأَلُنِي فَأُعْطِيَهُ؟ ثُمَّ يَقُوْلُ: مَنْ يُقْرِضُ غَيْرَ عَدِيْمٍ وَلَا ظَلُوْمٍ؟

رَوَاهُ مُسْلِمٌ.

53/5. According to Abū Hurayra ﵁, Allah's Messenger ﷺ said,

"Allah descends during the half or last third of the night and says, 'Who calls upon Me that I may respond to him? Who asks of Me that

[52] Set forth by •Muslim in *al-Ṣaḥīḥ:* Bk.: *Ṣalāt al-musāfirīn wa qaṣruhā* [The Traveler's Prayer and Shortening It], Ch.: "The Encouragement to Supplicate and Recite Words of Remembrance," 1:522 §758; •al-Nasāʾī in *al-Sunan al-kubrā*, 6:123 §10312, and in •*ʿAmal al-yawm wa al-layla*, 1:339 §478; •al-Ṭabarānī in *al-Duʿāʾ*, 1:63 §146; •al-Bayhaqī in *Faḍāʾil al-awqāt*, 1:168 §51.

[53] Set forth by •Muslim in *al-Ṣaḥīḥ:* Bk.: *Ṣalāt al-musāfirīn wa qaṣruhā* [The Traveler's Prayer and Shortening It], Ch.: "The Encouragement to Supplicate and Recite Words of Remembrance," 1:522 §758; •al-Bayhaqī in *al-Sunan al-kubrā*, 3:2 §4428; •Abū ʿAwāna in *al-Musnad*, 1:127 §§377,378; •al-Mizzī in *Tahdhīb al-kamāl*, 27:261.

I may give him? Who is it that will loan money to One who is neither indigent nor unjust?'"

Reported by Muslim.

٥٤/ ٦. عَنْ سَعْدِ بْنِ سَعِيدٍ بِهَذَا الْإِسْنَادِ وَزَادَ ثُمَّ يَبْسُطُ يَدَيْهِ تَبَارَكَ وَتَعَالَى يَقُولُ: مَنْ يُقْرِضُ غَيْرَ عَدُومٍ وَلَا ظَلُومٍ؟

رَوَاهُ مُسْلِمٌ.

54/6. According to Saʿd b. Saʿīd:

This tradition is reported through another chain with this addition: Allah ﷻ calls out extending His Hand, "Who will lend to One who is neither indigent or unjust?"

Reported by Muslim.

٥٥/ ٧. عَنْ أَبِي سَعِيدٍ وَأَبِي هُرَيْرَةَ ﵄ قَالَا: قَالَ رَسُوْلُ اللهِ ﷺ: إِنَّ اللهَ يُمْهِلُ حَتَّى إِذَا ذَهَبَ ثُلُثُ اللَّيْلِ الْأَوَّلُ نَزَلَ إِلَى السَّمَاءِ الدُّنْيَا فَيَقُوْلُ: هَلْ مِنْ مُسْتَغْفِرٍ؟ هَلْ مِنْ تَائِبٍ؟ هَلْ مِنْ سَائِلٍ؟ هَلْ مِنْ دَاعٍ؟ حَتَّى يَنْفَجِرَ الْفَجْرُ.

رَوَاهُ مُسْلِمٌ وَأَحْمَدُ وَالنَّسَائِيُّ.

55/7. According to Abū Saʿīd and Abū Hurayra ﵄, Allah's Messenger ﷺ said,

---

54 Set forth by •Muslim in *al-Ṣaḥīḥ:* Bk.: *Ṣalāt al-musāfirīn wa qaṣruhā* [The Traveler's Prayer and Shortening It], Ch.: "The Encouragement to Supplicate and Recite Words of Remembrance," 1:522 §758.

55 Set forth by •Muslim in *al-Ṣaḥīḥ:* Bk.: *Ṣalāt al-musāfirīn wa qaṣruhā* [The Traveler's Prayer and Shortening It], Ch.: "The Encouragement to Supplicate and Recite Words of Remembrance," 1:523 §758; •Aḥmad b. Ḥanbal in *al-Musnad*, 3:34 §11313; •al-Nasāʾī in *al-Sunan al-kubrā*, 6:124 §10315; •ʿAbd b. Ḥumayd in *al-Musnad*, 1:272 §861; •Ibn Abī Shayba in *al-Muṣannaf*, 6:72 §29556; •ʿAbd al-Razzāq in *al-Muṣannaf*, 10:444 §19654; •al-Ṭabarānī in *al-Muʿjam al-kabīr*, 22:370 §927; and cited by •Ibn ʿAbd al-Barr in *al-Istidhkār*, 2:68

"Indeed, Allah Most High lets the night pass until the first third of the night passes, and then descends to the lower heaven and says, 'Is there anyone seeking forgiveness? Is there anyone turning in repentance? Is there anyone asking? Is there anyone supplicating?' And this is until the appearance of dawn."

Reporteded by Muslim, Aḥmad and al- Nasā'ī.

٥٦/٨. عَنْ أَبِي هُرَيْرَةَ رضي الله عنه أَنَّ رَسُوْلَ اللهِ ﷺ قَالَ: يَنْزِلُ اللهُ إِلَى السَّمَاءِ الدُّنْيَا كُلَّ لَيْلَةٍ حِينَ يَمْضِي ثُلُثُ اللَّيْلِ الْأَوَّلُ فَيَقُوْلُ: أَنَا الْمَلِكُ. مَنْ ذَا الَّذِي يَدْعُونِي فَأَسْتَجِيْبَ لَهُ؟ مَنْ ذَا الَّذِي يَسْأَلُنِي فَأُعْطِيَهُ؟ مَنْ ذَا الَّذِي يَسْتَغْفِرُنِي فَأَغْفِرَ لَهُ؟ فَلَا يَزَالُ كَذَلِكَ حَتَّى يُضِيءَ الْفَجْرُ.

رَوَاهُ التِّرْمِذِيُّ وَالنَّسَائِيُّ وَابْنُ حِبَّانَ، وَقَالَ التِّرْمِذِيُّ: حَدِيثُ أَبِي هُرَيْرَةَ رضي الله عنه حَدِيثٌ حَسَنٌ صَحِيْحٌ وَقَدْ رُوِيَ هَذَا الْحَدِيثُ مِنْ أَوْجُهٍ كَثِيرَةٍ عَنْ أَبِي هُرَيْرَةَ عَنِ النَّبِيِّ ﷺ وَرُوِيَ عَنْهُ أَنَّهُ قَالَ: يَنْزِلُ اللهُ حِيْنَ يَبْقَى ثُلُثُ اللَّيْلِ الْآخِرُ وَهُوَ أَصَحُّ الرِّوَايَاتِ.

56/8. According to Abū Hurayra رضي الله عنه, Allah's Messenger ﷺ said,

"When the first third of each night passes, Allah descends to the lower heaven and says, 'I am the King. Who is it that calls upon Me that I may respond to him? Who is it that asks of Me that I may give him? Who is it that seeks My forgiveness that I may forgive him?' And this is until the appearance of dawn."

Reported by al-Tirmidhī, al-Nasā'ī and Ibn Ḥibbān. According to al-Tirmidhī, "Abū Hurayra's tradition is fine authentic and has been narrated by him through several other chains in these words that the Prophet ﷺ said, 'When one third of the night

[56] Set forth by •al-Tirmidhī in *al-Sunan:* Bk.: *al-Ṣalāh* [The Prayer], Ch.: "The Lord's Descending to the Lowest Heaven Every Night," 2:307 §446; •Ibn Ḥibbān in *al-Ṣaḥīḥ*, 3:201 §921; •al-Nasā'ī in *al-Sunan al-kubrā*, 6:125 §10319; •al-Lālikā'ī in *I'tiqād ahl al-Sunna*, 3:440 §752.

remains, Allah ﷻ descends . . .' This is the most authentic of the various narrations."

٥٧/ ٩. عَنْ عَائِشَةَ رضي الله عنها قَالَتْ: فَقَدْتُ رَسُوْلَ اللهِ ﷺ لَيْلَةً فَخَرَجْتُ فَإِذَا هُوَ بِالْبَقِيْعِ. فَقَالَ: أَكُنْتِ تَخَافِيْنَ أَنْ يَحِيْفَ اللهُ عَلَيْكِ وَرَسُوْلُهُ؟ قُلْتُ: يَا رَسُوْلَ اللهِ، إِنِّي ظَنَنْتُ أَنَّكَ أَتَيْتَ بَعْضَ نِسَائِكَ. فَقَالَ: إِنَّ اللهَ سبحانه وتعالى يَنْزِلُ لَيْلَةَ النِّصْفِ مِنْ شَعْبَانَ إِلَى السَّمَاءِ الدُّنْيَا فَيَغْفِرُ لِأَكْثَرَ مِنْ عَدَدِ شَعْرِ غَنَمِ كَلْبٍ.

رَوَاهُ التِّرْمِذِيُّ وَابْنُ مَاجَه وَابْنُ حُمَيْدٍ.

57/9. According to ʿĀʾisha رضي الله عنها,

"One night I did not find Allah's Messenger ﷺ, so I went out (to look for him), and lo and behold, he was in al-Baqīʿ Cemetery. He asked (me), 'Were you afraid that Allah and His Messenger would infringe on your rights?' I said, 'O Messenger of Allah, I thought that you had gone to visit one of your other wives.' He said, 'Allah ﷻ descends on the night of the fifteenth of Shaʿbān to the lower heaven (befitting His Glory) and forgives more people than the hairs on a flock of sheep of Banū Kalb tribe.'"

Reported by al-Tirmidhī, Ibn Mājah and Ibn Ḥumayd.

٥٨/ ١٠. عَنْ عَلِيِّ بْنِ أَبِـي طَالِبٍ رضي الله عنه قَالَ: قَالَ رَسُوْلُ اللهِ ﷺ: إِذَا كَانَتْ لَيْلَةُ النِّصْفِ مِنْ شَعْبَانَ فَقُوْمُوْا لَيْلَهَا وَصُوْمُوْا نَهَارَهَا فَإِنَّ اللهَ يَنْزِلُ فِيْهَا لِغُرُوْبِ الشَّمْسِ إِلَى سَمَاءِ الدُّنْيَا فَيَقُوْلُ: أَلَا مِنْ مُسْتَغْفِرٍ لِي فَأَغْفِرَ لَهُ؟ أَلَا مُسْتَرْزِقٌ فَأَرْزُقَهُ؟ أَلَا مُبْتَلًى

[57] Set forth by •al-Tirmidhī in *al-Sunan:* Bk.: *al-Ṣawm* [Fasts], Ch.: "The Night of Fifteenth of Shaʿbān," 3:116 §739; •Ibn Mājah in *al-Sunan:* Bk.: *Iqāmat al-ṣalāh wa al-sunna fīhā* [Establishing the Prayer and the Sunna Therein], Ch.: "The Night of Fifteenth of Shaʿbān," 1:444 §1389; •ʿAbd b. Ḥumayd in *al-Musnad*, 1:437 §1509; •al-Bayhaqī in *Shuʿab al-īmān*, 3:379 §3825, and in •*Faḍāʾil al-awqāt*, 1:130 §28; •al-Ḥusaynī in *al-Bayān wa al-taʿrīf*, 1:193 §505.

فَأُعَافِيَهُ؟ أَلَا كَذَا أَلَا كَذَا؟ حَتَّى يَطْلُعَ الْفَجْرُ.

رَوَاهُ ابْنُ مَاجَه.

58/10. According to ʿAlī b. Abī Ṭālib ﷺ, Allah's Messenger ﷺ said,

"See to it that you pray during the night of the fifteenth of Shaʿbān and fast during its day, for when the sun sets on that day, Allah descends to the lower heaven and says, 'Is there not someone who seeks forgiveness that I may forgive him? Is there not someone who seeks provision that I may provide for him? Is there not someone who suffers affliction that I may grant him well-being? Is there not so-and-so who seeks such-and-such?' This continues until dawn."

Reported by Ibn Mājah.

٥٩/ ١١. عَنْ عَائِشَةَ ﵂ قَالَتْ: فَقَدْتُ النَّبِيَّ ﷺ ذَاتَ لَيْلَةٍ فَخَرَجْتُ أَطْلُبُهُ فَإِذَا هُوَ بِالْبَقِيْعِ رَافِعٌ رَأْسَهُ إِلَى السَّمَاءِ. فَقَالَ: يَا عَائِشَةُ، أَكُنْتِ تَخَافِيْنَ أَنْ يَحِيفَ اللهُ عَلَيْكِ وَرَسُوْلُهُ؟ قَالَتْ: قَدْ قُلْتُ: وَمَا بِي ذَلِكَ وَلَكِنِّي ظَنَنْتُ أَنَّكَ أَتَيْتَ بَعْضَ نِسَائِكَ. فَقَالَ: إِنَّ اللهَ تَعَالَى يَنْزِلُ لَيْلَةَ النِّصْفِ مِنْ شَعْبَانَ إِلَى السَّمَاءِ الدُّنْيَا فَيَغْفِرُ لِأَكْثَرَ مِنْ عَدَدِ شَعَرِ غَنَمِ كَلْبٍ.

رَوَاهُ أَحْمَدُ وَابْنُ مَاجَه وَابْنُ رَاهَوَيْهِ.

59/11. According to ʿĀʾisha ﵂ said,

---

58 Set forth by •Ibn Mājah in *al-Sunan:* Bk.: *Iqāmat al-ṣalāh wa al-sunna fīhā* [Establishing the Prayer and the Sunna Therein], Ch.: "The Night of the Fifteenth of Shaʿbān," 1:444 §1388; •al-Bayhaqī in *Shuʿab al-īmān*, 3:378 §3822, and in •*Faḍāʾil al-awqāt*, 1:122 §24; •al-Fākihī in *Akhbār Makka*, 3:84 §1837; •al-Daylamī in *Musnad al-firdaws*, 1:259 §1007; •al-Mundhirī in *al-Targhīb wa al-tarhīb*, 2:74 §1550.

59 Set forth by •Aḥmad b. Ḥanbal in *al-Musnad*, 6:238 §26060; •Ibn Mājah in *al-Sunan :* Bk.: *Iqāmat al-ṣalāh wa al-sunna fīhā* [Establishing the Prayer and the Sunna Therein], Ch.: "The Night of the Fifteenth of Shaʿbān," 1:444 §1389; •Ibn Rāhawayh in *al-Musnad*, 2:326 §850; •ʿAbd b. Ḥumayd in *al-*

"One night I did not find Allah's Messenger ﷺ, so I went out to look for him, and lo and behold, he was in al-Baqīʿ Cemetery raising his head upward toward the heavens. He asked me, 'Were you afraid that Allah and His Messenger ﷺ would act wrongly towards you?' I said, 'No, O Messenger of Allah, rather, I thought that you had gone to visit one of your other wives.' He said, 'Allah ﷻ descends on the night of the fifteenth of Shaʿbān to the lower heaven and forgives greater number of people than the hairs on a flock of sheep of Banu Kalb tribe.'"

Reported by Aḥmad, Ibn Mājah and Ibn Rāhawayh.

٦٠/ ١٢. عَنْ أَبِـي مُوْسَى الْأَشْعَرِيِّ رضي الله عنه عَنْ رَسُوْلِ اللهِ ﷺ قَالَ: إِنَّ اللهَ لَيَطَّلِعُ فِي لَيْلَةِ النِّصْفِ مِنْ شَعْبَانَ فَيَغْفِرُ لِـجَمِيْعِ خَلْقِهِ إِلَّا لِـمُشْرِكٍ أَوْ مُشَاحِنٍ.

رَوَاهُ ابْنُ مَاجَه وَابْنُ حِبَّانَ وَالطَّبَرَانِيُّ وَابْنُ أَبِـي عَاصِمٍ.

60/12. According to Abū Mūsā al-Ashʿarī رضي الله عنه, Allah's Messenger ﷺ said,

"Indeed, Allah manifests on the night of the fifteenth of Shaʿbān and forgives His entire creation, save a polytheist or a slanderer."

Reported by Ibn Mājah, Ibn Ḥibbān, al-Ṭabarānī and Ibn Abī ʿĀṣim.

Musnad, 1:437 §1509; •al-Ḥusaynī in *al-Bayān wa al-taʿrīf*, 1:193 §505; •al-Suyūṭī in *al-Durr al-manthūr*, 7:402.

60 Set forth by •Ibn Mājah in *al-Sunan* : Bk.: *Iqāmat al-ṣalāh wa al-sunna fīhā* [Establishing the Prayer and the Sunna Therein], Ch.: "The Night of the Fifteenth of Shaʿbān," 1:445 §1390; •Ibn Ḥibbān in *al-Ṣaḥīḥ*, 12:481 §5665; •al-Ṭabarānī in *al-Muʿjam al-awsaṭ*, 7:36 §6776; •Ibn Abī ʿĀṣim in *al-Sunna*, 1:224 §512; •al-Bayhaqī in *Shuʿab al-īmān*, 5:272 §6628; •Ibn ʿAsākir in *Tārīkh Dimashq*, 38:235.

اَلْبَابُ الْعَاشِرُ

رَحْمَةُ اللهِ تَعَالَى لِلْعُصَاةِ وَالْمُذْنِبِيْنَ

Chapter Ten

On Allah's Mercy for the Dissolute and Sinful

٦١/ ١. عَنْ أَبِي هُرَيْرَةَ ﵁ قَالَ: قَبَّلَ رَسُوْلُ اللهِ ﷺ الْحَسَنَ بْنَ عَلِيٍّ ﵄ وَعِنْدَهُ الأَقْرَعُ بْنُ حَابِسٍ التَّمِيْمِيُّ جَالِسًا. فَقَالَ الأَقْرَعُ: إِنَّ لِي عَشَرَةً مِنَ الْوَلَدِ. مَا قَبَّلْتُ مِنْهُمْ أَحَدًا. فَنَظَرَ إِلَيْهِ رَسُوْلُ اللهِ ﷺ، ثُمَّ قَالَ: مَنْ لَا يَرْحَمُ لَا يُرْحَمُ.

مُتَّفَقٌ عَلَيْهِ.

61/1. According to Abū Hurayra ﵁,

"Once, the Prophet ﷺ kissed al-Ḥasan b. ʿAlī [his grandson] ﵁ and al-Aqraʿ b. Ḥābis al-Tamīmī was sitting in his presence. Al-Aqraʿ said, 'I have ten children and have not kissed a single one of them.' Upon hearing this, Allah's Messenger ﷺ looked at him and said, 'He who does not show mercy shall not receive mercy.'"

Agreed upon by al-Bukhārī and Muslim.

٦٢/ ٢. عَنْ أَبِي هُرَيْرَةَ ﵁ أَنَّ الْأَقْرَعَ بْنَ حَابِسٍ أَبْصَرَ النَّبِيَّ ﷺ وَهُوَ يُقَبِّلُ حُسَيْنًا، فَقَالَ: إِنَّ لِي عَشَرَةً مِنَ الْوَلَدِ. مَا فَعَلْتُ هَذَا بِوَاحِدٍ مِنْهُمْ. فَقَالَ رَسُوْلُ اللهِ ﷺ: مَنْ لَا يَرْحَمُ لَا يُرْحَمُ.

رَوَاهُ الْبُخَارِيُّ وَأَبُوْ دَاوُدَ وَاللَّفْظُ لَهُ.

---

[61] Set forth by •al-Bukhārī in *al-Ṣaḥīḥ:* Bk.: *al-Adab* [Good Manners], Ch.: "Being Merciful Toward One's Children and Kissing and Hugging Them," 5:2235 §5651; •Muslim in *al-Ṣaḥīḥ:* Bk.: *al-Faḍāʾil* [The Virtues], Ch.: "His Mercy ﷺ Toward Children and Family Members, and His Humbleness ﷺ, and the Virtue of All of That," 4:1808 §2315; •Aḥmad b. Ḥanbal in *al-Musnad*, 2:241 §7287; •Ibn Ḥibbān in *al-Ṣaḥīḥ*, 2:202 §457; •al-Bukhārī in *al-Adab al-mufrad*, 1:46 §§91,99; •al-Bayhaqī in *al-Sunan al-kubrā*, 7:100 §13354; •al-Mundhirī in *al-Targhīb wa al-tarhīb*, 3:142 §3419.

62/2. According to Abū Hurayra ◌,

"Once, al-Aqraʿ b. Ḥābis saw the Prophet ◌ kissing al-Ḥusayn ◌ and said, 'I have ten children and have not kissed any of them.' Upon hearing this, Allah's Messenger ◌ said, 'He who does not show tenderness shall not receive tenderness.'"

Reported by al-Bukhārī and Abū Dāwūd (the wording is His).

٣ / ٦٣. عَنْ جَرِيرِ بْنِ عَبْدِ اللهِ ◌ قَالَ: قَالَ رَسُولُ اللهِ ◌: لَا يَرْحَمُ اللهُ مَنْ لَا يَرْحَمُ النَّاسَ.

رَوَاهُ الْبُخَارِيُّ.

63/3. According to Jarīr b. ʿAbd Allāh ◌, Allah's Messenger ◌ said,

"Allah will not be merciful to those who are not merciful to the people."

Reported by al-Bukhārī.

٤ / ٦٤. عَنْ جَرِيرِ بْنِ عَبْدِ اللهِ ◌ قَالَ: قَالَ رَسُولُ اللهِ ◌: مَنْ لَا يَرْحَمِ النَّاسَ لَا يَرْحَمْهُ اللهُ.

رَوَاهُ مُسْلِمٌ.

---

[62] Set forth by •al-Bukhārī in *al-Ṣaḥīḥ*: Bk.: *al-Adab* [Good Manners], Ch.: "Being Merciful Toward One's Children and Kissing and Hugging Them," 5:2235 §5651; •Aḥmad b. Ḥanbal in *al-Musnad*, 2:241 §7287; •Abū Dāwūd in *al-Sunan*: Bk.: *al-Adab* [Good Manners], Ch.: "A Man Kissing His Child," 4:355 §5218; •Ibn Ḥibbān in *al-Ṣaḥīḥ*, 2:202 §457; •al-Bayhaqī in *al-Sunan al-kubrā*, 7:100 §13354; •al-Bukhārī in *al-Adab al-mufrad*, 1:46 §91.

[63] Set forth by •al-Bukhārī in *al-Ṣaḥīḥ*: Bk.: *al-Tawḥīd* [Divine Unity], Ch.: "The Word of Allāh: ⟨Say: "Call Allāh or call the Most Merciful."⟩, 6:2686 §6941, and in •*al-Adab al-mufrad*, 1:48 §96; •Ibn Abī Shayba in *al-Muṣannaf*, 5:214 §25356; •al-Quḍāʿī in *Musnad al-shihāb*, 2:66 §894; •al-Bayhaqī in *al-Sunan al-kubrā*, 9:41 §17682.

64/4. According to Jarīr b. ʿAbd Allāh ﵁, Allah's Messenger ﷺ said,

"Those who do not show mercy to others will not be shown mercy by Allah."

Reported by Muslim.

٦٥/ ٥. عَنْ عَائِشَةَ ﵂ قَالَتْ: قَالَ رَسُوْلُ اللهِ ﷺ: إِنَّ اللهَ يُحِبُّ الرِّفْقَ فِي الْأَمْرِ كُلِّهِ.

مُتَّفَقٌ عَلَيْهِ.

65/5. According to ʿĀʾisha ﵂, Allah's Messenger ﷺ said,

"Allah loves gentleness in all things."

Agreed upon by al-Bukhārī and Muslim.

٦٦/ ٦. عَنْ عَائِشَةَ ﵂ قَالَتْ: قَالَ رَسُوْلُ اللهِ ﷺ: يَا عَائِشَةُ، إِنَّ اللهَ رَفِيْقٌ يُحِبُّ الرِّفْقَ فِي الْأَمْرِ كُلِّهِ.

66/6. According to ʿĀʾisha ﵂, Allah's Messenger ﷺ said,

---

[64] Set forth by •Muslim in *al-Ṣaḥīḥ:* Bk.: *al-Faḍāʾil* [Virtues], Ch.: "Mercy Toward Children and Family Members," 4:1809 §2319; •al-Bukhārī in *al-Adab al-Mufrad*, 1:48 §96; •Ibn Abī Shayba in *al-Muṣannaf*, 5:214 §25356; •al-Quḍāʿī in *Musnad al-shihāb*, 2:66 §894; •al-Bayhaqī in *al-Sunan al-kubrā*, 9:41 §17682.

[65] Set forth by •al-Bukhārī in *al-Ṣaḥīḥ:* Bk.: *al-Adab* [Good Manners], Ch.: "There Should Be Gentleness in Everything," 5:2242 §5678, and in Bk.: *al-Istiʾdhān* [Asking for Permission to Enter], Ch.: "How to Return the Greeting of Non-Muslim Citizens," 5:2308 §5901, and in Bk.: *al-Daʿawāt* [Supplications], Ch.: "Supplicate to Allāh Against the Polytheists," 5:2349 §6032; •Muslim in *al-Ṣaḥīḥ:* Bk.: *al-Salām* [Salutations], Ch.: "The Prohibition of Greeting the People of the Book First and How to Return Their Greetings,"4:1706 §2165; •Aḥmad b. Ḥanbal in *al-Musnad*, 6:37 §24136; •al-Tirmidhī in *al-Sunan:* Bk.: *al-Istiʾdhān ʿan Rasūl Allāh* ﷺ [How Allāh's Messenger ﷺ Taught Us to Ask for Permission Before Entering], Ch.: "How to Greet Non-Muslim Citizens," 5:60 §2701; •al-Nasāʾī in *al-Sunan al-kubrā*, 6:102 §10213; •ʿAbd al-Razzāq in *al-Muṣannaf*, 6:11 §9839; •al-Bukhārī in *al-Adab al-mufrad*, 1:164 §462; •al-Mundhirī in *al-Targhīb wa al-tarhīb*, 3:278 §4047.

[66] Set forth by •al-Bukhārī in *al-Ṣaḥīḥ:* Bk.: *Istitāba al-murtaddīn wa*

"O ʿĀʾisha! Allah is Gentle and He loves gentleness in all things."

٦٧/ ٧. وفي رواية: إِنَّ اللهَ رَفِيْقٌ وَيُحِبُّ الرِّفْقَ وَيُعْطِي عَلَى الرِّفْقِ مَا لَا يُعْطِي عَلَى الْعُنْفِ.

مُتَّفَقٌ عَلَيْهِ.

67/7. Another report reads,

"Indeed, Allah is Gentle and He loves gentleness. He gives for gentleness what He does not give for harshness."

Agreed upon by al-Bukhārī and Muslim.

٦٨/ ٨. عَنْ جَرِيْرٍ ﵁ عَنِ النَّبِيِّ ﷺ قَالَ: مَنْ يُحْرَمِ الرِّفْقَ يُحْرَمِ الْخَيْرَ.

رَوَاهُ مُسْلِمٌ وَأَبُوْ دَاوُدَ وَابْنُ مَاجَه.

68/8. According to Jarīr (b. ʿAbd Allāh) ﵁, the Prophet ﷺ said,

---

al-muʿānidīn wa qitālihim [Asking Apostates and Rebels to Repent and Fighting Them], Ch.: "When a Non-Muslim Citizen or Someone Else Slanders the Prophet ﷺ Indirectly Without Being Explicit Such as Saying: *'al-sām ʿalaykum,'*" 6:2539 §6528; •Muslim in *al-Ṣaḥīḥ:* Bk.: *al-Birr wa al-ṣila wa al-ādāb* [Piety, Keeping Family Ties and Good Manners], Ch.: "The Virtue of Gentleness," 4:2003 §2593; •Aḥmad b. Ḥanbal in *al-Musnad*, 1:112 §902; •Abū Dāwūd in *al-Sunan:* Bk.: *al-Adab* [Good Manners], Ch.: "Gentleness," 4:254 §4807; •Ibn Mājah in *al-Sunan:* Bk.: *al-Adab* [Good Manners], Ch.: "Gentleness," 2:1216 §3688; •Mālik in *al-Muwaṭṭaʾ*, 2:979 §1767.

[67] Set forth by •al-Bukhārī in *al-Ṣaḥīḥ:* Bk.: *Istitāba al-murtaddīn wa al-muʿānidīn wa qitālihim* [Asking Apostates and Rebels to Repent and Fighting Them], Ch.: "When a Non-Muslim Citizen or Someone Else Slanders the Prophet ﷺ Indirectly Without Being Explicit Such as Saying: *'al-sām ʿalaykum,'*" 6:2539 §6528; •Muslim in *al-Ṣaḥīḥ:* Bk.: *al-Birr wa al-ṣila wa al-ādāb* [Piety, Keeping Family Ties and Good Manners], Ch.: "The Virtue of Gentleness," 4:2003 §2593; •Aḥmad b. Ḥanbal in *al-Musnad*, 1:112 §902; •Abū Dāwūd in *al-Sunan:* Bk.: *al-Adab* [Good Manners], Ch.: "Gentleness," 4:254 §4807; •Ibn Mājah in *al-Sunan:* Bk.: *al-Adab* [Good Manners], Ch.: "Gentleness," 2:1216 §3688; •Mālik in *al-Muwaṭṭaʾ*, 2:979 §1767.

[68] Set forth by •Muslim in *al-Ṣaḥīḥ:* Bk.: *al-Birr wa al-ṣila wa al-ādāb* [Piety,

"He who is denied gentleness is denied all good."

Reported by Muslim, Abū Dāwūd and Ibn Mājah.

٦٩/ ٩. عَنْ عَبْدِ اللهِ بْنِ عَمْرٍو ﵄ قَالَ: قَالَ رَسُوْلُ اللهِ ﷺ: اَلرَّاحِمُوْنَ يَرْحَمُهُمُ الرَّحْمَنُ. اِرْحَمُوْا مَنْ فِي الْأَرْضِ يَرْحَمْكُمْ مَنْ فِي السَّمَاءِ. اَلرَّحِمُ شُجْنَةٌ مِنَ الرَّحْمَنِ فَمَنْ وَصَلَهَا وَصَلَهُ اللهُ وَمَنْ قَطَعَهَا قَطَعَهُ اللهُ.

رَوَاهُ أَحْمَدُ وَالتِّرْمِذِيُّ وَابْنُ أَبِي شَيْبَةَ، وَقَالَ التِّرْمِذِيُّ: هَذَا حَدِيثٌ حَسَنٌ صَحِيحٌ.

69/9. According to ʿAbd Allāh b. ʿAmr ﵄, Allah's Messenger ﷺ said,

"Those who show mercy [*al-rāḥimūn*] shall be shown mercy by the All-Merciful [al-Raḥmān]; so show mercy to those on earth and you will be shown mercy by Him Who is in heaven. The word for womb [*raḥim*] derives from al-Raḥmān; so whoever keeps it, Allah will keep him, and whoever severs it, Allah will sever him."

Reported by Aḥmad, al-Tirmidhī and Ibn Abī Shayba. According to al-Tirmidhī, "This is a fine authentic tradition."

٧٠/ ١٠. عَنْ عَبْدِ اللهِ بْنِ عَمْرٍو ﵄ يَبْلُغُ بِهِ النَّبِيَّ ﷺ: اَلرَّاحِمُوْنَ يَرْحَمُهُمُ الرَّحْمَنُ. اِرْحَمُوْا أَهْلَ الْأَرْضِ يَرْحَمْكُمْ مَنْ فِي السَّمَاءِ.

رَوَاهُ أَبُوْ دَاوُدَ وَابْنُ أَبِي شَيْبَةَ، وَقَالَ الْمُنْذِرِيُّ: هَذَا حَدِيْثٌ حَسَنٌ

Keeping Family Ties and Good Manners], Ch.: "The Virtue of Gentleness," 4:2003 §2592; •Abū Dāwūd in *al-Sunan:* Bk.: *al-Adab* [Good Manners], Ch.: "Gentleness," 4:255 §4809; •Aḥmad b. Ḥanbal in *al-Musnad*, 4:362; •Ibn Mājah in *al-Sunan:* Bk.: *al-Adab* [Good Manners], Ch.: "Gentleness," 21:1216 §3687; •Ibn Ḥibbān in *al-Ṣaḥīḥ*, 2:308 §598.

69 Set forth by •Aḥmad b. Ḥanbal in *al-Musnad*, 2:160 §6494; •al-Tirmidhī in *al-Sunan:* Bk.: *al-Birr wa al-ṣila ʿan Rasūl Allāh* ﷺ [Piety and Keeping of Family Ties as Taught by Allāh's Messenger ﷺ], Ch.: "Having Mercy Towards People," 4:323 §1924; •Ibn Abī Shayba in *al-Muṣannaf*, 5:214 §25355; •al-Ḥākim in *al-Mustadrak*, 4:175 §7274.

صَحِيْحٌ. وَقَالَ ابْنُ قُدَامَةَ: هَذَا حَدِيْثٌ حَسَنٌ صَحِيْحٌ.

70/10. According to ʿAbd Allāh b. ʿAmr ﷺ, tracing it back, told that the Prophet ﷺ said,

"Those who show mercy [*al-rāḥimūn*] shall be shown mercy by the All-Merciful [al-Raḥmān]; so show mercy to those on earth and you will be shown mercy by Him Who is in heaven."

Reported by Abū Dāwūd and Ibn Abī Shayba. According to al-Mundhirī and Ibn Qudāma, "This is a fine authentic tradition."

٧١/ ١١. عَنْ حُذَيْفَةَ ﷺ قَالَ: قَالَ رَسُوْلُ اللهِ ﷺ: تَلَقَّتِ الْـمَلَائِكَةُ رُوْحَ رَجُلٍ مِمَّنْ كَانَ قَبْلَكُمْ. فَقَالُوْا: أَعَمِلْتَ مِنَ الْـخَيْرِ شَيْئًا؟ قَالَ: لَا. قَالُوْا: تَذَكَّرْ. قَالَ: كُنْتُ أُدَايِنُ النَّاسَ فَآمُرُ فِتْيَانِي أَنْ يُنْظِرُوْا الْـمُعْسِرَ وَيَتَجَوَّزُوْا عَنِ الْـمُوْسِرِ. قَالَ: قَالَ اللهُ ﷻ: تَجَوَّزُوْا عَنْهُ.

رَوَاهُ مُسْلِمٌ وَأَحْمَدُ وَالنَّسَائِيُّ.

71/11. According to Ḥudhayfa ﷺ, Allah's Messenger ﷺ said,

"There was once a man from the communities before you whose soul the angels seized. They asked, 'Did you ever perform good actions?' He replied, 'No.' The angels said, 'Try to recall.' He then said, 'I used to loan money to people and I would order my servant to

[70] Set forth by •Abū Dāwūd in *al-Sunan:* Bk.: *al-Adab* [Good Manners], Ch.: "Mercy," 4:285 §4941; •Ibn Abī Shayba in *al-Muṣannaf*, 5:214 §25355; •al-Bayhaqī in *al-Sunan al-kubrā*, 9:41 §17683, and in •*Shuʿab al-īmān*, 7:476 §11048; •Ibn Qudāma in *Ithbāt ṣifat al-ʿuluww*, 1:45; •al-Daylamī in *Musnad al-Firdaws*, 2:288 §3328; •al-Mundhirī in *al-Targhīb wa al-tarhīb*, 3:140 §3412.

[71] Set forth by •Muslim in *al-Ṣaḥīḥ:* Bk.: *al-Musāqa* [Watering], Ch.: "The Virtue of Giving Time for Someone Who Is Unable to Pay His Debt," 3:1194 §1560; •Aḥmad b. Ḥanbal in *al-Musnad*, 2:361 §8715; •al-Nasāʾī in *al-Sunan:* Bk.: *al-Buyūʿ* [Trade], Ch.: "Fair Dealings With People and Gentleness in Asking for One's Rights," 7:318 §4694, and in •*al-Sunan al-kubrā*, 4:60 §6293; •al-Dārimī in *al-Sunan*, 2:324 §2546.

give respite to the one of straitened means and to pardon the one who was unable.' Allah then said (to the angels), 'Leave him.'"

Reported by Muslim, Aḥmad and al-Nasāʾī.

٧٢/ ١٢. عَنْ أَبِي هُرَيْرَةَ ﷺ عَنْ رَسُوْلِ اللهِ ﷺ أَنَّهُ قَالَ: نَزَعَ رَجُلٌ لَمْ يَعْمَلْ خَيْرًا قَطُّ غُصْنَ شَوْكٍ عَنِ الطَّرِيْقِ إِمَّا كَانَ فِي شَجَرَةٍ فَقَطَعَهُ وَأَلْقَاهُ وَإِمَّا كَانَ مَوْضُوْعًا فَأَمَاطَهُ فَشَكَرَ اللهُ لَهُ بِهَا فَأَدْخَلَهُ الْجَنَّةَ.

رَوَاهُ أَحْمَدُ وَأَبُوْ دَاوُدَ وَابْنُ حِبَّانَ.

72/12. According to Abū Hurayra ﷺ, Allah's Messenger ﷺ said,

"There was a man who never performed good deeds, except that he removed a thorny branch from a road—one that was cut off a tree and thrown away or was lying there for some other reason—and appreciative of his act, Allah placed him in Paradise."

Reported by Aḥmad, Abū Dāwūd and Ibn Ḥibbān.

٧٣/ ١٣. عَنْ عَبْدِ اللهِ بْنِ يَزِيدَ ﷺ عَنِ النَّبِيِّ ﷺ أَنَّهُ نَهَى عَنِ النُّهْبَةِ وَالْمُثْلَةِ.

رَوَاهُ الْبُخَارِيُّ.

73/13. According to ʿAbd Allāh b. Yazīd ﷺ,

"The Prophet ﷺ forbade plundering and mutilation."

---

[72] Set forth by •Aḥmad b. Ḥanbal in *al-Musnad*, 2:286 §7834; •Abū Dāwūd in *al-Sunan:* Bk.: *al-Adab* [Good Manners], Ch.: "Removing Harmful Things from the Pathway," 4:362 §5245; •Ibn Ḥibbān in *al-Ṣaḥīḥ*, 2:297 §540; •al-Ṭabarānī in *al-Muʿjam al-awsaṭ*, 3:276 §3133; •al-Daylamī in *Musnad al-Firdaws*, 3:99 §4276.

[73] Set forth by •al-Bukhārī in *al-Ṣaḥīḥ:* Bk.: *al-Dhabāʾiḥ wa al-ṣayd* [The Slaughtered Animals and Game], Ch.: "The Offensiveness of Cutting Parts of Living Animals or Seizing Them for Targeting," 5:2100 §5197; •Aḥmad b. Ḥanbal in *al-Musnad*, 4:307 §§18762, 18764; •Ibn Abī Shayba in *al-Muṣannaf*, 4:481 §22321; •Ibn al-Jaʿd in *al-Musnad*, 1:85 §476; •Ibn Abī ʿĀṣim in *al-Āḥād wa al-mathānī*, 4:137 §2117; •al-Ṭabarānī in *al-Muʿjam al-kabīr*, 4:124 §3872.

Reported by al-Bukhārī.

٧٤/ ١٤. عَنْ بُرَيْدَةَ ﷺ قَالَ جَاءَ مَاعِزُ بْنُ مَالِكٍ ﷺ إِلَى النَّبِيِّ ﷺ فَقَالَ: يَا رَسُوْلَ اللهِ، طَهِّرْنِي. فَقَالَ: وَيْحَكَ، ارْجِعْ، فَاسْتَغْفِرِ اللهَ، وَتُبْ إِلَيْهِ. قَالَ: فَرَجَعَ غَيْرَ بَعِيْدٍ، ثُمَّ جَاءَ فَقَالَ: يَا رَسُوْلَ اللهِ، طَهِّرْنِي. فَقَالَ رَسُوْلُ اللهِ ﷺ: وَيْحَكَ، ارْجِعْ، فَاسْتَغْفِرِ اللهَ، وَتُبْ إِلَيْهِ. قَالَ: فَرَجَعَ غَيْرَ بَعِيْدٍ، ثُمَّ جَاءَ فَقَالَ: يَا رَسُوْلَ اللهِ، طَهِّرْنِي. فَقَالَ النَّبِيُّ ﷺ: مِثْلَ ذَلِكَ، حَتَّى إِذَا كَانَتِ الرَّابِعَةُ قَالَ لَهُ رَسُوْلُ اللهِ ﷺ: فِيْمَ أُطَهِّرُكَ؟ فَقَالَ: مِنَ الزِّنَى. فَسَأَلَ رَسُوْلُ اللهِ ﷺ: أَبِهِ جُنُوْنٌ؟ فَأُخْبِرَ أَنَّهُ لَيْسَ بِمَجْنُوْنٍ. فَقَالَ: أَشَرِبَ خَمْرًا؟ فَقَامَ رَجُلٌ: فَاسْتَنْكَهَهُ، فَلَمْ يَجِدْ مِنْهُ رِيْحَ خَمْرٍ. قَالَ: فَقَالَ رَسُوْلُ اللهِ ﷺ: أَزَنَيْتَ؟ فَقَالَ: نَعَمْ. فَأَمَرَ بِهِ، فَرُجِمَ، فَكَانَ النَّاسُ فِيْهِ فِرْقَتَيْنِ. قَائِلٌ يَقُوْلُ: لَقَدْ هَلَكَ. لَقَدْ أَحَاطَتْ بِهِ خَطِيْئَتُهُ. وَقَائِلٌ يَقُوْلُ: مَا تَوْبَةٌ أَفْضَلَ مِنْ تَوْبَةِ مَاعِزٍ أَنَّهُ جَاءَ إِلَى النَّبِيِّ ﷺ فَوَضَعَ يَدَهُ فِي يَدِهِ ثُمَّ قَالَ: اقْتُلْنِي بِالْحِجَارَةِ. قَالَ: فَلَبِثُوْا بِذَلِكَ يَوْمَيْنِ أَوْ ثَلَاثَةً، ثُمَّ جَاءَ رَسُوْلُ اللهِ ﷺ، وَهُمْ جُلُوْسٌ، فَسَلَّمَ ثُمَّ جَلَسَ. فَقَالَ: اسْتَغْفِرُوْا لِمَاعِزِ بْنِ مَالِكٍ. قَالَ: فَقَالُوْا: غَفَرَ اللهُ لِمَاعِزِ بْنِ مَالِكٍ. قَالَ: فَقَالَ رَسُوْلُ اللهِ ﷺ: لَقَدْ تَابَ تَوْبَةً لَوْ قُسِمَتْ بَيْنَ أُمَّةٍ لَوَسِعَتْهُمْ.

رَوَاهُ مُسْلِمٌ وَالنَّسَائِيُّ وَالدَّارَقُطْنِي وَأَبُوْ عَوَانَةَ وَالطَّبَرَانِيُّ.

74/14. Burayda ﷺ said,

"Māʿiz b. Mālik came to the Prophet ﷺ and said, 'O Messenger of Allah, purify me!' The Prophet ﷺ said, 'Woe to you! Go back and seek Allah's forgiveness and repent to Him.' So he went away—but

[74] Set forth by •Muslim in *al-Ṣaḥīḥ:* Bk.: *al-Ḥudūd* [Prescribed Punishments], Ch.: "Concerning the One Who Confesses to Adultery," 3:1321–1322 §1690; •al-Nasāʾī in *al-Sunan al-kubrā*, 4:286 §7163; •al-Dāraquṭnī in *al-Sunan*, 3:91 §49; •Abū ʿAwāna in *al-Musnad*, 4:134–135 §6292; •al-Ṭabarānī in *al-Muʿjam al-awsaṭ*, 5:118 §4843; •al-Bayhaqī in *al-Sunan al-kubrā*, 6:83 §11231.

not far—and then returned, saying, 'O Messenger of Allah, purify me!' The Prophet ﷺ said, 'Woe to you! Go back and seek Allah's forgiveness and repent to Him.' So he went back—but not far—and then returned, saying, 'O Messenger of Allah, purify me!' Allah's Messenger repeated what he said twice before, and when Māʿiz came back for the fourth time the Prophet ﷺ asked him, 'From what shall I purify you?' He replied, 'From adultery.' Allah's Messenger ﷺ asked, 'Is he insane?' The Companions informed him that he was not insane. Then he asked, 'Did he drink alcohol?' A man stood up and smelled him but did not smell the stench of alcohol. So Allah's Messenger ﷺ asked, 'Did you commit adultery?' 'Yes,' the man replied. Allah's Messenger ﷺ then ordered that he be stoned to death, and after he was stoned the people took two views with regard to him. One group opined: 'He destroyed himself and was encompassed by his sins.' The other group said: 'There is no repentance better than that of Māʿiz's. He came to the Prophet ﷺ and placed his hand in his, saying, "Stone me."' The contention between the two groups remained for two or three days. Allah's Messenger ﷺ came out as they were sitting and greeted them and sat down among them. He said, 'Seek forgiveness for Māʿiz b. Mālik.' The Companions ﷺ then said, 'May Allah forgive Māʿiz b. Mālik.' Then Allah's Messenger ﷺ said, 'He repented with such a sincere repentance that, were it to be divided among a people, it would suffice them all.'"

Reported by Muslim, al-Nasāʾī, al-Dāraquṭnī, Abū ʿAwāna and al-Ṭabarānī.

١٥/٧٥. عَنْ عِمْرَانَ بْنِ حُصَيْنٍ رضي الله عنه أَنَّ امْرَأَةً مِنْ جُهَيْنَةَ أَتَتْ نَبِيَّ اللهِ ﷺ وَهِيَ حُبْلَى مِنَ الزِّنَى. فَقَالَتْ: يَا نَبِيَّ اللهِ، أَصَبْتُ حَدًّا فَأَقِمْهُ عَلَيَّ. فَدَعَا نَبِيُّ اللهِ ﷺ وَلِيَّهَا فَقَالَ: أَحْسِنْ إِلَيْهَا. فَإِذَا وَضَعَتْ فَأْتِنِي بِهَا. فَفَعَلَ. فَأَمَرَ بِهَا نَبِيُّ اللهِ ﷺ فَشُكَّتْ عَلَيْهَا ثِيَابُهَا ثُمَّ أَمَرَ بِهَا فَرُجِمَتْ. ثُمَّ صَلَّى عَلَيْهَا. فَقَالَ لَهُ عُمَرُ: تُصَلِّي عَلَيْهَا، يَا نَبِيَّ اللهِ، وَقَدْ زَنَتْ؟ فَقَالَ: لَقَدْ تَابَتْ تَوْبَةً لَوْ قُسِمَتْ بَيْنَ سَبْعِيْنَ مِنْ أَهْلِ الْمَدِيْنَةِ، لَوَسِعَتْهُمْ. وَهَلْ وَجَدْتَ تَوْبَةً أَفْضَلَ مِنْ أَنْ جَادَتْ بِنَفْسِهَا لِلّٰهِ تَعَالَى؟

رَوَاهُ مُسْلِمٌ وَالدَّارِمِيُّ.

75/15. According to ʿImrān b. Ḥuṣayn ﷺ,

"Once, a woman from Juhayna came to the Prophet ﷺ and was pregnant with a child out of fornication. She said, 'O Prophet of Allah! I have committed an offence that calls for the prescribed punishment, so establish it against me! Allah's Prophet ﷺ called for her guardian [*walī*] and said, 'Treat her well and bring her back to me after she has given birth.' The guardian did as he was told. Then Allah's Prophet ﷺ pronounced his judgment over her and her clothes were tied around her and then he commanded and she was stoned to death. He then prayed [the funeral prayer] over her. ʿUmar said to him, 'O Prophet of Allah! Are you praying over her even though she committed adultery?' The Prophet ﷺ replied, 'Certainly, she has repented in such a way that, if her repentance were to be divided among seventy people of Medina, it would be enough for them. Have you found any repentance better than this? She sacrificed her life for Allah Most High.'"

Reported by Muslim and al-Dārimī.

---

[75] Set forth by •Muslim in *al-Ṣaḥīḥ:* Bk.: *al-Ḥudūd* [Prescribed Punishments], Ch.: "Confessing One's Adultery," 3:1324 §1696; •al-Dārimī in *al-Sunan*, 2:235§2325; •al-Ṭabarānī in *al-Muʿjam al-awsaṭ*, 5:117 §4843; •al-Mizzī in *Tahdhīb al-kamāl*, 34:325 §7654; •al-Shawkānī in *Nayl al-awṭār*, 7:280; •Ibn Ḥazm in *al-Muḥallā*, 11:127.

اَلْبَابُ الْحَادِي عَشَرَ

رَحْمَةُ اللهِ تَعَالَى لِلْحَيَوَانِ وَالطُّيُورِ وَغَيْرِهَا مِنَ الْخَلْقِ

CHAPTER ELEVEN

ON ALLAH'S MERCY FOR ANIMALS, BIRDS AND OTHER CREATURES

٧٦/ ١. عَنْ أَبِي هُرَيْرَةَ ؓ قَالَ: قَالَ النَّبِيُّ ﷺ: بَيْنَمَا كَلْبٌ يُطِيفُ بِرَكِيَّةٍ كَادَ يَقْتُلُهُ الْعَطَشُ إِذْ رَأَتْهُ بَغِيٌّ مِنْ بَغَايَا بَنِي إِسْرَائِيْلَ فَنَزَعَتْ مُوْقَهَا فَسَقَتْهُ فَغُفِرَ لَهَا بِهِ.

مُتَّفَقٌ عَلَيْهِ.

76/1. According to Abū Hurayra ؓ, the Prophet ﷺ said,

"Once, there was a panting dog near a well and it was on the verge of death due to severe thirst. A prostitute from the Children of Israel saw it and she took off her shoe, filled it with water and gave the dog drink. As a result she was forgiven."

Agreed upon by al-Bukhārī and Muslim.

٧٧/ ٢. عَنِ ابْنِ عُمَرَ ؓ عَنِ النَّبِيِّ ﷺ قَالَ: دَخَلَتِ امْرَأَةٌ النَّارَ فِي هِرَّةٍ رَبَطَتْهَا. فَلَمْ تُطْعِمْهَا وَلَمْ تَدَعْهَا تَأْكُلُ مِنْ خَشَاشِ الْأَرْضِ.

رَوَاهُ الْبُخَارِيُّ.

77/2. According to ʿAbd Allāh b. ʿUmar ؓ, the Prophet ﷺ said,

"Once, a woman entered the Hellfire due to a cat that she kept tied up. She neither fed it nor set it free so that it could eat of the vermin of the earth."

Reported by al-Bukhārī.

---

[76] Set forth by •al-Bukhārī in *al-Ṣaḥīḥ:* Bk.: *al-Musāqāt* [Watering], Ch.: "The Virtue of Providing Water," 2:834 §2236; •Muslim in *al-Ṣaḥīḥ:* Bk.: *al-Salām* [Salutations], Ch.: "The Unlawfulness of Killing Cats," 4:1760 §2242.

[77] Narrated by al-Bukhārī in *al-Ṣaḥīḥ:* Bk.: *Badʾu al-khalq* [On the Beginning of Creation], Ch.: "There are Five Injurious Animals that may be Killed in the Sacred Precint," 2:1205 §3140; •Ibn Mājah in *al-Sunan:* Bk.: *al-Zuhd* [The Renunciation], Ch.: "On Repentance," 2:1421 §4256; •ʿAbd al-Razzāq in *al-Muṣannaf*, 11:284 §20549.

٧٨/ ٣. عَنْ أَبِـي هُرَيْرَةَ ﵁ عَنْ رَسُوْلِ اللهِ ﷺ قَالَ: دَخَلَتِ امْرَأَةٌ النَّارَ فِي هِرَّةٍ رَبَطَتْهَا فَـلَا هِيَ أَطْعَمَتْهَا وَلَا هِيَ أَرْسَلَتْهَا تَأْكُلُ مِنْ خَشَاشِ الْأَرْضِ حَتَّى مَاتَتْ هَزْلًا.

رَوَاهُ مُسْلِمٌ.

78/3. According to Abū Hurayra ﵁, Allah's Messenger ﷺ said,

"Once, a woman entered the Hellfire due to a cat that she kept tied up. She neither fed it nor set it free so that it could eat of the vermin of the earth, so it died of starvation."

Reported by Muslim.

٧٩/ ٤. عَنْ أَبِـي هُرَيْرَةَ ﵁ أَنَّ رَسُوْلَ اللهِ ﷺ قَالَ: بَيْنَا رَجُلٌ يَمْشِي فَاشْتَدَّ عَلَيْهِ الْعَطَشُ فَنَزَلَ بِئْرًا فَشَرِبَ مِنْهَا ثُمَّ خَرَجَ فَإِذَا هُوَ بِكَلْبٍ يَلْهَثُ يَأْكُلُ الثَّرَى مِنَ الْعَطَشِ فَقَالَ: لَقَدْ بَلَغَ هَذَا مِثْلُ الَّذِي بَلَغَ بِـي فَمَلَأَ خُفَّهُ ثُمَّ أَمْسَكَهُ بِفِيْهِ ثُمَّ رَقِيَ فَسَقَى الْكَلْبَ فَشَكَرَ اللهُ لَهُ فَغَفَرَ لَهُ. قَالُوْا: يَا رَسُولَ اللهِ، وَإِنَّ لَنَا فِي الْبَهَائِمِ أَجْرًا؟ قَالَ: فِي كُلِّ كَبِدٍ رَطْبَةٍ أَجْرٌ.

رَوَاهُ الْبُخَارِيُّ وَمَالِكٌ.

79/4. According to Abū Hurayra ﵁, the Messenger of Allah ﷺ said,

---

[78] Narrated by •Muslim in *al-Ṣaḥīḥ:* Bk.: *al-Birr wa al-ṣila wa al-Adab* [Piety, Familial Integration and Good Manners], Ch.: "The Unlawfulness of Tormenting Cats and other Non-injurious Animals," 4:2110 §2619.

[79] Set forth by •al-Bukhārī in *al-Ṣaḥīḥ:* Bk.: *al-Musāqāt* [The Watering], chapter, "The Virtue of Providing Water," 2:833 §2234, and in Bk.: *al-Maẓālim wa al-ghaṣb* [On Oppression and Wrongful Seizure of Land], chapter, "Allowing Wells on Pathways as long as They Do not Cause Inconveniance," 2:870 §2334; •Abū Dāwūd in *al-Sunan:* Bk.: *al-Jihād* [The Striving], chapter, "The Commands Pertaining to the Riding of Animals and Beasts of Burden," 2:28 §2550; •Mālik in *al-Muwaṭṭā*ʾ, 2:929 §1661

"While a man was walking he felt thirsty and went down a well and drank water from it. On coming out of it, he saw a dog panting and licking mud because of excessive thirst. The man said (within himself), 'This (dog) is suffering from the same agonizing thirst I did.' So he (went down the well), filled his leather socks with water, caught hold of it with his teeth, climbed up and watered the dog. Allah appreciated his (good) deed and forgave him. The people asked, 'O Messenger of Allah! Is there a reward for us in serving (the) animals?' He replied, 'Yes, there is a reward for serving any animate.'"

Reported by al-Bukhārī and Mālik.

٨٠/ ٥. عَنْ أَبِـي هُرَيْرَةَ ﵁ أَنَّ رَسُوْلَ اللهِ ﷺ قَالَ: بَيْنَمَا رَجُلٌ يَمْشِي بِطَرِيْقٍ اشْتَدَّ عَلَيْهِ الْعَطَشُ فَوَجَدَ بِئْرًا فَنَزَلَ فِيهَا فَشَرِبَ ثُمَّ خَرَجَ فَإِذَا كَلْبٌ يَلْهَثُ يَأْكُلُ الثَّرَى مِنَ الْعَطَشِ. فَقَالَ الرَّجُلُ: لَقَدْ بَلَغَ هَذَا الْكَلْبَ مِنَ الْعَطَشِ مِثْلُ الَّذِي كَانَ بَلَغَ مِنِّي. فَنَزَلَ الْبِئْرَ فَمَلَأَ خُفَّهُ مَاءً ثُمَّ أَمْسَكَهُ بِفِيهِ حَتَّى رَقِيَ، فَسَقَى الْكَلْبَ فَشَكَرَ اللهُ لَهُ فَغَفَرَ لَهُ. قَالُوْا: يَا رَسُوْلَ اللهِ، وَإِنَّ لَنَا فِي هَذِهِ الْبَهَائِمِ لَأَجْرًا؟ فَقَالَ: فِي كُلِّ كَبِدٍ رَطْبَةٍ أَجْرٌ.

رَوَاهُ مُسْلِمٌ وَأَحْمَدُ.

80/5. According to Abū Hurayra ﵁, Allah's Messenger ﷺ said,

"Once there was a severely thirsty man walking on a path. (As he was walking) he happened on a well, went down and drank from it. As he came out, he noticed a panting dog licking the wet earth due to severe thirst. The man said (to himself), 'This dog is just as thirsty as I was,' and he went down, filled his leather sock with water and held it

---

[80] Set forth by •Muslim in *al-Ṣaḥīḥ:* Bk.: *al-Salām* [The Salutations], chapter, "On Giving Food and Water to Honoured Animals," 4:1761 §2244; •Aḥmad b. Ḥanbal in *al-Musnad*, 2:375, 517, 521 §§§8861, 10710, 10762; •Abū Dāwūd in *al-Sunan:* Bk.: *al-Jihād* [The Striving], chapter, "The Commands Pertaining to the Riding of Animals and Beasts of Burden," 2:28 §2550; •Ibn Ḥibbān in *al-Ṣaḥīḥ*, 4:185 §7595; •al-Nawawī in *Sharḥ Ṣaḥīḥ Muslim*, 14:242.

in his mouth until he climbed up and made the dog drink it. Allah was gracious for his action and forgave him." The Companions ؓ asked, "O Messenger of Allah! Are we rewarded for our kind treatment we extend to animals?" He replied, "Yes, (goodness done to) everything that has a functioning liver (i.e., is animate,) is rewarded."

Reported by Muslim and Aḥmad.

٨١/ ٦. عَنْ أَبِـي هُرَيْرَةَ ؓ عَنِ النَّبِيِّ ﷺ أَنَّ امْرَأَةً بَغِيًّا رَأَتْ كَلْبًا فِي يَوْمٍ حَارٍّ يُطِيْفُ بِبِئْرٍ قَدْ أَدْلَعَ لِسَانَهُ مِنَ الْعَطَشِ فَنَزَعَتْ لَهُ بِمُوْقِهَا فَغُفِرَ لَهَا.

رَوَاهُ مُسْلِمٌ وَأَحْمَدُ وَأَبُوْ يَعْلَى وَابْنُ حِبَّانَ.

81/6. According to Abū Hurayra ؓ, the Prophet ﷺ said,

"A prostitute saw a dog moving around a well on a hot day and hanging out its tongue because of thirst. She drew water for it in her leather socks (and made it drink). She was pardoned (for this act of hers)."

Reported by Muslim, Aḥmad, Abū Yaʿlā and Ibn Ḥibbān.

٨٢/ ٧. عَنْ أَبِـي أُمَامَةَ ؓ قَالَ: قَالَ رَسُوْلُ اللهِ ﷺ: مَنْ رَحِمَ وَلَوْ ذَبِيْحَةَ عُصْفُوْرٍ رَحِمَهُ اللهُ يَوْمَ الْقِيَامَةِ.

رَوَاهُ الطَّبَرَانِيُّ وَالْبَيْهَقِيُّ وَالْبُخَارِيُّ فِي الْأَدَبِ، وَقَالَ الْـهَيْثَمِيُّ: رَوَاهُ الطَّبَرَانِيُّ وَرِجَالُهُ ثِقَاتٌ.

82/7. According to Abū Umāma ؓ, Allah's Messenger ﷺ said,

---

81 Set forth by •Muslim in *al-Ṣaḥīḥ:* Bk.: *al-Salām* [The Salutations], chapter, "On Giving Food and Water to Honoured Animals," 4:1761 §2245; •Aḥmad b. Ḥanbal in *al-Musnad*, 2:507 §10591; •Abū Yaʿlā in *al-Musnad*, 10:423 §6035; •Ibn Ḥibbān in *al-Ṣaḥīḥ*, 2:110 §386.

82 Set forth by •al-Ṭabarānī in *al-Muʿjam al-kabīr*, 8:234 §7915; •al-Bayhaqī in *Shuʿab al-īmān*, 7:482 §11070; •al-Bukhārī in *al-Adab al-mufrad*, 1:138 §181.

"Whoever shows mercy, even when slaughtering a sparrow, Allah will show mercy to him on the Day of Resurrection."

Reported by al-Ṭabarānī, al-Bayhaqī and al-Bukhārī in *al-Adab al-mufrad*. According to al-Haythamī, "Al-Ṭabarānī reported it with authentic sources."

٨ / ٨٣. عَنِ ابْنِ عُمَرَ ﴿ لَعَنَ النَّبِيُّ ﷺ مَنْ مَثَّلَ بِالْحَيَوَانِ.

رَوَاهُ الْبُخَارِيُّ وَالنَّسَائِيُّ.

83/8. According to Ibn ʿUmar ﴿,

"The Holy Prophet ﷺ cursed the one who mutilates animals."

Reported by al-Bukhārī and al-Nasāʾī.

٩ / ٨٤. عَنِ ابْنِ عُمَرَ ﴿ أَنَّهُ مَرَّ عَلَى قَوْمٍ وَقَدْ نَصَبُوْا دَجَاجَةً حَيَّةً يَرْمُوْنَهَا فَقَالَ: إِنَّ رَسُوْلَ الله ﷺ لَعَنَ مَنْ مَثَّلَ بِالْبَهَائِمِ.

رَوَاهُ أَحْمَدُ.

84/9. According to Ibn ʿUmar ﴿,

"He passed by some people who had fixed a chicken in the ground and were practising archery on it. He said: 'Indeed Allah's Messenger ﷺ has cursed the one who mutilates animals.'"

Reported by Aḥmad.

١٠ / ٨٥. عَنْ سَعِيْدِ بْنِ جُبَيْرٍ ﴿ يَقُوْلُ: خَرَجْتُ مَعَ ابْنِ عُمَرَ ﴿ فِي طَرِيْقٍ مِنْ

---

83 Set forth by •al-Bukhārī in *al-Ṣaḥīḥ*: Bk.: *al-Dhabāʾiḥ wa al-Ṣayd* [Slaughtering and Hunting], chapter, "The prohibition of mutilation of live animals," 5:2100 §5196; •al-Nasāʾī in *al-Sunan*: Bk.: *al-Ḍaḥāyā* [Slaughtering], chapter, "The prohibition setting up animals in a cage as a target," 7:238 §4442; •al-Dārimī in *al-Sunan*, 2:113 §1973; •Ibn Ḥibbān in *al-Ṣaḥīḥ*, 12:434 §5617.

84 Set forth by •Aḥmad b. Ḥanbal in *al-Musnad*, 2:13 §4622.

طُرُقِ الْـمَدِيْنَةِ فَإِذَا غِلْمَةٌ يَرْمُوْنَ دَجَاجَةً. فَقَالَ ابْنُ عُمَرَ: مَنْ فَعَلَ هَذَا؟ فَتَفَرَّقُوْا فَقَالَ: إِنَّ رَسُوْلَ اللهِ ﷺ لَعَنَ مَنْ يُمَثِّلُ بِالْـحَيَوَانِ.

رَوَاهُ الدَّارِمِيُّ، وَقَالَ الْـحَاكِمُ: هَذَا حَدِيْثٌ صَحِيْحٌ عَلَى شَرْطِ الشَّيْخَيْنِ.

85/10. According to Saʿīd b. Jubayr رضي الله عنه,

"I was once treading a road in Medina in the company of Ibn ʿUmar رضي الله عنهما when we saw some boys shooting arrows at a chicken tied as a target. So Ibn ʿUmar رضي الله عنهما said: 'Who has done it?' (Hearing this) the boys dispersed. He said: 'Indeed, Allah's Messenger ﷺ has cursed the one who mutilates animals.'"

> Reported by al-Dārimī. According to al-Ḥākim, this is an authentic tradition in conformity with the stipulations of Shaykhayn.

٨٦/ ١١. عَنْ هِشَامِ بْنِ زَيْدٍ قَالَ: دَخَلْتُ مَعَ أَنَسٍ رضي الله عنه عَلَى الْـحَكَمِ بْنِ أَيُّوْبَ فَرَأَى غِلْـمَانًا أَوْ فِتْيَانًا نَصَبُوْا دَجَاجَةً يَرْمُوْنَهَا. فَقَالَ أَنَسٌ رضي الله عنه: نَهَى النَّبِيُّ ﷺ أَنْ تُصْبَرَ الْبَهَائِمُ.

رَوَاهُ الْبُخَارِيُّ.

86/11. According to Hishām b. Zayd,

"Anas رضي الله عنه and I went to see al-Ḥakam b. Ayyūb and (upon entering) Anas رضي الله عنه saw some boys or lads who had set up a chicken and were

---

85 Set forth by •al-Dārimī in *al-Sunan*, 2:113 §1973; •al-Ḥākim in *al-Mustadrak*, 4:261 §7575; •Abū Nuʿaym in *Ḥilya al-Awliyāʾ*, 4:296.

86 Set forth by •al-Bukhārī in *al-Ṣaḥīḥ:* Bk.: *al-Dhabāʾiḥ wa al-ṣayd* [Sacrificial Animals and Game], Ch.: "The Offensiveness of Cutting Parts of Living Animals or Seizing Them for Targeting," 5:2100 §5194; •Aḥmad b. Ḥanbal in *al-Musnad*, 3:171 §12769; •Abū Dāwūd in *al-Sunan:* Bk.: *al-Ḍaḥāyā* [Sacrificial Animals], Ch.: "The Prohibition of Seizing Animals for Targeting and the Order to Slaughter Gently," 3:100 §2816; •al-Bayhaqī in *al-Sunan al-kubrā*, 9:86 §17908.

shooting arrows at it. Anas ؓ said, 'The Prophet ﷺ forbade tying up animals so that they could be shot and killed.'"

Reported by al-Bukhārī.

٨٧ / ١٢ . عَنِ ابْنِ عُمَرَ ﭬ أَنَّهُ دَخَلَ عَلَى يَحْيَى بْنِ سَعِيدٍ وَغُلَامٌ مِنْ بَنِي يَحْيَى رَابِطٌ دَجَاجَةً يَرْمِيهَا. فَمَشَى إِلَيْهَا ابْنُ عُمَرَ حَتَّى حَلَّهَا ثُمَّ أَقْبَلَ بِهَا وَبِالْغُلَامِ مَعَهُ فَقَالَ: ازْجُرُوا غُلَامَكُمْ عَنْ أَنْ يَصْبِرَ هَذَا الطَّيْرَ لِلْقَتْلِ فَإِنِّي سَمِعْتُ النَّبِيَّ ﷺ نَهَى أَنْ تُصْبَرَ بَهِيمَةٌ أَوْ غَيْرُهَا لِلْقَتْلِ.

رَوَاهُ الْبُخَارِيُّ.

87/12. It is reported that Ibn ʿUmar ؓ went to see Yaḥyā b. Saʿīd and saw one of Yaḥyā's boys targeting stones at a chicken that was tied up. Ibn ʿUmar walked over to the chicken, untied it, and brought both the chicken and the young boy to Yaḥyā b. Saʿīd and said,

"You must forbid your son to tie up this bird and kill it, for I heard the Prophet ﷺ prohibit the tying up of animals and killing them."

Reported by al-Bukhārī.

١٣ / ٨٨ . عَنْ سَعِيدِ بْنِ جُبَيْرٍ ﭬ قَالَ: كُنْتُ عِنْدَ ابْنِ عُمَرَ ﭬ فَمَرُّوا بِفِتْيَةٍ أَوْ بِنَفَرٍ نَصَبُوا دَجَاجَةً يَرْمُونَهَا فَلَمَّا رَأَوْا ابْنَ عُمَرَ ﭬ تَفَرَّقُوا عَنْهَا وَقَالَ ابْنُ عُمَرَ: مَنْ فَعَلَ هَذَا؟ إِنَّ النَّبِيَّ ﷺ لَعَنَ مَنْ فَعَلَ هَذَا.

رَوَاهُ الْبُخَارِيُّ.

88/13. According to Saʿīd b. Jubayr ؓ,

---

[87] Set forth by •al-Bukhārī in al-Ṣaḥīḥ: Bk.: al-Dhabāʾiḥ wa al-ṣayd [Slaughtered Animals and Game], Ch.: "The Offensiveness of Cutting Parts of Living Animals and Seizing Animals for Targeting," 5:2100 §5195; •Aḥmad b. Ḥanbal in al-Musnad, 2:94 §5682; •Abū ʿAwāna in al-Musnad, 5:53 §7765; •al-Bayhaqī in al-Sunan al-kubrā, 9:334 §19268.

[88] Set forth by •al-Bukhārī in al-Ṣaḥīḥ: Bk.: al-Dhabāʾiḥ wa al-ṣayd [The

"I was once in the company of Ibn ʿUmar ؓ when he and his companions passed by some young men or a group who were shooting arrows at a chicken tied as a target. When they saw Ibn ʿUmar ؓ, they dispersed and Ibn ʿUmar called out, 'Who did this? Indeed, the Prophet ﷺ cursed the one who does this!'"

Reported by al-Bukhārī.

٨٩/ ١٤. عَنْ سَعِيْدِ بْنِ جُبَيْرٍ ؓ قَالَ: مَرَّ ابْنُ عُمَرَ ؓ بِفِتْيَانٍ مِنْ قُرَيْشٍ قَدْ نَصَبُوْا طَيْرًا وَهُمْ يَرْمُوْنَهُ وَقَدْ جَعَلُوْا لِصَاحِبِ الطَّيْرِ كُلَّ خَاطِئَةٍ مِنْ نَبْلِهِمْ؟ فَلَمَّا رَأَوْا ابْنَ عُمَرَ ؓ تَفَرَّقُوْا. فَقَالَ ابْنُ عُمَرَ ؓ: مَنْ فَعَلَ هَذَا؟ لَعَنَ اللهُ مَنْ فَعَلَ هَذَا. إِنَّ رَسُوْلَ اللهِ ﷺ لَعَنَ مَنِ اتَّخَذَ شَيْئًا فِيْهِ الرُّوْحُ غَرَضًا.

رَوَاهُ مُسْلِمٌ وَالتِّرْمِذِيُّ وَالنَّسَائِيُّ.

89/14. According to Saʿīd b. Jubayr ؓ,

"Once Ibn ʿUmar ؓ passed by a group of young men from Quraysh who were shooting arrows at a tied bird. Every arrow that they missed came into the possession of the owner of the bird. When they saw Ibn ʿUmar ؓ, they dispersed. He exclaimed, 'Who did this? May Allah curse whoever did this! Indeed, Allah's Messenger ﷺ cursed the one who takes a sentient being as a target.'"

Reported by Muslim, al-Tirmidhī and al-Nasāʾī.

٩٠/ ١٥. عَنْ عَبْدِ اللهِ ؓ قَالَ: كُنَّا مَعَ رَسُوْلِ اللهِ ﷺ فِي سَفَرٍ فَانْطَلَقَ لِحَاجَتِهِ. فَرَأَيْنَا حُمَرَةً مَعَهَا فَرْخَانِ. فَأَخَذْنَا فَرْخَيْهَا فَجَاءَتِ الْحُمَرَةُ فَجَعَلَتْ تَفْرِشُ. فَجَاءَ النَّبِيُّ ﷺ فَقَالَ: مَنْ فَجَعَ هَذِهِ بِوَلَدِهَا؟ رُدُّوْا وَلَدَهَا إِلَيْهَا. وَرَأَى قَرْيَةَ نَمْلٍ قَدْ حَرَّقْنَاهَا.

Slaughtered Animals and Game], Ch.: "The Offensiveness of Cutting Parts of Living Animals or Seizing Animals for Targeting," 5:2100 §5196; •Ibn al-Sarāyā in *Silāḥ al-muʾmin fī al-duʿāʾ*, 1:229 §412; •al-Ḥusaynī in *al-Bayān wa al-taʿrīf*, 2:162 §1367; •al-ʿAsqalānī in *al-Wuqūf ʿalā al-mawqūf*, 1:105 §134.

89

فَقَالَ: مَنْ حَرَّقَ هَذِهِ؟ قُلْنَا: نَحْنُ. قَالَ: إِنَّهُ لَا يَنْبَغِي أَنْ يُعَذِّبَ بِالنَّارِ إِلَّا رَبُّ النَّارِ.

رَوَاهُ أَبُو دَاوُدَ.

90/15. According to ʿAbd Allāh ☙,

"Once we were with Allah's Messenger ☙ on a journey and he went to relieve himself. (When he was away) we saw a sparrow with her two young hatchlings. We took the two hatchlings from it, and (greatly upset) she came and began to spread out her wings. When the Prophet ☙ returned, he asked, 'Who tormented this bird by taking her young ones? Give them back to her.' Also, he saw an anthill that we had set on fire and said, 'Who set this on fire?' When we told him that we did it, he said, 'It is not fitting for anyone to punish with fire save the Lord of the Fire.'"

Reported by Abū Dāwūd.

١٦/٩١. عَنْ عَبْدِ الله ابْنِ مَسْعُودٍ ☙ قَالَ: كُنَّا مَعَ رَسُولِ الله ☙ فِي سَفَرٍ وَمَرَرْنَا بِشَجَرَةٍ فِيهَا فَرْخَا حُمَّرَةٍ، فَأَخَذْنَاهُمَا. قَالَ: فَجَاءَتِ الْحُمَّرَةُ إِلَى النَّبِيِّ ☙ وَهِيَ تَصِيحُ، فَقَالَ: مَنْ فَجَعَ هَذِهِ بِفَرْخَيْهَا؟ قَالَ: فَقُلْنَا: نَحْنُ. قَالَ: رُدُّوهُمَا.

رَوَاهُ الْحَاكِمُ وَالْبَيْهَقِيُّ، وَقَالَ الْحَاكِمُ: هَذَا حَدِيثٌ صَحِيحُ الْإِسْنَادِ.

91/16. According to ʿAbd Allāh b. Masʿūd ☙,

"Once when we were on a journey with Allah's Messenger ☙, we passed by a tree that had two hatchlings of a lark in it and we took them. Afterwards, the sparrow [mother] went to the Prophet ☙,

---

90 Set forth by •Abū Dāwūd in al-Sunan: Bk.: al-Jihād [Striving], Ch.: " The Offensiveness of Burning the Enemy with Fire," 3:55 §2675, and in Bk.: al-Adab [Good Manners], Ch.: "Killing Small Ants," 4:367 §5268; and cited by •al-Dhahabī in al-Kabāʾir, 1:206; •al-Zaylaʿī in Naṣb al-rāya, 3:407; •al-Nawawī in Riyāḍ al-ṣāliḥīn, 367 §367.

91 Set forth by •al-Ḥākim in al-Mustadrak: Bk.: al-Dhabāʾiḥ [Slaughtered Animals], Ch.: "4:267 §7599; •al-Bayhaqī in Dalāʾil al-nubuwwa, 1:321; •al-Hannād in al-Zuhd, 2:620 §1337; •al-Jazarī in al-Nihāya, 4:121.

screaming. The Prophet ﷺ asked, 'Who tormented this bird by taking her young ones?' When we told him that we did it, he said, 'Give them back to her.'"

Reported by al-Ḥākim and al-Bayhaqī. According to al-Ḥākim: "This tradition has an authentic chain of transmission."

٩٢/ ١٧. عَنْ عَبْدِ اللهِ رضي الله عنه أَنَّهُ قَالَ: نَزَلَ النَّبِيُّ ﷺ مَنْزِلًا فَانْطَلَقَ لِحَاجَتِهِ فَجَاءَ وَقَدْ أَوْقَدَ رَجُلٌ عَلَى قَرْيَةِ نَمْلٍ إِمَّا فِي الْأَرْضِ وَإِمَّا فِي شَجَرَةٍ. فَقَالَ رَسُوْلُ اللهِ ﷺ: أَيُّكُمْ فَعَلَ هَذَا؟ فَقَالَ رَجُلٌ مِنَ الْقَوْمِ: أَنَا، يَا رَسُوْلَ اللهِ. قَالَ: اطْفُهَا اطْفُهَا.

رَوَاهُ أَحْمَدُ، وَقَالَ الْهَيْثَمِيُّ: رَوَاهُ أَحْمَدُ وَرِجَالُهُ رِجَالُ الصَّحِيْحِ.

92/17. According to ʿAbd Allāh رضي الله عنه,

"The Prophet ﷺ dismounted during a journey for a break and went to relieve himself. (Upon returning, he found that) a man set an ant colony on fire—one that was either on the ground or on a tree. Allah's Messenger ﷺ said, 'Who among you did this?' A man from them said, 'I did it, O Messenger of Allah.' The Prophet ﷺ said, 'Put the fire out. Put the fire out.'"

Reported by Aḥmad and according to al-Haythamī, Aḥmad's sources are authentic.

[92] Set forth by •Aḥmad b. Ḥanbal in *al-Musnad*, 1:396 §3763; •al-Ṭayālisī in *al-Musnad*, 1:46 §345; •al-Fākihī in *Akhbār Makka*, 5:141; •al-Haythamī in *Majmaʿ al-zawāʾid*, 4:41.

Bibliography

The Holy Qur'ān.

Ibn ʿAbd al-Barr, Abū ʿUmar Yūsuf b. ʿAbd Allāh b. Muhammad (368–463/979–1071), *al-Istidhkār,* Beirut, Lebanon: Dār al-Kutub al-ʿIlmiyya, 2000.

—. *al-Tamhīd,* Morocco: Wazāt ʿUmūm al-Awqāt wa'ṣ-Su'ūn al-Islāmiyya, 1387 AH.

ʿAbd b. Ḥumayd, Abū Muhammad b. Naṣr al-Kasī (d. 249/863), *al-Musnad,* Beirut, Lebanon: Dār al-Kutub al-ʿIlmiyya + Cairo, Egypt: Maktaba al-Sunna, 1408/1988.

ʿAbd al-Razzāq, Abū Bakr b. Hammām b. Nāfiʿ al-Ṣanʿānī (126–211/744–826), *al-Muṣannaf,* Beirut, Lebanon: al-Maktab al-Islāmī, 1403 AH.

Ibn ʿAdī, ʿAbd Allāh b. ʿAdī b. ʿAbd Allāh b. Muhammad Abū Aḥmad al-Jurjānī (277–365/890–976), *al-Kāmil fī Ḍuʿafā' al-Rijāl,* Beirut, Lebanon: Dār al-Fikr.

Aḥmad b. Ḥanbal, Abū ʿAbd Allāh b. Muhammad (164–241/780–855), *al-Musnad,* Beirut, Lebanon: al-Maktab al-Islāmī, 1398/1978.

al-Albānī, Muhammad Nāṣir al-Dīn (1333–1420/1914–1999), *Silsilat al-Aḥādīth al-Ṣaḥīḥa,* Oman: al-Maktab al-Islāmī.

—. *Ẓilal al-Janna fī takhrīj al-Sunna li Ibn Abī Āṣim,* Beirut, Lebanon: al-Maktab al-Islāmī, 1400 AH.

al-Andalusī, Muhammad b. ʿAlī b. Aḥmad al-Wādyāshī (723–804 AH), *Tuḥfat al-Muḥtāj ilā Adillat al-minhāj*, Mecca, Saudi Arabia: Dār Ḥirā', 1406 AH.

Ibn ʿAsākir, Abū al-Qāsim ʿAlī b. al-Ḥasan b. Hibat Allāh b. ʿAbd Allāh b. al-Ḥusayn al-Dimashqī (499–571/1105–1176), *Tārīkh Dimashq al-Kabīr,* generally known as *Tārīkh Ibn ʿAsākīr,* Beirut, Lebanon: Dār al-Iḥyā' al-Turāth al-ʿArabī, 1421/2001.

Al-Aṣbahānī, Ismāʿīl b. Muhammad (457–535 AH), *Dalā'il al-Nubuwwa,* Riyadh, Saudi Arabia: Dār Ṭayba, 1409 AH.

Ibn Abī ʿĀṣim, Abū Bakr b. ʿAmr al-Ḍaḥḥāk b. Makhlad al-Shaybānī (206–287/822–900), *al-Āḥād wa al-Mathānī,* Riyadh, Saudi Arabia: Dār al-Rāya, 1411/1991.

—. *al-Sunna,* Beirut, Lebanon: al-Maktab al-Islāmī 1400 AH.

Abū ʿAwāna, Yaʿqūb b. Isḥāq b. Ibrāhīm b. Zayd al-Naysabūrī (230–316/845–928), *al-Musnad,* Beirut, Lebanon: Dār al-Maʿrifa, 1998.

al-ʿAynī, Badr al-Dīn Abū Muhammad Maḥmūd b. Aḥmad b. Mūsā b. Aḥmad b. Ḥusayn b. Yūsuf b. Maḥmūd (762–855/1361–1451), *ʿUmdat al-Qārī Sharḥ ʿalā Ṣaḥīḥ al-Bukhārī,* Beirut, Lebanon: Dār al-Fikr, 1399/1979.

al-Azdī, Rabīʿ b. Ḥabīb b. ʿAmr al-Baṣrī (95–153/713–770), *al-Jāmiʿ al-Ṣaḥīḥ—Musnad al-Imām al-Rabīʿ b. al-Ḥabīb,* Beirut, Lebanon: Dār al-Ḥikma, 1415 AH.

al-ʿAẓīm Ābādī, Abū al-Ṭayyab Muhammad Shams al-Ḥaqq, *ʿAwn al-Maʿbūd Sharḥ Sunan Abī Dāwūd,* Beirut, Lebanon: Dār al-Kutub al-ʿIlmiyya, 1415 AH.

al-Baghawī, Abū Muhammad al-Ḥusayn b. Masʿūd b. Muhammad (436–516/1044–1122), *Sharḥ al-Sunna,* Beirut, Lebanon: al-Maktab al-Islāmī, 1403/1983.

—. *Sharḥ al-Sunna,* Beirut, Lebanon: al-Maktab al-Islāmī, 1403/1983.

al-Bayhaqī, Abū Bakr Aḥmad b. al-Ḥusayn b. ʿAlī b. ʿAbd Allāh b. Mūsā (384–458/994–1066), *Dalāʾil al-Nubuwwa*, Beirut, Lebanon: Dār al-Kutub al-ʿIlmiyya, 1405/1985.

—. *Faḍāʾil al-awqāt*, Mecca, Saudi Arabia: Maktaba al-Mināra, 1410/1989.

—. *al-Iʿtiqād*, Beirut, Lebanon: Dār al-Āfāq al-Jadīd, 1401 AH.

—. *Shuʿab al-Īmān*, Beirut, Lebanon: Dār al-Kutub al-ʿIlmiyya, 1410/1990.

—. *al-Sunan al-Kubrā*, Mecca, Saudi Arabia: Maktaba Dār al-Bāz, 1410/1990.

—. *al-Sunan al-Ṣughrā*, Medina, Saudi Arabia: Maktaba al-Dār, 1410/1989.

al-Bazzār, Abū Bakr Aḥmad b. ʿAmr b. ʿAbd al-Khāliq al-Baṣrī (210–292/825–905), *al-Musnad*, Beirut, Lebanon: 1409 AH.

al-Bukhārī, Abū ʿAbd Allāh Muhammad b. Ismāʿīl b. Ibrahīm b. Mughīra (194–256/810–870), *al-Adab al-Mufrad*, Beirut, Lebanon: Dār al-Bashāʾir al-Islāmiyya, 1409/1989.

—. *al-Tārīkh al-Kabīr,* Beirut, Lebanon: Dār al-Kutub al-ʿIlmiyya.

—. *al-Ṣaḥīḥ*, Beirut, Lebanon, Damascus, Syria: Dār al-Qalam, 1401/1981.

al-Dāraquṭnī, Abū al-Ḥasan ʿAlī b. ʿUmar b. Aḥmad b. al-Mahdī b. Masʿūd b. al-Nuʿmān (306–385/918–995), *al-Sunan*, Beirut, Lebanon: Dār al-Maʿrifa, 1386/1966.

al-Dārimī, Abū Muhammad ʿAbd Allāh b. ʿAbd al-Raḥmān (181–255/797–869), *al-Sunan*, Beirut, Lebanon: Dār al-Kitāb al-ʿArabī, 1407 AH.

Abū Dāwūd, Sulaymān b. Ashʿath b. Isḥāq b. Bashīr al-Sijistānī (202–275/817–889), *al-Sunan*, Beirut, Lebanon: Dār al-Fikr, 1414/1994.

al-Daylamī, Abū Shujāʿ Shīrawayh b. Shardār b. Shīrawayh al-Daylamī al-Hamdānī (445–509/1053–1115), *Musnad al-Firdaws*, Beirut, Lebanon: Dār al-Kutub al-ʿIlmiyya, 1986.

al-Dhahabī, Shams al-Dīn Muhammad b. Aḥmad al-Dhahabī (673748/1274–1348), *Mīzān al-Iʿtidāl fī Naqd al-Rijāl*, Beirut, Lebanon: Dār al-Kutub al-ʿIlmiyya, 1995.

—. *Siyar Aʿlām al-Nubalāʾ*, Beirut, Lebanon: Muʾassisa al-Risāla, 1413 AH.

—. *Al-Kabāʾir*. Beruit: Dār al-Nadwa al-Jadīda, n.d.

Ibn Abī al-Dunyā, Abū Bakr ʿAbd Allāh b. Muhammad b. al-Qurashī (208–281 AH), *al-Awliyāʾ*, Beirut, Lebanon: Muʾassisa al-Kutub al-Thaqāfiyya, 1413 AH.

—. *al-ʿIyāl*, Saudi Arabia: Dār Ibn al-Qayyim, 1410 AH.

al-Fakihī, Abū ʿAbd Allāh Muhammad b. Isḥāq b. ʿAbbās al-Makkī (217–275 AH), *Akhbār Makka fī Qadīm al-Dahr wa Ḥadīthi-hī*, Beirut, Lebanon: Dār Khiḍar, 1414 AH.

al-Faryābī, Abū Bakr Jaʿfar b. Muhammad b. al-Ḥasan (207–301 AH), *Dalāʾil al-Nubuwwa*, Mecca, Saudi Arabia, Dār Ḥirāʾ, 1406 AH.

Ibn Ḥajar al-ʿAsqalānī, Aḥmad b. ʿAlī b. Muhammad b. Muhammad b. ʿAlī b. Aḥmad al-Kinānī (773–852/1372–1449), *al-Dirāya fī Takhrīj Aḥādīth al-Hidāya*, Beirut, Lebanon, Dār al-Maʿrifa.

—. *Fatḥ al-Bārī Sharḥ Ṣaḥīḥ al-Bukarī*, Lahore, Pakistan: Dār Nashr al-Kutub al-Islāmiyya, 1401/1981.

—. *al-Iṣāba fī Tamyīz al-Ṣaḥāba*, Beirut, Lebanon: Dār al-Jīl, 1412/1992.

—. *Lisān al-Mīzān,* Beirut, Lebanon: Muʾassisa al-Aʿlamī li al-Maṭbūʿāt, 1406/1986.
—. *al-Maṭālib al-ʿĀliya*, Beirut, Lebanon: Dār al-Maʿrifa, 1407/1987.
—. *Taghlīq al-Taʿlīq ʿalā Ṣaḥīḥ al-Bukhārī,* Beirut, Lebanon: al-Maktab al-Islāmī & Oman, Jordan: Dār Ammār, 1405 AH.
—. *Tahdhīb al-Tahdhīb,* Beirut, Lebanon: Dār al-Fikr, 1404/1984.
—. *Talkhīṣ al-Ḥabīr fī Aḥādīth al-Rāfiʿī al-Kabīr,* Medina, Saudi Arabia: 1384/1964.
—. *al-Wuqūf ʿalā al-mawqūf,* Beirut, Lebanon: Muʾassisa al-Risāla, 1406 AH.
al-Ḥākim, Abū ʿAbd Allāh Muhammad b. ʿAbd Allāh b. Muhammad (321–405/933–1014), *al-Mustadrak ʿalā al-Ṣaḥīḥayn*, Mecca, Saudi Arabia: Dār al-Bāz.
al-Ḥakīm al-Tirmidhī, Abū ʿAbd Allāh Muhammad b. ʿAlī bin al-Ḥasan b. Bashir, *Nawādir al-Uṣūl fī Aḥadīth al-Rasūl,* Beirut, Lebanon: Dār al-Jīl, 1992.
al-Ḥamawī, Yāqūt b. ʿAbd Allāh al-Ḥamawī Abū ʿAbd Allāh (d. 626 AH), *Muʿjam al-Buldān,* Beirut, Lebanon: Dār al-Fikr.
Hammām b. Munabbih al-Ṣanʿānī (d. 132 AH), *al-Ṣaḥīfa*, Beirut, Lebanon: al-Maktab al-Islāmī, 1407/1987.
al-Ḥārith, Ibn Abī Usāma (186–282/802–895), *Baghyat al-Bāḥith ʿan Zawāʾid Musnad al-Ḥārith*, Medina, Saudi Arabia: Markz Khidma al-Sunna wa al-Sīra al-Nabawiyya, 1413/1992.
al-Haythamī, Nūr al-Dīn Abū al-Ḥasan ʿAlī b. Abī Bakr b. Sulaymān (735–807/1335–1405), *Majmaʿ al-Zawāʾid*, Cairo, Egypt: Dār al-Riyān li al-Turāth & Beirut Lebanon: Dār al-Kitab al-ʿArabī, 1407/1987.
—. *Mawārid al-Zamʾān ilā Zawāʾid Ibn Ḥibbān,* Beirut, Lebanon: Dār al-Kutub al-ʿIlmiyya.
Ibn Ḥayyān, ʿAbd Allāh b. Muhammad b. Jaʿfar b. Ḥayyan al-Aṣbahānī Abū Muhammad (274–369 AH), *Ṭabaqāt al-Muḥaddithīn bi-Aṣbahān,* Beirut, Lebanon: Muʾassisa al-Risāla, 1412 AH.
Ibn Ḥazm, ʿAlī b. Aḥmad b. Saʿīd b. Ḥazm al-Andalusī (384–456/994–1064), *Ḥujja al-wadāʿ*, Riyadh, Saudi Arabia: Bayt al-Afkār ak-Duwaliyya, 1988.
—. *al-Muḥallā,* Beirut, Lebanon: Dār al-Āfāq al-Jadīd.

Ibn Ḥibbān, Abū Ḥātim Muhammad b. Ḥibbān b. Aḥmad b. Ḥibbān (270–354/884–965), *al-Ṣaḥīḥ*, Beirut, Lebanon: Muʾassisa al-Risāla, 1414/1993.

al-Hindī, ʿAlāʾ al-Dīn ʿAlī al-Muttaqī (d. 975 AH), *Kanz al-ʿUmmāl fī Sunan al-Afāl wa al-Aqwāl*, Beirut, Lebanon: Muʾassisa al-Risāla, 1399/1979.

al-Ḥusaynī, Ibrahīm b. Muhammad (1054–1120 AH), *al-Bayān wa al-Taʿrīf*, Beirut, Lebanon: Dār al-Kitāb al-ʿArabī 1401 AH.

Ibn al-Jaʿd, Abū al-Ḥasan ʿAlī b. Jaʿd b. ʿUbayd Hāshimī (133–230/750–845), *al-Musnad*, Beirut, Lebanon: Muʾassisa Nādir, 1410/1990.

Ibn al-Jārūd, Abū Muhammad ʿAbd Allāh b. ʿAlī (d. 307/919), *al-Muntaqā min al-Sunan al-Musnadā*, Beirut, Lebanon: Muʾassisa al-Kitāb al-Thaqāfiyya, 1418/1988.

Ibn al-Jawzī, Abū al-Faraj ʿAbd al-Raḥmān b. ʿAlī b. Muhammad b. ʿAlī b. ʿUbayd Allāh (510–579/1116–1201), *Ṣifa al-Ṣafwa*, Beirut, Lebanon: Dār al-Kutub al-ʿIlmiyya, 1409/1989.

Ibn Abī Ḥātim, ʿAbd al-Raḥmān b. Muhammad Idrīs. *Tafsīr al-Qurʾān al-ʿAẓīm*. Sayda: al-Maktaba al-ʿAṣriyya, n.d.

al-Jurjānī, Abū al-Qāsim Ḥamza b. Yūsuf (345/428 AH), *Tārīkh Jurjān*, Beirut, Lebanon: ʿĀlim al-Kutub, 1401/1981.

al-Jazarī, Abū al-Saʿādāt al-Mubārak b. Muhammad (544–606), *al-Nihāya fī Gharīb al-Athar*, Beirut, Lebanon: al-Maktaba al-ʿIlmiyya, 1399 AH.

Ibn Kathīr, Abū al-Fidāʾ Ismāʿīl b. ʿUmar (701–774/1301–1373), *al-Bidāya wa al-Nihāya*, Beirut, Lebanon: Dār al-Fikr, 1419/1998.

—. *Tafsīr al-Qurʾān al-ʿAẓīm*, Beirut, Lebanon: Dār al-Maʿrifa, 1400/1980.

al-Khaṭīb al-Baghdādī, Abū Bakr Aḥmad b. ʿAlī b. Thābit b. Aḥmad b. al-Mahdī b. Thābit (392–463/1002–1071), *Mawḍaḥ awhām al-jamʿ wa al-tafrīq*, Beirut, Lebanon: Dār al-Maʿrifa, 1407.

—. *Tārīkh Baghdād*, Beirut, Lebanon: Dār al Kutāb al-ʿIlmiyya.

al-Khilāl, Aḥmad b. Muhammad b. Hārūn b. Yazīd al-Khilāl Abū Bakr (311–334 AH), *al-Sunna*, Riyad, Saudi Arabia, 1410 AH.

Ibn Khuzayma, Abū Bakr Muhammad b. Isḥāq (223–311/838–924), *al-Ṣaḥīḥ*, Beirut, Lebanon: al-Maktab al-Islāmī, 1390/1970.

al-Kinānī, Aḥmad b. Abī Bakr b. Ismāʿīl (762–840 AH), *Miṣbāḥ al-Zujāja fī Zawaʾīd b. Māja,* Beirut, Lebanon: Dār al-ʿArabiyya, 1403 AH.

al-Lālakāʾī, Abū al-Qāsim Hibat Allāh b. al-Ḥasan b. al-Manṣūr (d. 418 AH), *Karāmāt al-Awliyāʾ,* Riyadh, Saudi Arabia, Dār al-Ṭayba, 1412 AH.

—. *Sharḥ Uṣūl Iʿtiqād Ahl al-Sunna wa al-Jamaʿa min al-Kitāb wa al-Sunna aw Ijmāʿ al-Ṣaḥāba,* Riyadh, Saudi Arabia, Dār al-Ṭayba, 1402 AH.

al-Maḥāmilī, Ḥusayn b. Ismāʿīl al-Ḍabbī Abū ʿAbd Allāh (235–330/849–941), *al-Amālī,* Damam & Jordan: Dār Ibn al-Qayyim, 1412 AH.

Ibn Mājah, Abū ʿAbd Allāh Muhammad b. Yazīd al-Qazwīnī (209–273/824–887), *al-Sunan,* Beirut, Lebanon: Dār al-Kutub al-ʿIlmiyya, 1419/1998.

Mālik, Ibn Anas b. Mālik b. Abī ʿĀmir b. ʿAmr b. Ḥārith al-Aṣbaḥī (93–179/712–795), *al-Muwaṭṭāʾ,* Beirut, Lebanon: Dār Iḥyāʾ al-Turāth al-ʿArabī.

Ibn Manda, Abū ʿAbd Allāh Muhammad b. Isḥāq b. Yaḥyā (310–395/922–1005), *al-Īmān,* Beirut, Lebanon: Muʾassisa al-Risāla, 1406 AH.

Ibn Manẓūr, Muhammad b. Mukarram b. ʿAlī b. Aḥmad b. Abī Qāsim b. Ḥabqa al-Ifrīqī (630–711/1232–1311), *Lisān al-ʿArab,* Beirut, Lebanon: Dār Sādir.

al-Maqdisī, Muhammad b. ʿAbd al-Wāḥid al-Ḥanbalī, (567–643 AH), *al-Aḥādīth al-Mukhtāra,* Syria: Dār al-Fikr, 1405 AH.

—. *al-Targhīb fī al-duʿāʾ*, Beirut, Lebanon: Dār Ibn Ḥazm, 1416/1995.

al-Marwazī, Muhammad b. Naṣr b. al-Ḥajjāj Abū ʿAbd Allāh (d. 202–294 AH), *Musnad Abī Bakr* ﷺ, Beirut, Lebanon: al-Maktab al-Islāmī.

—. *Taʿẓīm Qadr al-Ṣalāt,* Medina, Saudi Arabia, Maktaba al-Dār, 1406 AH.

al-Mizzī, Abū al-Ḥajjāj Yūsuf b. Zakī ʿAbd al-Raḥmān b. Yūsuf b. ʿAbd al-Malik b. Yūsuf b. ʿAlī (654–742/1256–1341), *Tahdhīb al-Kamāl,* Beirut, Lebanon: Muʾassisa al-Risāla, 1400/1980.

—. *Tuḥfat al-Ashrāf bi-Maʿrifat al-Aṭrāf,* Mumbai, India: al-Dār al-Qayyyima & Beirut, Lebanon: Maktab al-Islāmī, 1403/1983.

Ibn al-Mubārak, Abū ʿAbd al-Raḥmān ʿAbd Allāh b. Wāḍiḥ al-Marwazī (118–181/736–798), *al-Musnad,* Riyadh, Saudi Arabia: Maktaba al-Maʿārif, 1407 AH.

—. *Kitāb al-Zuhd,* Beirut, Lebanon: Dār al-Kutub al-ʿIlmiyya.

al-Mubārakfūrī, Muhammad ʿAbd al-Raḥmān b. ʿAbd al-Raḥīm (1283–1353 AH), *Tuḥfa al-Aḥwadhī fī Sharḥ Jāmiʿ al-Tirmidhī,* Beirut, Lebanon: Dār al-Kutub al-ʿIlmiyya.

al-Munāwī, ʿAbd al-Rawf b. Tāj al-Ārifīn b. ʿAlī b. Zayn al-ʿAbidīn (952–1031/1545–1621), *Fayḍ al-Qadīr Sharḥ al-Jāmiʿ al-Ṣaghīr,* Egypt: Maktaba al-Tujjāriyya al-Kubrā, 1356 AH.

al-Mundhirī, Abū Muhammad ʿAbd al-Aẓīm b. ʿAbd al-Qawī b. ʿAbd Allāh b. Salama b. Saʿd (581–656/1185–1258), *al-Targhīb wa al-Tarhīb,* Beirut, Lebanon: Dār al-Kutub al-ʿIlmiyya, 1417 AH.

Muslim, Ibn al-Ḥajjāj Abū al-Ḥasan al-Qushayrī al-Naysābūrī (206–261/821–875), *al-Ṣaḥīḥ,* Beirut, Lebanon: Dār al-Iḥyāʾ al-Turāth al-ʿArabī.

al-Nasāʾī, Aḥmad b. Shuʿayb Abū ʿAbd al-Raḥmān (215–303/830–915), *ʿAmal al-Yawm wa al-Layla,* Beirut, Lebanon: Muʾassisa al-Risāla, 1407/1987.

—. *al-Sunan,* Beirut, Lebanon: Dār al-Kutub al-ʿIlmiyya, 1416/1995.

—. *al-Sunan al-Kubrā,* Beirut, Lebanon: Dār al-Kutub al-ʿIlmiyya, 1411/1991.

al-Nasafī, ʿAbd Allāh b. Maḥmūd b. Aḥmad (d. 710 AH), *Madārik al-tanzīl,* Beirut, Labanon: Dār Iḥyāʾ al-Turāth al-ʿArabī.

al-Nawawī, Abū Zakariyyā Yaḥyā b. Sharaf b. Murrī b. al-Ḥasan b. al-Ḥusayn b. Muhammad b. Jumuʿa b. Ḥizām (631–677/1233–1278), *al-Majmūʿ*, Beirut, Lebanon: Dār al-Fikr, 1997 AD.

—. *Riyāḍ al-Ṣāliḥīn min Kalām Sayyid al-Mursalīn* ﷺ, Beirut, Labanon: Dār al-Khayr, 1412/1991.

—. *Sharḥ Ṣaḥīḥ Muslim,* Karachi, Pakistan: Qādīmī Kutub Khāna, 1375/1956.

Abū Nuʿaym, Aḥmad b. ʿAbd Allāh b. Aḥmad b. Isḥaq b. Mūsā b. Mihrān al-Aṣbahānī (336–430/948–1038), *Ḥilya al-Awliyāʾ wa*

Ṭabaqāt al-Aṣfiyā', Beirut, Lebanon: Dār al-Kitāb al-ʿArabī, 1400/1980.

—. *al-Musnad al-Mustakhraj ʿalā Ṣaḥīḥ al-Imām Muslim,* Beirut, Lebanon: Dār al-Kutub al-ʿIlmiyya, 1996.

—. *Tārīkh Aṣbahān,* Beirut, Lebanon: Dār al-Kutub al-ʿIlmiyya, 1410/1990.

al-Qāḍī ʿIyāḍ, Abū al-Faḍl ʿIyāḍ b. Mūsā b. ʿIyāḍ b. ʿAmr b. Mūsā b. ʿIyāḍ b. Muhammad b. Mūsā b. ʿIyāḍ al-Yaḥṣubī (476–544/1083–1149), *al-Shifāʾ bi-Taʿrīf Ḥuqūq al-Muṣṭafā* ﷺ, Beirut, Lebanon: Dār al-Kitab al-ʿArabī.

—. *Mashāriq al-Anwār*, al-Maktaba al-ʿAtīqa.

Ibn Qāniʿ, Abū al-Ḥusayn ʿAbd al-Bāqī b. Qāniʿ (265/351 AH), *Muʿjam al-Ṣaḥāba,* Medina, Saudi Arabia: Maktaba al-Ghurabā' al-Athariyya, 1418 AH.

al-Qazwīnī, ʿAbd al-Karīm b. Muhammad Rāfiʿī, *al-Tadwīn fī Akhbār Qazwīn,* Beirut, Lebanon: Dār al-Kutub al-ʿIlmiyya, 1987.

al-Qudāʿī, Abū ʿAbd Allāh Muhammad b. Salama b. Jaʿfar b. ʿAlī (d. 454/1062), *Musnad al-Shihāb,* Beirut, Lebanon: Mu'assisa al-Risāla, 1407 AH.

Ibn Qudāma, Abū Muhammad ʿAbd Allāh b. Aḥmad al-Maqdasī (d. 620 AH), *Ithbāt ṣifat al-ʿuluww*, Kuwait: al-Dār al-Salafiyya, 1406 AH.

al-Qurṭubī, Abū ʿAbd Allāh Muhammad b. Aḥmad b. Muhammad b. Yaḥyā b. Mufarraj al-Umawī (d. 671 AH), *al-Jāmiʿ li-Ahkām al-Qur'ān,* Beirut, Lebanon: Dār al-Iḥyā' al-Turāth al-ʿArabī.

Ibn Qutayba, ʿAbd Allāh b. Muslim b. Qutayba Abū Muhammad al-Daynūrī (213–276/828–889), *Ta'wīl Mukhtalif al-Ḥadīth,* Beirut, Lebanon, Dār al-Jīl, 1393/1972.

Ibn Rāhawayh, Abū Yaʿqūb Isḥāq b. Ibrahīm b. Makhlad b. Ibrahīm b. ʿAbd Allāh (161–237/778–851), *al-Musnad,* Medina, Saudi Arabia: Maktaba al-Īmān, 1412/1991.

Ibn Saʿd, Abū ʿAbd Allāh Muhammad (168–230/784–845), *al-Ṭabaqāt al-Kubrā,* Beirut, Lebanon: Dār Beirut li al-Ṭabat wa al-Nashr, 1398/1978.

al-Ṣanᶜānī, Muhammad b. Ismāᶜīl al-Amīr (773–852 AH), *Subul al-Salām Sharḥ Bulūgh al-Marām*, Beirut, Lebanon: Dār al-Iḥyāʾ al-Turāth al-ᶜArabī, 1379 AH.

al-Sarakhsī, Shams al-Dīn, *al-Mabsūṭ*, Beirut, Lebanon: Dār al-Maᶜrifa, 1978 AD.

Ibn al-Sarāyā, Muhammad b. Muhammad b. ᶜAlī (677–745 AH), *Silāḥ al-muʾmin fī al-duᶜāʾ*, Damascu, Syria: Dār Ibn Kathīr, 1414/1993.

Abū Saᶜūd, Muhammad b. Muhammad al-ᶜImādī (898–982/1493–1575), *Irshād al-ᶜaql al-salīm ilā mazāyā al-Qurʾān al-karīm*, Beirut, Lebanon: Dār al-Iḥyāʾ al-Turāth al-ᶜArabī.

al-Shāfiᶜī, Abū ᶜAbd Allāh Muhammad b. Idrīs b. ᶜAbbās b. ᶜUthmān b. al-Shāfiᶜ al-Qurashī (150–204/767–819), *al-Musnad*, Beirut, Lebanon: Dār al-Kutub al-ᶜIlmiyya.

al-Shāṭibī, Abū Isḥāq Ibrāhīm b. Mūsā (d. 790 AH), *al-Muwāfaqāt*, Beirut, Lebanon: Dār al-Maᶜrifa.

al-Shawkānī, Muhammad b. ᶜAlī b. Muhammad (1173–1250/1760–1834), *Fatḥ al-Qadīr*, Beirut, Lebanon, Dār al-Fikr, 1402/1982.

—. *Nayl al-Awtār Sharḥ Muntaqā al-Akhbār*, Beirut, Lebanon: Dār al-Fikr, 1402/1982.

Ibn Abī Shayba, Abū Bakr ᶜAbd Allāh b. Muhammad b. Ibrahīm b. ᶜUthmān al-Kūfī (159–235/776–850), *al-Muṣannaf*, Riyadh, Saudi Arabia: Maktaba al-Rushd, 1409 AH.

Ibn al-Sunnī, Aḥmad b. Muhammad al-Daynūrī (284–364 AH), *ᶜAmal al-Yawm wa al-Layla*, Beirut, Lebanon: Dār Ibn Ḥazm, 1425/2004.

al-Suyūṭī, Jalāl al-Dīn Abū al-Faḍl ᶜAbd al-Raḥmān b. Abī Bakr b. Muhammad b. Abī Bakr b. ᶜUthmān (849–911/1445–1505), *al-Ashbāh wa al-naẓāʾir*, Beirut, Lebanon: Dār al-Kutub al-ᶜIlmiyya, 1403 AH.

—. *al-Dībāj ᶜalā Ṣaḥīḥ Muslim*, al-Khūbar, Saudi Arabia: Dār Ibn ᶜAffān, 1416/1996.

—. *al-Durr al-Manthūr fi al-Tafsīr bi al-Maʾthūr*, Beirut, Lebanon: Dār al-Maᶜrifa.

—. *al-Jāmiᶜ al-Ṣaghīr fī Aḥadīth al-Bashīr al-Nadhīr*, Beirut, Lebanon: Dār al-Kutub al-ᶜIlmiyya.

—. *Sharḥ ᶜalā Sunan al-Nasāʾī*, Ḥalb, Syria: Maktab al-Maṭbūᶜāt al-Islamiyya, 1406/1986.

al-Ṭabarānī, Abū al-Qāsim Sulaymān b. Aḥmad b. Ayyūb b. Maṭīr al-Lakhmī (260–360/873–971), *Kitāb al-Duʿā'*, Beirut, Lebanon: Dār al-Kutub al-ʿIlmiyya, 1421/2001.

—. *al-Muʿjam al-Awsaṭ*, Riyadh, Saudi Arabia: Maktaba al-Maʿārif, 1405/1985.

—. *al-Muʿjam al-Kabīr*, Mosul, Iraq: Matbaʿa al-Zahrā' al-Ḥadītha.

—. *al-Muʿjam al-Kabīr*, Cairo, Egypt: Maktaba Ibn Taymiyya.

—. *al-Muʿjam al-Ṣaghīr*, Beirut, Lebanon: Dār al-Kutub al-ʿIlmiyya, 1403/1983.

—. *Musnad al-Shāmiyyīn*, Beirut, Lebanon: Mu'assisa al-Risāla, 1405/1985.

al-Ṭabarī, Abū Jaʿfar Aḥmad Muhammad b. Jarīr b. Yazīd (224–310/839–923), *Jāmiʿ al-Bayān fī tafsīr al-Qur'ān*, Beirut, Lebanon: Dār al-Fikr, 1405 AH.

—. *Tārīkh al-Umam wa al-Mulūk*, Beirut, Lebanon: Dār al-Kutub al-ʿIlmiyya, 1407 AH.

al-Ṭaḥāwī, Abū Jaʿfar Aḥmad b. Muhammad b. Salama b. Salma b. ʿAbd al-Malik b. Salma (229–321/853–933), *Sharḥ Maʿānī al-Āthār*, Beirut, Lebanon: Dār al-Kutub al-ʿIlmiyya, 1399 AH.

al-Ṭayālisī, Abū Dāwūd Sulaymān b. Dāwūd al-Jārūd (133–204/751–819), *al-Musnad*, Beirut, Lebanon: Dār al-Maʿrifa.

Ibn Taymiyya, Aḥmad b. ʿAbd al-Ḥalīm b. ʿAbd al-Salām al-Ḥarānī (661–728/1263–1328), *Majmūʿ Fatāwā*, Maktaba Ibn Taimiyya.

al-Tirmidhī, Abū ʿĪsā Muhammad b. ʿĪsā b. Sūra b. Mūsā (210–279/825–892), *al-Sunan*, Beirut, Lebanon: Dār al-Gharb al-Islāmī, 1998.

Abū Yaʿlā, Aḥmad b. ʿAlī b. Mathnā b. Yaḥyā b. ʿĪsā b. al-Hilāl al-Mūṣilī al-Tamīmī (210–307/825–919), *al-Muʿjam*, Faislabad, Pakistan: Idārat al-ʿUlūm al-Athriyya, 1407 AH.

—. *al-Musnad*, Damascus, Syria: Dār al-Ma'mūn li al-Turāth, 1404/1984.

Yaḥyā b. Muʿīn, Abū Zakariyyā (158–233 AH), *al-Tārīkh*, Damascus, Syria: Dār al-Ma'mūn li al-Turāth, 1400 AH.

Al-Zamakhsharī, Jār Allāh Abū al-Qāsim Maḥmūd b. ʿUmar (427–538 AH), *Al-Kashshāf ʿan ḥaqā'iq ghawāmiḍ al-Tanzīl*. Cairo, Egypt, 1373/1953.

al-Zaylaʿī, Abū Muhammad ʿAbd Allāh b. Yūsuf al-Ḥanafī (d. 762/1360), *Naṣb al-Rāya li-Aḥadīth al-Hidāya,* Egypt: Dār al-Ḥadīth, 1357/1938.

—. *Takhrīj al-Aḥādith wa al-Āthār*, Riyadh, Saudi Arabia: Dār Ibn Khuzayma, 1414 AH.

Zayn al-Dīn, ʿAbd al-Raʾūf b. Tāj al-ʿĀrifīn b. ʿAlī (d. 1031 AH), *al-Ittiḥāfāt al-Saniyya,* Beirut, Lebanon: Muʾassisa al-Risāla.

al-Zurqānī, Abū ʿAbd Allāh Muhammad b. ʿAbd al-Bāqī b. Yūsuf b. Aḥmad b. ʿAlwān Egyptian Azharī Mālikī (1055–1122/1645–1710), *Sharḥ al-Mawāhib al-Laduniyya,* Beirut, Lebanon: Dār al-Kutub al-ʿIlmiyya, 1417/1996.

Index

Also available by Shayh-ul-Islam Dr Muhammad Tahir-ul-Qadri

Title: The Glorious Qur'ān
Format: Hardback, 1100 pages 4 colour [Gold embossed Cover]
Date of publication: September 2011
ISBN–13: 978–1–908229–00–7
Price: £24.99 or $39.95 [+ P&P]

Title: Prophetic Virtues & Miracles
Format: Hardback, 384 pages
Date of publication: January 2012
ISBN–13: 978–1–908229–01–4
Price: £29.99 or $45.95 [+ P&P]

Title: Righteous Character & Social Interactions
Format: Hardback, 640 pages
Date of publication: January 2012
ISBN–13: 978–1–908229–02–1
Price: £34.99 or $49.95 [+ P&P]

Title: Fatwa on Terrorism & Suicide Bombings
Format: Hardback, 512 pages
Date of publication: January 2011
ISBN–13: 978–0–95518–889–3
Price: £24.99 or $39.95 [+ P&P]

Title: Muhammad ﷺ: The Merciful
Format: Hardback & Paperback, 432 pages
Date of publication: December 2013
ISBN–13: 978–1–908229–18–2 (hbk)
ISBN–10: 978–1–908229–23–6 (pbk)
Price (hbk): £29.99 or $45.95 [+ P&P]
Price (pbk): £17.99 or $29.95 [+ P&P]

Title: Mawlid al-Nabi ﷺ: Celebration and Permissibility
Format: Hardback & Paperback, 750 pages
Date of publication: January 2014
ISBN–13: 978–1–908229–14–4 (hbk)
ISBN–10: 978–1–908229–24–3 (pbk)
Price (hbk): £34.99 or $49.95 [+ P&P]
Price (pbk): £19.99 or $34.95 [+ P&P]

Order Online

www.minhajpublications.com | info@minhajpublications.com

+44 (0) 208 534 5243